For all sincere men seeking light, both those within the Craft,
and those considering entry. May the truth, spoken here
in love, bring them freedom.

I AM THE LIGHT OF THE WORLD;
HE THAT FOLLOWETH ME SHALL NOT WALK IN DARKNESS,
BUT SHALL HAVE THE LIGHT OF LIFE.

JOHN 8:12

33 Degrees *of* DECEPTION

An Exposé of Freemasonry

Tom C. McKenney

BRIDGE LOGOS
FOUNDATION

Alachua, Florida 32615

Bridge-Logos
Alachua, FL 32615 USA

33 Degrees of Deception
by Tom C. McKenney

Printed in the United States of America.

Library of Congress Catalog Card Number: pending
International Standard Book Number: 978-0-88270-438-8

Scripture quotations taken from the *King James Version* of the Bible.

In Memoriam

To the memory of the late Reverend James D. Shaw, who loved Freemasonry with all his heart, pursued its knowledge and served its institutions with all his mind and strength. He labored devotedly in the Craft, receiving some of its highest honors. And, unlike the rich young ruler, he forsook it all to follow Jesus; and, having laid his hand to the plow, he never looked back. He selflessly spent the remainder of his life sharing with others—inside and outside the Craft—the truth that had set him free. And to the memory of Jim's late wife Bonnie, who shared the journey with Jim, paying with him the price of massive rejection and all the years of fear, persecution, danger, and pain. Having been severely injured when their car was sabotaged, Bonnie was bed-fast and in pain for the rest of her life.

****

And to the memory of my late friend, Wing Commander Mick Oxley, Royal Air Force (Ret), who, like Jim Shaw, spent much of his life sincerely and actively searching for God in the wrong places. In his worldwide service with the RAF, Mick sought "light"—first in Islam, then Eastern Mysticism, and finally in Freemasonry (English Constitution). In 1967 he finally found the true Light in Jesus Christ and devoted the rest of his life to proclaiming the liberating truth of Jesus, and revealing the error and wickedness in false religions, especially those where he himself had once wandered in darkness.

Acknowledgements

This book would probably not have been written had it not been for the persistent encouragement and assistance of the Rev. Pierce Dodson of Lebanon, Tennessee, a warrior for the truth, who was determined to see this book published. He never lost his zeal and sense of urgency concerning this message of truth and freedom; and he never wavered, even when I, weary and distracted by the pressure of other commitments, gave him little encouragement. Pierce saw the need—especially now, when the world's attention is on the books by Dan Brown, and on the constant flood of television "documentaries," such as those on the History Channel, glorifying the mysterious aspects of Freemasonry and its supposed ancient origins.

My daughter, Melissa Harris of Pass Christian, Mississippi, not only labored mightily in the preparation of the manuscript, but she, quite literally, made it possible. I could not have completed the project without her extreme competence and heroic effort, as she labored under the most difficult of circumstances, in the most difficult and painful time in her life, expending time and strength she did not have. Only she and her Lord will ever know how difficult it was.

Finally, I am grateful to Lloyd and Peggy Hildebrand, apostles of Truth, and their staff at Bridge-Logos Foundation, for making this possible, for their gracious patience with me, and for making the process as pleasant as such a difficult task can be.

Contents

Author's Preface

My personal Masonic library consists of more than 200 volumes, most of which I am "not supposed to have." I have read the most significant ones carefully, referring to them over and over, as both of my previous books on the subject were being prepared, and during the preparation of this book. I would like for those Masons who care enough to have an opinion of me to know that I did not set out in an anti-Masonic, doctrinal rage, slashing blindly right and left as I clawed my way through the bewildering, often contradictory literature of the Masonic institution. In fact, I referred so often to the works of some of these men that I began to feel that I knew them. For one of them, Henry Wilson Coil, I came to have a certain amount of respect.

A few of these men have been genuinely evil, steeped in anti-Christian, Luciferian esoterica, knowingly serving the Prince of Darkness. I believe that even these, however, were not deliberately attempting to deceive the innocent readers of their writings; I believe that even they, for the most part, believed that what they were writing was the truth. Most of these men were philosophically honorable men who were blinded to the truth of Jesus and who were, as Paul wrote to Timothy about the Last Days, "deceiving and being deceived." They represent, on a grand, international scale, what Jesus so crisply summarized as "the blind, leading the blind."

Candidates for the first three degrees (the local lodge/Blue Lodge) are almost always assured that Masonry is based upon the Bible (it isn't—it is based upon the Kabalah, and Egyptian paganism, and we will come back to that). And, if they profess to be Christians, they are told that it will make them better Christians (it won't—it will do just the opposite). When these men read or hear of my books, their first response is usually anger. For those who get beyond the anger, their next very natural, and reasonable, response is often, "But if what you are saying is true, why would my father, my uncles, my pastor and other good men in my lodge, deceive me?" The answer, always, is that those honest, honorable, Christian men who told you these things did so because they believed them to be true. The natural follow-on question, then, is, "Why then did those men of that still-earlier generation deceive my father, my pastor and the others, who then deceived me?" Again, the answer is the same: generation after generation, good men convince other good men to enter and embrace the Lodge because those who have gone before them also believed that it was good.

With this book, I am praying to break that self-perpetuating cycle of hereditary deception and misplaced trust. Once the light of truth is allowed to penetrate the darkened lodge hall with its painted-over, or boarded-up windows, the chain of deception can be broken, and sincere, good men can cease to be its victims.

The Deadly Deception

In 1988 I wrote a book entitled *The Deadly Deception*, the real life story of the Reverend James D. Shaw and his experience of Freemasonry. I wrote the book in the first person, the way he told it to me, as if Jim were telling the story to the reader; and, in a very real sense, he was. It is the compelling story of a man who had longed for a family, and who had hungered since childhood to find, know and worship God. He had lived to adulthood, success in business and service in World War II, without either. Then, in the system of Freemasonry, Jim believed that he had finally found both family and spiritual fulfillment. As a devoted member of the Craft he studied voraciously, and moved up "through the chairs" of the offices of the Blue Lodge, becoming Worshipful Master. And, all the while, he also moved up through the "higher degrees" of the Scottish Rite, became a member of the Order of the Eastern Star, and entered and rose to prominence in the Shrine. Jim and Bonnie, his wife, enjoyed the rich social life in the Masonic family, and he believed that he had found all that he had ever longed for. He was made a Knight Commander of the Court of Honor, the stepping stone to the 33rd Degree, the top of the Masonic Mountain. His cup was running over.

But then he began to have troubling questions about Freemasonry. He asked those men who should have had the answers, but he received none. And then he was introduced to Jesus, the living Christ, and his life was changed forever. In the book, *The Deadly Deception* Jim's story went around the World, published in the US and in Europe. Many lives were changed, always amidst heated controversy with Freemasonry and its passionate defenders.

Please Tell Me

Six years later, in 1994, I wrote a second book about Freemasonry, a thematic book in question-and-answer format. It was based on questions that people had asked, repeatedly, as I was interviewed on hundreds of radio and television talk shows. This book was entitled, *Please Tell Me*, and was essentially a book of systematic information about Freemasonry, based entirely (and exclusively) on official Masonic sources. In that book, not a single non-Masonic source was cited or quoted as an authority. Except for a few references to news publications and the testimony of a Past Grand Chaplain, every source cited was a Masonic publication. *Please Tell Me* became a reference book for churches and schools, and for family libraries.

Both books were best-sellers and, by the grace of God, the truth in them changed many lives; but both went out of print when the publisher declared bankruptcy.

This New Book

Now, thanks to the leadership of Bridge-Logos Publishing Company, the life-changing truth of these two books is again available to the public. This new book includes the entire content of both *The Deadly Deception* and *Please Tell Me*; but it also contains much more. Dramatic and significant changes have taken place in the world of Freemasonry since 1994 and, in this re-birth of the two original books, that additional new information brings the reader up to date concerning what is happening in the world of Freemasonry today. This is a book that you can keep in your home library, give to your church library, or give to a friend who needs it.

A Note Concerning the Use of the Word "Doctrine"

Among researchers in the field of Freemasonry there has been a debate over what, in Masonic publications, constitutes doctrine. Some insist strongly that Masonic doctrine can only be derived from, or supported by, the published rituals. Others believe that doctrine may also be derived from or supported by other publications, such as monitors and other "official" Masonic publications of jurisdictions, rites and bodies. Still others argue that doctrine may also be derived from the writings of Masonic philosophers which are approved and recommended by various jurisdictions, but which are "unofficial," such as the writings of revered Masonic philosophers Albert Pike, J.D. Buck, and Albert Mackey.

So that we understand one another from the start, for purposes of this book, there will be no such attempt to define "doctrine." My intention is to demonstrate, simply and clearly, the generally accepted beliefs, teachings and practices which are found in the vast, complex world of Masonic literature, citing ritual, "official" sources bearing the imprimatur of the relevant jurisdiction, and the "unofficial" Masonic classics by revered Masonic philosophers, which are lauded by Masonic officialdom and which are included in curricula for the education of candidates for the various degrees, and continuing education in the Lodge. My goal is to state simply the most significant beliefs and practices of the world of Freemasonry, and to present the underlying Masonic literature from which they flow.

A Special Word to the Masonic Reader

This book is not "anti-Masonic"; this book is simply the truth—spoken, I pray, in love. I have lived some things and learned some things that most Freemasons don't know—things that they need to know. And I have attempted to set them down in an orderly way as honestly and simply as I can. I am not the enemy of Masons—I am their friend, their advocate, seeking only to tell them the truth about the system that deceives them, uses them, and makes merchandise of their sincere commitment and their loyalty. What I oppose is that system—**not you.**

Many, many times, at the end of a talk show interview, I have been asked, "Tom, what one last thing would you like to say?" My reply is always the same: To the non-Masons, and especially those thinking of becoming Masons, I say, "Please learn the facts before making the decision to join the Lodge; arm yourself with the truth before you commit." And to the Mason, if he will listen to just one thing I say, it is this: "Don't be afraid of the truth"; Jesus promised that if we give it a chance, the truth will set us free."

Except for news items and testimonies, **every reference and every quotation in this book is from a Masonic book, or from your own Masonic Bible.** All of these references are to be found in your Monitor, in your Masonic Bible, in your copy of *Morals and Dogma*, or in your lodge library.

And to the Mason I say again, don't be afraid of the truth; it is only the lie that can hurt you.

The Library of the Grand Lodge of Iowa

If your lodge library doesn't have some of these Masonic books you can order them, free of charge, from the Library of the Grand Lodge of Iowa. The Library of the Grand Lodge of Iowa is one of the finest Masonic libraries in the World, and they are very generous in lending them at no charge and mailing them to you. Call them at (319) 365-1438; e-mail at librarian@gl-ia.org.

And, now, with all this in mind, may you be blessed, and may lives be changed, by the truth contained in this new book.

Tom C. McKenney
Ocean Springs, Mississippi
2011

Part One

Into the Light: An Odyssey

One Man's Wholehearted Search for God

AND YE SHALL SEEK ME, AND FIND ME, WHEN YE SHALL
SEARCH FOR ME WITH ALL YOUR HEART.
JEREMIAH 29:13

THIS LODGE HALL WAS ONCE A CHURCH. Its stained glass windows flooded the sanctuary with beautiful light. Its large doors were thrown wide open, inviting all who hunger and thirst for answers to life, death and eternity to come in and partake of the water of life freely. Now, however, it is converted to a Lodge Hall. Its windows are boarded up, painted over, and its large doors permanently closed. The one remaining entrance, a small blue door, is locked. If there is a meeting underway it is also guarded by a man with a sword. It now says to the "profane" world, "You cannot come in here unless you become one of us, sworn on your life to protect the secrets of life, death and eternity; they are only for us--the elite few."

And, to the black man walking past, it is saying, "You can *never* come in here, for you are inferior and can never be one of us."

✳✳✳

Foreword to Part One

BY DUANE WASHUM, PAST WORSHIPFUL MASTER, VEGAS
LODGE NUMBER 32, IN LAS VEGAS, NEVADA

There was never any person in my entire life whom I loved and admired more than my dad. When he passed away, I lost more than my dad; I lost my hero, my mentor, and my best friend. And because my best friend had once said that Freemasonry made him a better man, I was motivated to become a Freemason. Besides, for the Washum family, becoming a Mason was a family tradition. However, shortly after serving the lodge I was once a member of, as its Worshipful Master, I was convicted by the Holy Spirit. And upon conviction, I prayed to God for His forgiveness and accepted Jesus Christ as my Lord and Savior. I knew that day, that when I found Christ, my search for Light was over, because He is the Light of the World (John 8:12). I also learned in the days to follow that Freemasonry was not a family tradition—it was a family tragedy.

My journey into Freemasonry did not extend as far as Jim Shaw's travels carried him, but, like Jim, the day came when I realized that Freemasonry was nothing I could continue being a part of. When a man turns to Freemasonry and whatever it is he feels the Craft has to offer, he is turning his back to the True and Living God.

> "For what is a man profited, if he shall gain the whole world, and lose his own soul? or what shall a man give in exchange for his soul?" (Matthew 16:26)

3

Freemasonry has caused divisions within families. Even more so, it has caused divisions within the Body of Christ. I pray for more men like Tom McKenney, who has willingly "put on the full armor of God" in order to expose the truth about Freemasonry and its incompatibility with the Christian faith.

In Christ,
Duane Washum
Ex Masons For Jesus

Introduction to Part One

Freemasonry, *sincerely* entered into, is a search for light; any knowledgeable Mason can tell you this. Yet, beneath the surface of this search for light—a search for spiritual knowledge and understanding—there is much, much more. Like an island, rising from the surface of the sea, whose peak is 1,000 feet above sea level, what we see is actually but the very top of a huge mountain, which may rise for four or five miles from the sea floor. The vast majority of that giant mountain is seldom seen, and then only by a small number of committed scholars and explorers, with sophisticated, undersea equipment.

Freemasonry is a lot like that. Most Masons see and know only of the small peak which is above the "sea level" of Masonic knowledge—that which consists of the Blue Lodge experience and the "higher" degrees of the York and Scottish Rites. Only a very small percentage of Masons is even aware of this unseen knowledge and its occult, religious significance; and, of these, only a dedicated few will pursue and study it.

As a matter of fact, the vast majority of Masons live out their lives, either unaware of the deeper significance in Masonry, or, if they have some vague awareness that there is more meaning to what they have seen, heard, and done, they don't bother to look into it. Their entire understanding of Freemasonry is limited to what they have been taught in their Blue Lodge experience; and, quite naturally, they settle for that. They believe what they have been taught, trust the system with their whole hearts, and give it no further thought. In fact, even among the relative few

5

who go on into the "higher" degrees of the York and Scottish Rites, only a very small percentage of them will look beyond the degrees for their true meaning. Some will continue to pay dues and attend meetings and social functions, but do nothing more. Still others will take the first three degrees to "get their tickets punched," for social, political or other purposes, and soon become inactive. Intellectually and philosophically they leave it behind and go on with life.

Jim Shaw was the rare exception. He was not satisfied with social fulfillment, political advantage or surface knowledge; he sensed the deeper, true meaning of the promised "light," and he sought it with all his heart, mind and strength. His ardent quest carried him through the chairs of leadership in the Blue Lodge, the Scottish Rite, the Order of the Eastern Star, and the Mystic Shrine. He pursued the writings of the Masonic philosophers, in an unending search for enlightenment, for intellectual and spiritual fulfillment; he climbed the mountain of Masonic knowledge, searching for that ultimate "light" in all its fullness. He became a Degree Master in the Scottish Rite and was made a Knight Commander of the Court of Honor, the very stepping stone to the 33rd Degree, the top of the Masonic Mountain. But then he began to have troubling questions about it all. He asked insightful questions of those who should have had the answers; but they could give him no satisfactory answers. And then he was introduced to Jesus, the living Christ, and his life was changed forever.

There, in the rarified air at the top of the spiritual mountain, he broke through the clouds at last and found the full revelation, the true meaning of Light and Life. This is his story.

Come and make that pilgrimage to Truth with Jim, here in Part One, "Into the Light: An Odyssey."

On My Own

My mother married for the second time when I was two years old. I was, of course, too young to understand that my father had deserted us when I was only a few months old. I have never seen him.

As time passed, my stepfather developed a growing dislike for me that I accepted as normal, having no knowledge or experience against which to judge life. He really loved my mother, I think, in his own imperfect way. But his resentment of me created problems for her almost from the start.

My Christian grandmother was a beloved and powerful influence in my life. She loved me. Our mutual love and her obvious dislike of my stepfather contributed to his ever-increasing hatred and rejection of me.

However my origin, my grandmother and our love for one another impacted on my problems at home, these took a giant leap for the worse with the birth of my little half-sister. It was only natural that my stepfather would favor her, which he definitely and obviously did. If there was anything remaining of our father-son relationship, it vanished with her coming.

After my little sister, three boys were born. With the coming of each one, my stepfather's life was increasingly fulfilled with his own babies. Simultaneously, I grew older, losing any "little boy" advantage with which I may have begun our relationship. I just became, obviously and completely, an unwanted, adolescent ugly duckling, an entirely unwelcome complication in his home.

Work Begins Early

Unpleasant as all this was for me, I accepted it. I had never known anything else. And I was busy. My stepfather had decreed I must work and support myself. So I did, beginning with my first newspaper route at age five. Soon I was buying all my own clothes, books and school supplies.

During elementary school I had a newspaper route which I delivered early in the morning before going to school and a second job working in the neighborhood drugstore after school. In the evenings I walked, doing my paper route collections, and selling extra papers up and down the streets. I kept up with my school work, worked at my jobs and stayed out of trouble—except at home.

Living With Physical Abuse

Things really didn't seem so bad. I just did what I had to do and thought my life was fairly normal—except for one thing. The beatings I took from my stepfather didn't seem normal to me. They were frequent, whenever he could find the slightest excuse—and they were nothing like the loving chastening a godly father should give his child. They were beatings. But I took them, not seeing any alternative, and made the best of things. I could cling to the belief that my mother and grandmother loved me. This was my life through the age of 12.

The Beatings Come to an End

I was 13 the day I saw my stepfather hit my mother with his fist. I didn't take time to think. I just reacted in a reflex built way down deep inside my very nature. I jumped him, pulled him away from her, and a wild fight followed. Although he was much larger than I, and I was only a boy, I fought with the fury of a son rescuing his beloved mother, and with the pent-up anger of a lifetime of physical and emotional abuse. I fought him to the floor. He got up and left the house. Although I didn't realize it, this part of my life had come to an end.

"You must go"

The next afternoon, when I came home from working at the drugstore, my mother was waiting for me in the front yard. She was crying. She stopped me short of the house and said, "Jimmie, Joe says you must pack up and leave. He says he can't stand having you around here anymore, and you must go." She was choking on the words. And as the reality of what I was hearing came into focus in my mind, weeping rose up within me and spilled over. We wept there, standing in the front yard, but this was something we both had to face. She now had four younger children besides me and a life she had to live.

The Seed Is Planted

As I shouldered my school books and what little clothing I had, my mother went on to say, "Now, Jimmie, I want you to get a room near your work; and since you have been supporting yourself anyway, maybe it won't be too difficult for you. Jimmie, I want you to try to be a man. Try to be like your Uncle Irvin [her brother]; he is a good man and a Mason. He goes to church and is good to his family and if you get to know him better maybe you can grow up to be a good man and a Mason like he is."

My mother knew nothing of what Freemasonry is, but she knew her brother as a hard-working, church-going, good man.

My stepfather had forbidden that anyone in our family attend church services, saying that all the people in the churches were hypocrites. I believe that the fact that Uncle Irvin was an active member of the Methodist Church was the main reason my mother looked up to him. She wanted me to be like him. The seed that would later germinate, spring up, and grow to full fruit in ardent commitment to Freemasonry, taking me to its high levels of service and leadership, was planted.

Although I didn't realize it then, the course of much of my life already was set. But I wouldn't just become a good Mason like my Uncle Irvin; I would go far beyond him in the Craft—far, far beyond him, for it would become the center of knowledge, wisdom, and religious fulfillment in my life.

My life would come to be built around my search for light and the fellowship I found in the Masonic Order and its various bodies.

As we stood there in the front yard that pivotal, painful day she went on to advise me. "Stay out of pool rooms," she said, and I always have. "Don't smoke cigarettes," she said, and I never have. She added, "If you must smoke, smoke cigars like your Uncle Irvin;" and for many years of my life, I did.

As she spoke, I began to realize the enormity of what was happening. With this realization growing within me and blinded with tears, I reached out to her, hugged her, turned and walked away. As I took each step up the street and away from mother, the weight of the world and of an unknown future settled down on my 13-year-old shoulders.

I was on my own.

In Search of a Future

The first thing I had to do after leaving home and my mother—now on my own for the first time in my life—was to find a place to live. Mother had suggested that I find a room near my work and I did, at a rooming house just down the street from the drugstore. The owner of the drugstore gave me longer hours to work so that I could give up the paper route. I began to adjust to my new life.

Working in the drugstore, going to school and studying filled my days and nights. But I was able to keep up with my school work and in this way finished elementary school and high school, including four years of ROTC.[1]

During those first years on my own, my grandmother was even more important in my life. She was a real rock of stability and support and we became even closer.

She tried to get Uncle Irvin to take me places and spend time with me because she knew I had never known a father. She wanted him to help fill that void in this growing boy's relatively empty life and I very much wanted that. But he was too busy—always too busy—with his Masonic Lodge activities, his work at the post office and his own family.

Mother had set him up as my father figure and role model, and I really wanted to know him; but he was too busy.

Alone Again

After high school graduation, with the encouragement and financial support of my grandmother, I began the study of law. In those days it was possible to enter the study of law directly out of high school, earn the LLB degree[2] from the state university and take the bar examination. But after only one year my grandmother died and I was forced to drop out of law school. My world suddenly became much more empty. My one real friend and supporter on earth was gone. I was alone again.

Bonnie Enters My Life

But my work kept me busy, and I got an additional job that summer, hoping that maybe I could earn enough money for another year of law school. I was definitely interested in girls and, although there was precious little time for them, I began to meet some and get to know them. That summer I met Bonnie and almost everything in my life changed! It was another turning point. But, as usual, I didn't realize it at the time.

Bonnie was wonderful. She seemed to return this sentiment and her family liked and approved of me. Things developed quickly, we decided to marry and soon did. Since my second job (in hopes of another year of law school) was in a restaurant and I was learning a good deal about the restaurant business, Bonnie's family suggested that we go into that business. They lent us the money to buy a place that was for sale. We cleaned, painted and decorated it nicely and were soon doing a good business. We were enjoying the work, prospering and were quite happy with it all, and with each other. Life was good.

Law school was disappearing on the road behind me now. The path of my life had taken a permanent turn in another direction.

My First Experience of Fraternal Orders

One day a man who was eating in our restaurant asked to see me. I went over to the side table where he was seated and asked him what he wanted. He said he was a representative of the Loyal Order of the Moose and that I had been selected to be a member. He also said that it would provide important social and business contacts and would be good for my restaurant business.

It sounded good to me and before long I was a member. At the same time, Bonnie joined the Women of the Moose. It was the beginning of our active involvement in fraternal orders and I had not the slightest idea of where it would eventually take me.

The Moose Lodge was quite different from the Masonic orders I would later know so well. For one thing, the Moose meetings were quite short. Our lodge met upstairs over a lunchroom and bar. When the relatively short meetings were over, nearly everyone went downstairs to the bar where things continued for a much longer time (sometimes it almost seemed that this was the real reason for meeting).

Still, I didn't attend the Moose meetings very often until I was approached about being an officer. Now, for the boy who had never felt accepted and had never been an officer in anything, this was pretty heady stuff; I immediately accepted, necessarily becoming much more active.

The lunchroom under the Lodge Hall belonged to the Lodge. The man who operated the business had to pay no rent, nor did he have any utility costs, which made his brisk business even more profitable. He was a member of the Lodge and I envied his advantage in business, compared with my own situation.

Mother's Last Goodbye

In all the time that Bonnie and I had operated the restaurant, Uncle Irvin had never been there, so I was surprised one day to see him coming in. He said that my grandfather was outside in the car but didn't feel well enough to come inside. I went out to the car to see him and could see at a glance that grandfather was very, very sick and weak. We visited briefly and then Uncle

13

Irvin drove away. It was the last time I saw grandfather alive; he died the following week.

At his funeral, I noticed that mother did not look well at all. She appeared pale and weak, struggling, it seemed, just to sit up. I had never seen her look so ill, but I thought it was just the pain and stress of losing her father. I didn't feel free to stay very close to her, since my stepfather was there. But I comforted her as best I could and, as we parted, she told me goodbye. How could I have suspected that it was her last goodbye? The following week she died, and the following Saturday, exactly one week after grandfather's funeral, we buried mother.

I have never been able to find out what caused her death. Even to this day, there is something mysterious about it as if something is being concealed; but it seems to have been a heart attack.

After the funeral service was completed, my stepfather came over to where Bonnie and I were standing and said, "Jim, I feel that I need to tell you something. I believe that your mother would still be alive had it not been for the way I treated you."

Then he said, emotionally, "I will never marry again!" Six months later he was remarried. But I do believe there was truth in what he told me about mother's death. He was never again any part of my life.

War Comes

Not long after mother's death, World War II came and ended the Great Depression. The Japanese bombed Pearl Harbor and America entered the conflict. We were in it at last and the operator of the lunchroom at the Moose Lodge was drafted. This opened up that position and the governing board asked me to take it over. Bonnie and I talked it over and decided I would probably also be drafted soon, so we sold our restaurant (in order to be ready) and were soon working full time at the Moose Lodge. Our lives were even more closely tied to fraternal orders now. Still we had no idea where it would lead.

More than a year went by. I tried to join the Navy but was turned down. We stayed busy with the lunchroom and lodge activities. I had really forgotten about the draft when the notice came. I had been drafted.

The Masonic Connection

I had been out of high school more than six years and married for five years when I entered the Army during World War II. Yet from the very first I began to remember what my mother had said to me, that awful day at age 13 when I had been forced to leave home.

Maybe it was because, once again, I was alone and entering into an unknown way of life. I remembered about my Uncle Irvin and his active involvement in the Masonic Lodge. As I went through basic training I noticed that many of the officers there wore Masonic rings.

Toward the end of basic training, two men from my unit were to be selected for Officer Candidate School to be trained as officers and commissioned second lieutenants. I was not selected and the two who were selected were both Masons. I thought about my four years of ROTC, my age, my experience and wondered why I had not been selected. I didn't realize then that these men had been selected by Masons because they were Masons. In later years I would understand very well. But at the time I could only wonder.

Climbing "Shaw Hill"

I was much older than the other men in my company. As a matter of fact, I was older than my company commander. In spite of my "advanced age," I had been assigned to the infantry, and was base plate man in the mortar platoon of a rifle company. We traveled on foot and I had the heaviest load to carry. The others called me "Pop," but I didn't mind. I carried my base plate, plus my own weapon and all my individual gear, and usually outdid the younger men.

As a matter of fact, during a training march from Camp Butner to Raleigh, North Carolina, I was the only man in the company able to carry another man to the top of a certain hill along the way.

My platoon commander congratulated me, named it "Shaw Hill," and that little honor meant a lot more to me than anyone else there could have known. I still think at times of that hill, about halfway between Camp Butner and Raleigh, and what Lieutenant Ram said that day about this abandoned little kid from the big city. The war came and went and, with that behind me, I was even more sure that I could make it in life. With Bonnie at my side, I knew that I could succeed. Mother would be pleased if she knew. I *really could* be a successful, good man like my Uncle Irvin.

ENDNOTES

1   Army ROTC (Reserve Officer Training Corps) is a training program that prepares young men and women to be officers in the Army. High School ROTC prepares the student for college ROTC, and that leads to a commission as second lieutenant.
2   Bachelor of Laws and Letters, the traditional law school degree until recent times.

Brought to the Light

The war was over and I was home again with Bonnie. We were supremely happy, and together we were about to enter into the Masonic fellowship that would become the center of our world.

I soon told Bonnie that I would really like to join the Masonic Lodge. I remembered the Masonic officers in basic training and I had a need to belong, a need for acceptance in a group, for friends, for a family.

Immediately I received a surprising revelation from Bonnie: she had been a member of the Order of the Eastern Star since age 18, and her father was a Mason! I was amazed; I had no idea of any of this. She had never attended a meeting or even mentioned it to me since I had known her. But she was happy that I wanted to be a Mason.

I was happy that we already had this little foundation laid, and now I earnestly pursued the idea.

Why All These Pennies?

I was still a member in good standing in the Moose Lodge. During the war, while I had been away, my dues had been suspended (it was the patriotic thing to do). We had many good friends in the Moose Lodge, I was made welcome there and it was as if I had never been away—except that we no longer operated the lunchroom.

I told a few friends in the Moose that I was thinking of joining the Masonic Lodge and discovered that there was no conflict at all. Three of my Moose brothers were also Masons. They were pleased that I wanted to be one too.

Each one of them gave me a penny and told me to "keep it handy," as I would be needing it.

They were a bit mysterious about it and didn't explain, so I wondered what all this penny business was about but didn't ask. I wondered even more as days passed, because every Mason I mentioned this to did the same thing! I soon had quite a few pennies and was certain that it was important to "keep it handy," but hadn't the slightest idea why. Then, the mysterious nature of Masonry was one of the things about it that attracted me. I began to look forward to entering in with increased anticipation.

As the Christmas season approached in late 1945 I found a temporary job at the post office. Uncle Irvin was assistant postmaster and could have helped me to get the job, but he didn't. I got the job without his help, was working the second shift, and Bonnie and I were getting along fine.

First Steps Toward the Light

Bonnie and I had two close friends, Mac and Merle, whom we had known before the war. Merle had worked for us at the restaurant and had later married Mac. One evening they invited us over to their home and, after dinner, when the ladies were in the kitchen, I asked Mac (who was a Mason) how I could get into the Masonic Lodge.

He was delighted, and replied, "All you have to do is ask. I will get a friend of mine at the Fire Department to recommend you, and with my recommend[3] that will get the ball rolling."

About two weeks passed and I had a phone call from a man who said he was on the Masonic Lodge committee that would be talking with me and asked if they might come over that evening.

I told him I would be glad for them to come and after dinner that evening, three men[4] came. We visited and they asked me questions about myself, including my reasons for wanting to join. They were pleasant, and Mac had already told me what to expect so I was at ease throughout the interview. They left in agreement that I would be taken into the Lodge.

Preparation for Initiation

A few days later I received a letter telling me to be at the Lodge Hall at 7 P.M. Tuesday evening. I arrived promptly and found that two others were to be initiated along with me.

We were met by the Lodge secretary who told us what the cost of the initiation would be and explained that these dues (fees that must be paid) would have to be paid for all three degrees before we could proceed with the first degree initiation. I paid my dues and, when the others had settled their business, we were taken to a room which I later knew very well as the "Preparation Room." But at the time I had no idea where I was or why I was there. In the Preparation Room we were told to remove all clothing, and were then given a two-piece garment made of thin, white material that looked like pajamas; and we were given one sandal each. We were told to put the sandal on the right foot, leaving the left foot bare. We were now prepared to receive the Entered Apprentice Degree, or the First Degree in Freemasonry.

A man called "The Senior Deacon" then entered and asked questions of us such as "Why do you wish to become Freemasons; do you join because you believe it will help you in your business, or help you to gain influence in your community?"

Now, to such questions the candidate is supposed to answer as if he had no such selfish motivation. But it has been my experience that the vast majority of Masons enter for these very self-serving reasons. As a matter of fact, although the theory is that Masons do not recruit, or advise prospects that there are business and professional advantages in being a Mason, both are commonly done. Again, Mac had prepared me by warning me about such questions and I gave satisfactory answers. But I was able to do so honestly, for I really did have an earnest desire to join and to belong—just to belong. Then the Senior Deacon left.

After the departure of the Senior Deacon, I was blindfolded. The blindfold is called a "hoodwink," and the candidate so prepared is said to be "hoodwinked," unable to see or know the nature of his surroundings or situation.

After the hoodwink was placed over my eyes, a heavy cloth was further placed under it and over my eyes to insure that I would not be able to see anything, not even a crack of light.

Then the light cloth shirt was arranged so that my left arm was out of it, and the left side of the shirt folded back and tucked under, leaving the left arm and left side of the torso bare. The left leg of the "pajama bottoms" was rolled up high, leaving the left foot and leg bare. A rope (I later learned that it was blue and was called a "cabletow") was tied around my neck. I was ready.

Although I very much wanted to be taken into the Masonic Lodge, I began to experience real fear. I couldn't see, didn't know where I was, was half-naked among an unknown number of strangers, being held by a rope around my neck, and I certainly didn't know what would happen next. There was a sense of unreality and helplessness and a rising groundswell of disorientation, insecurity and fear. Mac had told me (although he was under a terrible oath not to do so) a little of what to expect. I knew I would be blindfolded but expected to be able to see a little bit anyway. However, I could see nothing at all.

This being in total darkness produced a deep-down feeling of helplessness, and gave rise to thoughts of terrible things that might be done. The thing that kept me from being overwhelmed with fear was the knowledge that Mac, Uncle Irvin and my Masonic friends in the Moose Lodge were all alive and well. Since they all had somehow survived this, I believed that I would survive it too. But I was extremely uncomfortable.

Into the Holy Place

The Steward led me to the Lodge Hall door and instructed me to give three raps. Nothing happened at first and then there were three answering raps from inside and a voice asked, "Who comes here?"

The Steward, answering for me, replied, "A poor blind candidate who desires to be brought from darkness into light, and receiving a part of the rights, lights and benefits of this Worshipful Lodge dedicated to the Holy Saints John, as many a brother and fellow have done before him."

I was asked, "Is this an act of your own free will and accord?"

Prompted by the Steward, I replied, "It is."

It was already becoming apparent to me that, although I really wanted to be a Mason, this was not to be an honest exchange between me and these unseen persons; there were prearranged "right" answers to all their prearranged questions, and I would be told how to reply. The voice on the other side of the door asked if I were properly prepared and worthy and well-qualified. To both questions the Steward replied in the affirmative.

Then the other voice asked, "By what further right or benefit does he expect to gain admission?"

The Steward replied, for me, "By being a man, free born, of lawful age and well-recommended."[5] The voice on the other side then said, "Let him wait with patience until the Worshipful Master is informed and his answer returned."

After another period of waiting in the black silence, the door was opened before me and the voice said that I was to be allowed to enter and be received "in due and ancient form." I was led through the door. Although I didn't know where I was, I had passed through the protected portals and into the holy and secret place. I was inside a Lodge Hall for the first time in my life.

Brought to the Light

That same voice I heard from inside the door (it turned out to be the Senior Deacon) then said, from directly in front of me, "You are received into this Lodge of Entered Apprentices upon the point of a sharp instrument piercing your naked left breast, which is to teach you as this is an instrument of torture to the flesh, so the remembrance of it be to your mind and conscience, should you ever presume to reveal any of the secrets of Freemasonry unlawfully."

The "sharp instrument" was actually a large compass with the two sharp points brought together as one, and "sharp" it most certainly was. I *really did* feel pain as it was pressed into my flesh. When he said "presume," he emphasized the word by jabbing me again. This thing was becoming more and more serious and I was even more afraid. Yet, under the circumstances, I stood silently and made no reply.

I was then caused to walk again, led by the same man who was holding me by the rope around my neck and by my left arm. We stopped. Another voice (it was the Worshipful Master) ordered me taken to a place in the center of the room for prayer. I was led there, made to kneel, and the Master prayed a formal, generalized prayer, never mentioning Jesus, and ending with, "So mote it be."

After the prayer he came to where I was kneeling, placed his hand on my head and asked, "In whom do you place your trust?"

Except for the few times as a child with my grandmother, I had not been taken to church or taught about God and I really didn't know how to reply. I was awkwardly silent for what seemed a long time.

Finally the Senior Deacon leaned over and whispered in my ear that I should say "In God,"[6] and I did. The Master then said that since my trust was in God my faith was well-founded and I was to follow my "conductor" (the Senior Deacon, who was leading me around by the rope around my neck) and not be afraid. That helped a little but I was still far from being at ease.

I was then led to another place in the room where another man (the Junior Warden) asked the same questions as before my being allowed to enter the room. He then directed me to be led to still another place where the Senior Warden asked the very same questions and received the same replies. At each stop someone rapped once with a gavel.

It was all very strange and formal and the questions and answers were beginning to sound familiar. From there I was led to the position of "the Worshipful Master in the East" where he asked the *very same* questions and received the very same replies. It was really beginning to be repetitious. Then, at the direction of the Worshipful Master, I was instructed in the proper manner of "approaching the East."[7] The Senior Deacon, my principal escort, turned me around saying, "You will face the East. Take one step with your left foot, and bring the heel of your right foot to the hollow (instep) of your left foot, feet forming the angle of the oblong square."

He helped me do this because I could not see. He held on to me or I might have lost my balance. It was an unnatural way to stand and being blindfolded made it even more difficult. Then, suddenly, he shouted, "STAND ERECT!"[8]

I was startled and wondered what *that* was all about (I was already standing up, although my feet were somewhat twisted around). But I was beginning to expect such unexpected things and, although I certainly didn't know it, an even more startling surprise was just ahead.

The voice of the Worshipful Master, somewhere in front of me, said, "Friend, for the first time in your life you have advanced to the altar of Masonry; you stand before us a candidate seeking admission to our Order. But before going farther be warned of the solemnity and importance of the step you are about to take. If you are unwilling to proceed, withdraw while there is yet time."

There had been moments of fear when I wanted to leave, but felt trapped in what was taking place. And now, as I awkwardly stood there, blindfolded and disoriented, not knowing what (or how many) men may be looking at me, I began to feel a strange kind of numbness. I felt somewhat like a victim still, but really didn't want to leave. I was beginning to feel as if I were being carried along, propelled by a force I neither knew nor understood. The Master went on with remarks about the nature of the Order and of the high moral character required to belong.

Then I was placed in a kneeling position before the altar, "in due form." This was to kneel on the naked left knee, right leg extended to form the Tau Cross ("angle of a square"), left hand under the Bible on the altar (on top of which were the square and compass), right hand resting thereon and body erect. I was now ready to take the oath, although I certainly didn't know it, and I knew *nothing* of what would be *in* that oath.

Kissing Jesus Goodbye

The Master then assured me that the oath which I was about to take would in no way "conflict with religious, political or private pursuits be they what they may,"[9] and, asked me if I were willing to continue. I really didn't know what he was talking about but it sounded reassuring so I said, "I am."

I was then led to swear, repeating after the Worshipful Master, the oath of an Entered Apprentice Mason. He would speak a few words and I would repeat them, having no idea to what I was swearing until each small group of words was spoken for me to repeat.

As it progressed I realized that I was swearing to protect the secrets of the Lodge. Then I heard myself saying that I was "binding myself under no less penalty than that of having my throat cut from ear to ear, my tongue torn out by its roots, and buried in the sands of the sea a cable's length from shore, where the tide ebbs and flows twice in twenty-four hours, should I ever willingly, knowingly, or unlawfully violate this, my Entered Apprentice Oath, so help me God and keep me steadfast."

The awfulness of the oath dawned within me as I was speaking it and it was both frightening and repulsive to me. But, having begun, having "come this far," I just continued to the end.[10] The Master then told me that, in order to seal this oath, I was to kiss the open Bible before me. I had my hands on it so I knew where it was and I leaned forward and kissed it. I had no idea that I was actually kissing Jesus goodbye at the altar of Baal. I didn't know that throughout my lifetime in Masonry I would not be allowed to pray in His name, or even to hear or speak His name in the Lodge, even in Scripture readings.[11] But I didn't know Him then, so would have had no sense of loss even had I known this.

I Wanted a Glass of Water

The Worshipful master then directed that since I was now bound to the Lodge "by an oath which cannot be broken," I was to have the rope (cabletow) removed from my neck.

The Senior Deacon removed it.

Then the Master said to me, "My brother, in your present blind condition, what do you most desire?"

Well, I had been through a lot of stress by that time and was very thirsty. I assumed from his question that whatever I asked for, I would probably be given. So I thought it over briefly and was just about to say, "a cold glass of water," when the Senior Deacon leaned over and whispered in my ear, "Light."

So, a little disappointed, I said, "Light."

The big surprise was just about ready. The Master called the lodge members to the altar and they gathered in two rows, one on either side of me, aligned east-to-west. He then quoted from Genesis where God said, "Let there be light" and said, "In solemn imitation of Him I, in like manner, Masonically declare, 'let there be LIGHT!'"

When he shouted "LIGHT" all the other men present around me clapped their hands and stamped their feet simultaneously, startling me half to death and, at the same moment, the Senior Deacon ripped off the hoodwink and I was blinded with brilliant light.

The Worshipful Master then said, "And there is light."

I was stunned and dazzled momentarily. Then the Master went on talking, explaining the objects I was beginning to be able to focus my eyes on and see before me. He told me about the Bible[12], square, and compass, their meaning, and called them the "three great lights of Masonry." Then he referred to the three candles around the altar and said they represented the "three lesser lights" of Masonry, which in reality are the sun, the moon, and the Worshipful Master of the Lodge. None of this meant much to me at that time, except that I already had a vague idea that the Bible was supposed to be a sacred book.

Then the Worshipful Master showed me how to perform the dueguard (by holding my hands in the position in which they had been at the altar, left one palm-up and the right one over it, palm-down), and the sign. The sign was performed by drawing the open hand from the left ear, across the throat to the right ear, as if cutting the throat across. I was still kneeling at the altar. The Master then demonstrated the secret grip (pressing the knuckle of the right index finger) and gave me the secret word, ("Boaz").

He helped me to stand and instructed me to go and salute the Junior and Senior Wardens with the due-guard and sign. Led by the Senior Deacon, I did.

Returning then to the west side of the altar, I waited while the Master approached the altar and presented me with a lambskin apron. He explained that it was an emblem of innocence and the mark of a Mason. He further spoke of its importance and then told me to take it to the Senior Warden in the West who would instruct me in the way to wear it. I did it, thinking that there is a very great deal of moving around in these ceremonies.

The Senior Warden explained its use by ancient stonemasons and by members of the Lodge, or "speculative" Masons, including the way I should wear it (with the bib turned up). Then he put the apron on me, led me back to my place at the altar, we both saluted the Worshipful Master and he reported, "Your orders have been obeyed, Worshipful Master."

The Pennies Explained

At this point the Master asked me to deposit something of value of a metallic kind and directed me to search my person for such an object.

"The pennies," I thought, "this is what the pennies were about."

Well, I knew there was no use looking in those pajamas for a coin for they had no pockets. The Master then explained that all this was to remind me of my "poor and penniless condition," should I ever meet a friend, particularly a brother Mason, who is destitute. I was to give to him, as able to do so "without inconvenience."

Then I was sent to the preparation room to dress again and then return for further instruction.

I went, thinking, "This explains all that mysterious stuff about the pennies, and yet it doesn't. They said I would be *needing* them and I really don't." It was a partial truth—but not the clear, plain truth. I had actually been misled. I wondered if somehow this was an indication of deceptions to come. I had believed them completely and it had really not been true.

Upon my return, I saluted the Worshipful Master and was seated as a member of the Lodge. I watched, with growing understanding, as the other two candidates were initiated after me. I was a Mason at last—without any help from Uncle Irvin.

ENDNOTES

3   A recommendation for acceptance is called a "recommend"
in the Lodge, as is the case with Mormons seeking admission
to the secret rituals of the Mormon Temple. Joseph Smith,
founder of Mormonism and writer of the temple ritual, was a
Mason. Much of the Mormon Temple ritual is the same as in
Masonic ritual, having apparently been "borrowed" from it by
Smith. Two such "recommends" are required before admission
to the Masonic Lodge can he pursued.

4   These three men constituted the "Investigation Committee";
there are always three men, and they are elected each year to
this position.

5   Although essentially the same, the rituals for the first three
("Blue") degrees vary in small ways from state to state in the
USA. In most states the wording here includes "white," for
blacks and women are entirely excluded from the Masonic
brotherhood. There is a black Masonic system, called the
Prince Hall Lodge, but it is not associated in any way with
"white" Freemasonry. It is referred to as "clandestine"
Masonry, and is considered by the rest of Masonry to be a
spurious, illegitimate imitation.

6   Some really funny things do happen in these ceremonies.
Once, later on, when Jim was Worshipful Master, he placed his
hand on a candidate's head and asked him. "In whom do you
place your trust?" Without hesitation the man replied, "My
wife."

7   "The east" is the location within the Lodge Hall where the
Worshipful Master sits upon his throne/chair of authority.
In the ancient mystery religions, from which Freemasonry
springs, the Sun was worshipped, and the most sacred
direction was east, where the sun arose each morning to renew
life on earth.

8   This position of the feet is no coincidence when facing the
Worshipful Master "in the East." This position of the feet
forms the "Tau Cross," a phallic symbol from antiquity
associated with phallic worship and Sun worship in which the
Sun was viewed as the source of life (male), rising each day in
the east to impregnate the Earth (female) with new life. Such
worship was always done facing East. Here in the ritual, the
command "STAND ERECT" is also not a coincidence, and is

9 This is, at best, logically absurd. He could have no way of knowing this, for he had no knowledge of what such values, beliefs and standards Jim may have held, then or in the future. One clear exception to this false assurance, for example, is that all Christians are forbidden by Scripture from taking such oaths, particularly blood oaths of mutilation and murder.

10 There have been cases reported of men who stopped at the point of the terrible oath and refused to continue, but such cases are rare. By the time most men are at this point, nearly finished with the oath, they will, because of fear, their humbling position, the rope around the neck, and the hypnotic effect of the ceremony, proceed with the oath, although they may feel revulsion at it.

11 In a "well-ordered Lodge" the name of Jesus is not allowed to he spoken. Praying in His name is a serious offense and can even bring about the closing of a lodge. When New Testament Scriptures are read in the rituals, portions including the name of Jesus are simply omitted. Dr. Albert Mackey, the great 19th Century Masonic philosopher, called this removal of references to Jesus in Scripture quotations, "slight, but necessary, modifications."

12 In this part of the ritual the Worshipful Master tells the initiate," the Holy Bible is to be your rule and guide to your faith and practice." Years later, when Jim was a Worshipful Master, a friend who was an officer in the Lodge asked him, after an initiation, "Jim, if it is true that the Bible is to be our rule and guide, why don't we follow its teachings?" He had an excellent question, one for which Jim had no answer, and the man soon left Masonry.

of obvious symbolic meaning. In this regard, see Appendix B, "Masonic Symbolism."

I'm Going to Florida

After the three of us had been initiated into the Entered Apprentice Degree we were immediately assigned an instructor from among the experienced brothers in the Lodge. He was to meet with us at least once weekly at the Lodge Hall for several weeks[13] to instruct and coach us in the necessary memory work until we were ready to recite before the Lodge and actually have the degree conferred.

This memory work consisted of portions of the initiation ritual (in which we had been prompted during initiation, or had simply had them shown us or spoken for us), such as the secret word, dueguard, sign, grip, and the oath (obligation). Then, when we were ready, we would be examined orally before the Lodge, the questions being put to us by our instructor.

Our final examination for the Entered Apprentice Degree would be given on the same night that we would be initiated into the Fellowcraft Degree, making for a very long meeting on that night.

The instructor set a regular night for the three of us to meet with him and I was looking forward to it. I was definitely motivated, an eager beaver, ready to "get on with it." I wanted to take the oral exam for Entered Apprentice and be initiated into the Fellowcraft Degree as soon as possible.

Meanwhile, Roy, a friend with whom I had been in the Army, called me. He was living in South Florida in one side of a duplex house. The other side was empty. He urged Bonnie and me to leave the North, with its long, cold winters and come to Florida with him and his family. He painted a most appealing picture and said he was sure we could both find jobs there.

We really didn't want to leave, for the city was "home" to us. Both of us had grown up there and what families we had were there. So I just went ahead with my job at the post office and looked forward to the training sessions with our instructor at the Lodge Hall. I believed that I would soon be ready, with the other two men, to take the examination. I kept thinking about Roy and what he had suggested, but it was just too big a change to make so lightly.

One Cold Night

Christmas had come and gone, then New Year's Day, and the post office still kept me on. I was working second shift, from 3 to 11 P.M., on the south side of town where packages were handled. The weather was extremely cold.

One bitterly cold night, when my shift was over, I walked out to the parking lot to get into my car and drive home as I always did. When I tried to start the car it wouldn't do a thing; it was frozen. A lot of the gasoline being sold at the time had water in it and I was the victim of a tank full. The fuel line and the carburetor were frozen and it simply wouldn't start. I was stranded in the middle of a very cold winter night.

There was no one left in the lot to give me a ride, so there was nothing to do but walk to town where I could catch a streetcar home. I locked the car, wrapped my coat around me and set out for town, walking into a cold north wind. As I walked along on painfully cold feet I began thinking of Roy and his proposal. The more I thought of it, the more attractive the thoughts of that warm climate became.

Soon, with each step I was saying to myself, "I'm going to Florida, I'm going to Florida, I'm going to Florida," keeping cadence with my steps crunching on the frozen ground. With each step I was more determined to do it and by the time I reached town, and the first streetcar stop, the decision was made. We were going to Florida, and the sooner the better!

When I presented the idea to Bonnie she was willing and immediately we began to make preparations. Thoughts of how this would affect my progress as a Mason didn't have much impact; that could be worked out somehow. The cold weather and contrasting thoughts of palm trees, warm breezes and orange groves prevailed. We were going to Florida at least until the awful winter was over.

Within a few weeks we were on our way south. We drove through Kentucky, Tennessee and Georgia. The farther south we drove the warmer it was and the happier I became. It felt so "right."

A Temporary Standstill

In Florida we moved right into the other side of the duplex Roy and his family were in and settled down. I was in contact with the Lodge back home and they thought I would soon be back. So did I but I felt no compulsion to be in a hurry about it. My degree instructor finally wrote and told me that the other two men who had been initiated as Entered Apprentices with me were already Master Masons (had completed the first three degrees); he wanted to know when I would be coming back and was concerned that I would not be able to remember the material after so long a time. Actually, I did remember it—and very well—for I frequently went over all of it in my mind. I remembered it though I had not been able to attend even the first training session with the instructor before leaving for Florida.

It was suggested that I might be able to go on with the degree work right there in Florida so I inquired about it. I learned that, with a letter from the Lodge back home, I could continue in

Florida as a "courtesy candidate" and finish all three degrees right there. Since I had already paid for all three of the Blue Degrees[14], it wouldn't cost me anything to take the degrees in Florida. I was delighted, made the necessary arrangements, and immediately commenced the memory work with an instructor from the local lodge.

So Why Leave?

Meanwhile, I applied for a job with the City Port Authority and was accepted. Bonnie had a good job, already, and we were doing fine. Spring had come and cold weather was over back home but thoughts of returning to the North were rapidly losing their appeal. We talked it over, discussed it with Roy and his wife and considered the facts. We both had good jobs where we were, had no jobs back home, and liked Florida better each day. So, we reasoned, why leave? We decided to stay right where we were, at least for the foreseeable future.

Back Into the Craft

It may seem that my ardent seeking into Freemasonry had been interrupted, that it had been displaced in my life's goals and values, but it hadn't been—not at all. I had been preoccupied with the move to Florida and the search for a good job there, but actually all this had only involved a few months. I had continued to rehearse the secret degree work in my mind all the while and I had kept in touch with the Lodge in Indianapolis. There had been a little "time out," but no real change in my heart.

With my acceptance by the Florida Lodge as a courtesy candidate for the rest of the Blue Degrees, I stepped right back into my active pursuit of the Masonic mountaintop.

I was soon ready for the oral examination for the Entered Apprentice Degree and initiation into the Fellowcraft Degree. I had never ceased to remember and to prepare, and was anxious to proceed with it.

A Fellowcraft Mason

Although I was now in another Grand Lodge (each state is a separate "Grand Lodge" and, in many ways, independent of the others) and in the Southern Jurisdiction,[15] things were essentially the same in Florida and I felt a basic familiarity with what was happening as I was being prepared for the Fellowcraft initiation. When I arrived at the Lodge Hall and was led into the Preparation Room I was much more relaxed than I had been that first time a few months earlier in Indianapolis. There were three other men to be examined with me, including one who had previously taken the examination and failed it. We waited in our street clothes while the Worshipful Master opened the Lodge in the Master Mason's Degree (the Lodge is always opened in the Master Mason's degree when candidates are to be examined for the Blue Degrees). Then the Lodge was "called off" to the Entered Apprentice Degree for the examination and the Senior Deacon escorted us into the Lodge Hall, placing us near the altar.

Our instructor had now changed roles and become our examiner, as we had known he would do. He took his place at the west side of the altar, facing us, and began to ask us the questions for which we had been prepared. No one of us was asked all the questions; but, of course, it was necessary for each of us to know all the answers for we couldn't know which ones we would be asked.

We answered his questions in order, without a flaw, and were then escorted back to the Preparation Room to wait while the Lodge members voted on whether to award the degree to us.[16]

After a rather short time, the Junior Deacon came into the Preparation Room and told us that we had all been accepted and awarded the Entered Apprentice Degree. We were all pleased, but not too surprised, and were immediately told to remove our clothes to prepare for initiation into the Fellowcraft (Second) Degree. We undressed and were given pajama tops and bottoms, very similar to those I remembered from the Entered Apprentice initiation, and, again, one slipper. This time, however, we were told to put the one slipper on the left foot, leaving the right one bare. The right leg of the trousers was rolled up above the knee and the right arm left out of the top leaving the right side of the torso naked.

We were ready, but this time I was not to be first; the man who had failed and been forced to retake his examination was taken into the Lodge Room for initiation first.

When the first man had completed the initiation, put his street clothes back on and been seated in the Lodge Hall to watch the rest of us, it was my turn.

I was hoodwinked, just like before. But when the cabletow was tied onto me it was not put around my neck; instead, it was wound twice around my right arm. The Steward led me to the inner door and told me to give three raps. After a brief delay, there were three answering raps on the other side of the door. The Steward opened the door just enough to allow discussion and the question was asked (it was the Senior Deacon, as in the first degree), "Who comes here?" The Steward, who was holding onto me, replied, "A brother who has been regularly initiated an Entered Apprentice and now desires to receive additional light in Masonry by being passed to the degree of Fellowcraft."

I was then asked by the Senior Deacon, "Is this an act of your own free will and accord?" and I replied, "It is."

This time things were not so strange and new; in fact, I could anticipate some of it before it took place. I was much more relaxed. The Senior Deacon asked the Steward if I were duly and truly prepared and if I were well qualified.

To both, the Steward replied that I was.

The Senior Deacon asked the Steward if I had made suitable proficiency in the preceding degree, and was told that I had. The Senior Deacon then asked "by what further right or benefit" I expected to gain admission. The Steward replied, "By benefit of the Pass."

The Steward was then asked if I had the pass and replied that I did not, but that he had it for me.

The door was opened just enough for the Steward to whisper the password to the Senior Deacon who then said, "Let him wait until the Worshipful Master is informed of his request and his answer returned."

The door was closed. After a short delay the door was opened and the Senior Deacon said from right in front of me that it was the will of the Worshipful Master that I enter the Lodge of Fellowcrafts and that I be received "in due and ancient form." That part sounded very familiar.

The Senior Deacon then said to me, "My brother, it is the will of the Worshipful Master that you be received into this Lodge upon the angle of a square at your naked right breast, which is to teach you that the square of virtue should be a rule and guide to your conduct in all your future action with mankind and more especially with a brother Mason."

As he was saying this, he pressed the point of the square into my bare chest; it was uncomfortable, but nothing like as painful as the compass points pressed into me in the first initiation. He then took me firmly by my bare right arm and began to lead me around the room. It is awkward to walk in a strange place blindfolded, even when being led along; there is always the thought that you are about to run into something.

In this way I made my way around the Lodge Hall and, as we passed certain places, I heard tapping sounds, two each time. We seemed to be going around again, and this time stopped (at the station of the Junior Warden) and there were three taps. The same questions and answers that were exchanged at the door were repeated.

Then the Junior Warden asked, "Has he the password?"

The Senior Deacon replied, "He has it not; I have it for him."

Upon being told to advance and give the password, the Senior Deacon did so, saying "SHIBBOLETH." The Junior Warden replied, "Right. Pass on."

We began moving again and stopped as before (this time it was at the station of the Senior Warden). The same questions and answers were exchanged and the Senior Warden directed that I be conducted to the Worshipful Master in the East for final instruction. We began moving again and stopped at the Master's station. Here the very same questions were asked and the very same replies given. (The similarity with the Entered Apprentice initiation ritual was apparent to me, even at the time.) The Worshipful Master then directed that I be returned to the Senior Warden in the West who would instruct me in the proper manner in which to approach the East. So back to the Senior Warden's station we went and he said that the Senior Deacon should so instruct me.

The thought that this was a wasted trip flickered across my mind when the Senior Deacon turned me around (facing the East) and told me to step off with my left foot as an Entered Apprentice, then take a step with my right foot, bringing the heel of my left foot up to the hollow (instep) of the right one, forming the angle of an oblong square (the Tau Cross).

This was just the way I had done it in the first initiation, except that the extra step resulted in reversing the Tau Cross made with my feet. Then, as before, the Senior Deacon suddenly and loudly said in my ear, "STAND ERECT!" This time I rather expected it, so wasn't startled as I was the first time, but it still had a strange effect on me that I didn't understand.

Then the Worshipful Master began to speak from directly in front of me. He said that our knowledge as Masons is progressive and our obligation is similarly progressive and binding. But he gave me the same assurance as had been given in the Entered Apprentice initiation that nothing in my oath or obligation would conflict with my duty to my God, my country, my neighbor or myself, but said it would merely bind me more closely to the brothers of the Lodge.

He then asked me whether, with that assurance, I were willing to proceed, and I said, "I am." He then told the Senior

Deacon to place me "in due form" at the altar to be made a Fellowcraft.

The Senior Deacon said to me, "Advance! Kneel on your naked right knee, your left forming a square, your body erect, your right hand resting on the Holy Bible, square and compass, your left elbow forming a right angle, supported by the square." He helped me to get into this position, and then said to the Master, "The candidate is in due form, Worshipful Master." There were three raps of a gavel, some shuffling noises, and the Master said, "You will repeat your name and repeat after me: "I, James D. Shaw, of my own free will and accord, in the presence of Almighty God and this Worshipful Lodge, do hereby and hereon solemnly and sincerely promise and swear." I reaffirmed the oath that I had taken as an Entered Apprentice and swore not to reveal any of the secrets of a Fellowcraft Mason to any Entered Apprentice or to any "profane person."[17] I promised to abide by the laws, rules and regulations of a Fellowcraft Lodge and that I would respond to degree. Then I swore not to cheat or defraud, knowingly, a Fellowcraft Lodge or a brother of that degree.[18] To all this I swore, "binding myself under no less a penalty than that of having my left breast torn open, my heart plucked out and given to the beasts of the field and fowls of the air as a prey" should I ever knowingly or willingly violate the oath.

The Worshipful Master then said, "In token of your sincerity, kiss the Holy Bible open before you." As I had done in the first initiation, I leaned forward and kissed the Bible. It gave me a strange sensation.

The Master then told the Senior Deacon that, since I was bound to the Lodge by an oath which cannot be broken (a bond much stronger than any rope) that he was to remove the cabletow from my arm. As soon as it was removed, the Master asked me what I most desired. Prompted by the Senior Deacon, I replied, "Further light" (by this time, I knew better than to ask for cold water).

The Master then said, "Further light being your desire, you shall receive it." As in the first degree, the brothers came down and lined up on either side of me and, as they and the Master clapped their hands, the hoodwink was removed from my eyes. Then the Master called my attention to the fact that this time one point of the compass was hidden beneath the square, which was to teach me that there were still more secrets hidden from my view. He then approached the altar and demonstrated the due-guard and sign of a Fellowcraft Mason. The due-guard consisted of the right arm extended, just below the chest, palm-down, and the left arm raised to form a right angle, just as mine had been while taking the oath. The sign was given by raising the right hand to the left breast and drawing it swiftly across the chest as if tearing it open with claws and then dropping the hand to the side, all in one motion.

The Master then extended his right hand to me "in token of brotherly love and confidence" and demonstrated the pass grip by shaking hands and pressing his thumb between the first and second fingers where they join the hand. He gave me the word, the name of the pass grip, "SHIBBOLETH."

Next came the "real grip," made by putting the thumb on the first knuckle of the second finger so that each can stick the nail of his thumb into the knuckle of the other. The name was given to me as "JACHIN," spoken in the following manner.

While giving the grip, you say, "What is this?"; the answer is "A grip." Then, "A grip of what?"; the reply is "The grip of a Fellowcraft Mason." Question: "Has it a name?"; reply: "It has." Next you say, "Give it me." Reply: "I will letter it or halve it." Then you say, "Halve it and begin." Answer: "Nay, you begin." Again you say, "You begin." The reply: "Ja." My response: "Chin." Then he replies: "Jachin; right brother, I greet you." It was all so complicated but I could only accept it.

Then the Master got an apron and put it on me with appropriate remarks about its importance. The Senior Warden tucked the lower left corner under the top. I was then escorted by the Senior Deacon to the station of the Worshipful Master in the East who presented and explained the significance of "the tools of a Fellowcraft Mason," the plumb, square, and level, applying them to principles of virtue and morality.

He then said, "I further present you with three precious jewels; their names are Faith, Hope and Charity. They teach us to have faith in the Grand Architect of the Universe, hope in immortality and charity to all mankind, more especially a brother Mason."

Then he directed the Senior Deacon to conduct me "out of the Lodge Room" and to "reinvest him with that of which he has been divested" (in ordinary language, to take me back to the Preparation Room and let me put my clothes back on).

My Fellowcraft initiation was almost completed, and I was feeling pretty good about it.

When I had re-dressed I was readmitted to the Lodge Hall and seated. I was told that our forefathers, the ancient Masonic brethren, worked at the building of King Solomon's Temple and many other edifices, Masonic buildings, cathedrals and the like.

The Senior Deacon described the two columns (or pillars) of the Temple, said the name of the left one is Boaz, and that of the right one Jachin. He also went into considerable detail in describing the symbolic significance of the decorations on them.

Then the Master said that I had been admitted to the "Middle Chamber" of King Solomon's Temple for the explanation of the letter "G." He said that it denotes "Deity" before whom we ought all to bow in reverence to worship and adore. He said that it also denotes "Geometry" by means of which "we may track Nature through her various windings to her most concealed recesses." He said that by means of geometry we may better comprehend the perfection of Nature and the "goodness of the Great Artificer of the Universe."

With this brief lecture on the letter "G" my initiation ended and I watched as the remaining candidate was initiated. As was the case when I was initiated into the Entered Apprentice

Degree, my watching the other man not only helped me to understand it all better, but helped me to be off to a good start in memorizing it all for my coming examination in the degree. I was back on the Masonic pathway and picking up speed.

ENDNOTES

13   The exact amount of time required for this varies depending on how quickly the candidate can memorize the material required, but is usually completed in 4-6 weeks.

14   Basic Freemasonry consists of the first three degrees: Entered Apprentice, Fellowcraft, and Master Mason. These constitute the foundation of all Masonry and are conferred and conducted in the local, hometown lodge. The lodge is referred to as "Blue Lodge," and the first three degrees as the "Blue Degrees," because of the importance of the blue sky and its heavenly host of stars and planets. Astrology is extremely important to Masonry, and it is also important that ancient pagans worshiped on high places (hill tops) "under the starry canopy of heaven."

15   American Freemasonry (Blue Lodge and Scottish Rite) is divided into two jurisdictions. The Northern Jurisdiction includes 15 northern and northeastern states; the much-larger Southern Jurisdiction includes the other 35 states, plus all U.S. territories and trusts.

16   This voting is done with white and black balls, dropped into a box. A white ball is a "yes" vote, and a black ball is a "no" vote. If there is even one black ball in the box, the candidate is not accepted for the degree. All such voting is done while the Lodge is in session in the Master Mason (3rd) degree, and only 3rd Degree (Master) Masons can take part.

17   All non-Masons are, according to Masonic law and tradition, "profane" persons. This includes the Mason's wife, children and parents, unless they, too, are Masons. The English word "profane" is derived from the Latin word "profanus," meaning "before, or outside, the temple," hence not holy, not clean, debased and unworthy, a thing to be avoided for it would contaminate the holy and clean ones. If you are not a Mason,

this is what you are to the Masonic world. See, in this regard, I Timothy 1:9-11 for the Bible meaning of "profane."

18   Note that there is no promise not to cheat or defraud the "profane." That seems to be accepted in Masonic morality. See Appendix C, "Masonic Morality."

WHEN POSSIBLE, LODGE HALLS are on the uppermost floor of a building. This symbolizes the worship of the ancients on high places, under the starry heavens with their astrological significance. It also makes security and secrecy easier to maintain. In addition to the top-floor location, note the heavy blue drapes.

***

Master Mason

For the next two weeks the three of us attended training
sessions at the Lodge three nights a week. Once again, it
seemed easy and natural for me to learn the secret degree work.
I was glad to have the first two degrees behind me and was eager
to get on with the work and become a Master Mason. I really
liked the growing sense of acceptance my commitment to the
Lodge gave me; those men were devoting time and energy to
me and my progress in the Craft and the feeling of belonging
did something good for me—something I had wanted for a very
longtime and had not known.

At the end of two weeks (which passed very quickly) we
met at the Lodge for our examination in the Fellowcraft Degree
and initiation into the Master Mason Degree. Once again, we
waited in the Preparation Room in our street clothes while the
Worshipful Master opened the lodge in the Master Mason's
Degree and then "called it off' to the Fellowcraft Degree for
examination.

The Senior Deacon escorted us into the Lodge Hall and
placed us, as before, facing the altar and the Worshipful Master.
Our instructor, who was now our examiner, stood (as before)
facing us with his back to the altar. I felt a strange mixture of
apprehension and eager confidence—like a well-trained athlete
at the start of a race. I was ready.

The examiner questioned us in turn and we all gave the correct answers; although no one of us was asked all of the questions, I could have answered them all. We were then escorted back into the Preparation Room to await the voting by the membership.

They didn't take much time in the voting and the Junior Deacon came into the room to announce that we had all been accepted. There had been no black balls in the ballot box; "the ballot was clear." We were Fellowcraft Masons!

Immediately I was told to remove my clothes and prepare for initiation into the Master Mason degree. The others would be initiated in the following weeks; I was to be initiated alone. I put on the same pajama-like bottoms as before, but this time both legs were rolled up above the knees: and both feet were left bare. I was not given the shirt to put on and was left naked above the waist. The cabletow was wound about my body three times at the waist and then I was hoodwinked. I could see nothing at all—not even any light.

The same questions as before were asked and answered at the door and I was led through the door and into the Lodge Room. The Senior Deacon said, "Brother James, you are received into this Lodge of Master Masons upon the points of the compass extending from your right to left breast, which is to teach you that, as the most vital parts of the man are contained between the breasts, so are the most valuable tenets of Masonry contained between the two extreme points of the compass, which are virtue, morality and brotherly love." The compass points were sharp and I felt them as he made his teaching points.

After being received at the door, I was led to the Worshipful Master who asked for the password. The Senior Deacon, in a whisper, communicated it to him, for me, "Tubal- Cain." Then I was led by the Senior Deacon around the room as before, stopping at the station of the Junior Warden, who sent me to the Senior Warden, who then directed that I be placed at the altar in due form to receive the obligation. I was led to the altar and stood waiting.

From directly in front of me the Master spoke, giving again the assurance that there was nothing in the oath that would conflict with my other duties and commitments; and, once again, I had no way of knowing that what he was saying could not possibly be true.

Asked, as before, if I were willing to proceed with the oath, I replied "I am," and he directed the Senior Deacon to place me "in due form" at the altar to be made a Master Mason.

Taking the Master Mason Oath

The Senior Deacon placed me in position, kneeling this time on both bare knees, body erect, legs forming a square, both hands resting on the square and compass upon the Bible.

Told that I was "in due form" to receive the obligation, the Worshipful Master had me repeat after him, a few words at a time, the oath of obligation: "I, James D. Shaw, of my own free will and accord in the Presence of Almighty God and this Worshipful Lodge, do hereby and hereon solemnly promise and swear; that I will always hail, ever conceal and never reveal, any of the secret arts, parts or points of the Master Mason's degree to any person or persons whomsoever except it be to a true and lawful brother of this degree and not unto him or them until after due trial and strict examination I have found him or them justly entitled to receive the same. I furthermore promise and swear that I will conform and abide by all the laws, rules and regulations of the Master Mason's degree, and of the Lodge of which I shall hereafter become a member, and that I will ever maintain and support the constitution, laws and edicts of the Grand Lodge under whom the same shall work, so far as they shall come to my knowledge. Furthermore, that I will keep the secrets of a worthy Master Mason as inviolable as my own, when communicated to and received by me as such. Furthermore, I will aid and assist all worthy distressed brother Master Masons, their widows and orphans, I knowing them to be such, so far as their necessities may require and my ability will permit without material injury to myself. Furthermore, that I will not assist in, nor be present at, the initiating, passing or raising of a woman, an old man in his dotage, a young man in his non-age, a madman or a fool, I knowing them to be such. I furthermore promise and swear I will not visit a clandestine lodge of Freemasons, nor converse Masonically with a clandestine Mason or with one who has been expelled or suspended, while under that sentence, knowing them to be such.

"I furthermore promise and swear that I will not cheat, wrong or defraud a lodge of Master Masons or a brother of this degree, knowing them to be such, but will give them due and timely notice that they may ward off all approaching danger. I furthermore promise and swear that I will not violate the chastity of a Master Mason's wife, his mother, sister, or daughter, knowing them to be such.[19] I furthermore promise and swear that I will not give the Grand Masonic Word in any other manner than that in which I shall receive it, which shall be on the five points of fellowship and at low breath. I furthermore promise and swear that I will not give the Grand Hailing Sign of Distress except it be in case of most imminent danger, my life in peril, or within a lawfully constituted lodge of Masons. When I hear the words spoken and see the sign given, I will hasten to the aid of the one giving it if there be a greater possibility of saving his life than that of losing my own.

"To all of the which, I do most sincerely promise and swear with a firm and steadfast resolution to keep and perform the same, without the least equivocation, mental reservation or self-evasion whatever, binding myself under no less a penalty than that of having my body severed in twain, my bowels taken out and burned to ashes, the ashes scattered to the four winds of heaven that there should be no more remembrance among men and Masons forever of so vile a wretch as I should be, should I ever knowingly or wittingly violate or transgress this my solemn and binding Master Mason's obligation. So help me God and keep me steadfast."

As had been the case with the oaths of obligation of the first two degrees, I had no idea of what I would be swearing to do until I was actually hearing and repeating each line. Had I been able to hear or read the oath in advance, I might not have been able to say it. Even while taking it as I did, one might expect that the nature of parts of it would have made me hesitate; but I really wasn't thinking of the nature of the oath. I was thinking of Uncle Irvin and how I was now going to be a good and successful man as I supposed him to be. If mother were alive, she would be pleased.

But There Was More

Upon completion of the oath, the Master came down to the altar. He directed the Senior Deacon to remove the cabletow from around my waist since I was now bound by my obligation to the Lodge. He then asked me what I most desired; prompted, I replied "More light." He replied that, since that was my desire, that was what I should receive. As the hoodwink was suddenly removed, the brothers (assembled as before) clapped their hands in unison and my eyes were again dazzled by the sudden bright light. Even though this had happened to me twice before, it was still somewhat startling and disorienting. It was as if a susceptibility or fear had been planted in me the first time and it remained.

The Master then instructed me in making the sign which was made by dropping the left hand to my side, bringing the right hand to the left of my waist, palm-down, and then bringing it quickly across my waist as if severing my body in twain with my thumb, then dropping my right hand to the side.

I was shown to make the due-guard by extending the hands, palm-down, as they had been placed on the square and compass while taking the oath. The pass grip was shown me by grasping the hand in the normal (handshake) way, but pressing the thumb between the second and third joints of the fingers where they join the other's hand. The name of the pass was then given me: "Tubal-Cain."

Thinking I was just about finished with the Master Mason initiation, feeling I was "down to the short rows," I was both listening to the Worshipful Master and feeling a growing sense of pleasant release. I had it made, I thought, and it had been so easy!

I was given an apron and the Senior Warden helped me to put it on as a Master Mason with the "bib" hanging down in front. I was then returned to the preparation room and told to take off the initiation drawers I was in and put my street clothes back on, with the apron.

A plumb emblem, the Junior Warden's "Jewel," was put around my neck; I was now dressed as a Master Mason. I looked myself over as best I could, and was thinking, "Wow! I am a Master Mason at last!"

It was a heady moment and I was exhilarated. But my newfound sense of having arrived didn't last long. I was told that I must be returned to the Lodge Room for further instruction.

An Unexpected Disappointment

Back inside the Lodge Room, still feeling very pleased and proud to be a Master Mason, feeling the exciting newness of wearing the Master Mason's apron and with the plumb emblem around my neck, I was taken to a position before the Worshipful Master.

He said to me, "You have been taught to wear your apron as a Master Mason and you are doing so at the moment. This would imply you are a Master Mason and qualified to travel and work as such. Nay, more, I observe that you have upon your person the badge of office, the Jewel of the Junior Warden, one of the principal officers of the Lodge. This mark of distinction must be highly pleasing to you and doubtless you now consider yourself a Master Mason. Is that not so?"

Suddenly the exhilaration left me and fear took its place. Something was going on that I hadn't expected. I was afraid to say "yes," so I said nothing at all. The Senior Deacon then answered for me, saying, "He is of that opinion, Worshipful Master." The Master then said to me, "It is my duty to tell you that you are *not yet* a Master Mason, nor do I know that you will *ever* be. The road you must travel in order to prove yourself is a long, hard and rough one, upon which lives have been lost, and you may lose yours."

Well, that ended any doubts I had about whether my initiation was over; now I *knew* I was not yet finished. I was not yet a Master Mason and what he said about losing my life sounded ominous. With that strange fear still stirring within me, I was led to the altar and told to kneel and pray for myself, either silently or out loud. I had no idea how to pray, so I just knelt silently with my head bowed and waited.

Living Out the Legend

After kneeling and waiting silently, appearing to pray, I was told to remove all articles from my pockets, take off my watch, and to lay them all on the altar. The hoodwink was once again put over my eyes and I couldn't see a thing.

The Senior Deacon then said to me, "My brother, heretofore you have represented a candidate in search of MORE LIGHT; now you will represent another character, no less a personage than our Grand Master Hiram Abiff,[20] Grand Master and architect at the building of King Solomon's Temple. It was the custom of this great and good man, at high twelve, when the craft were called from labor to refreshment, to enter the Holy of Holies, to offer up his adorations to Deity and draw his designs upon his trestle board."

All the time he was telling me this, he was leading me around the room. Trying to listen and understand while stumbling along blindfolded was difficult and awkward for me.

He continued, "He then passed out by way of the South Gate to talk to the workmen, as you will do now."

After being led a few more steps, I was accosted by a brother representing the character Jubela, (it was actually the Junior Warden). He spoke to me as if I were actually Hiram Abiff, and grabbed me by the lapels. He said that I had promised to reveal the secret word of a Master Mason when the Temple was completed, that it was nearly completed, and demanded that I give him the secret word then and there. All the while, as he spoke roughly to me, he was jerking me around and really roughing me up.

The Senior Deacon, speaking for me, said, "Craftsman, this is neither the time nor the place. Wait until the Temple is finished and then you shall have the secrets of a Master Mason."

Jubela then got even more violent, demanding the secret word, right then! Again speaking for me, the Senior Deacon said, "Craftsman, I cannot and will not give them," upon which Jubela struck a blow across my throat with the 24-inch gauge. It hurt and startled me and I was immediately hurried a few steps farther where I was stopped and grabbed by a second "ruffian," called Jubelo. This one *really* jerked me around, and said, "Grand Master Hiram Abiff, the craft are waiting and many are exceedingly anxious to receive the secrets of a Master Mason, and we see no good reason why we are put off so long. We have determined that we will wait no longer. I therefore *demand* of you the secrets of a Master Mason!"

Again speaking for me, the Senior Deacon said, "Craftsman, why all this violence? When the Temple is finished, you shall receive this secret word; I cannot, nor will not, give them to you at this time."

Jubelo then became even more furious and again demanded the word, upon which the Senior Deacon answered for me, "I cannot give them nor can they be given except in the presence of three: Solomon, King of Israel; Hiram, King of Tyre; and myself."

Jubelo, becoming *still more* violent, reminded me that there was no one there to help me and threatened to kill me if I didn't give him the word.

For me, the Senior Deacon replied, "My life you may take, but my integrity, *never!*"

Jubelo then struck a heavy blow across my chest with the square. It hurt, but I was immediately jerked away and led a few more steps when I was grabbed a third time and shaken. This was all very real, even though it was obvious that parts were being acted out. I was being jerked about, shoved, shouted at and hit by people I couldn't see. I had great difficulty in keeping my balance (if the "ruffians" hadn't been holding onto my coat I would have fallen several times), and the violence was even more shocking because I couldn't see it coming.

The third "ruffian," Jubelum, said as he was shaking me that he had heard me speaking to Jubela and Jubelo and saw that I had escaped, but said I would *not* escape from him *ever*. He said that what he said, he would do, and that he held in his hand "an instrument of death." He said that if I didn't give him the secrets of a Master Mason immediately he would kill me.

Speaking for me again, the Senior Deacon replied as he had already replied to Jubela and Jubelo. Jubelum then shouted at me, "For the last time, Grand Master Hiram, give me the secret word or I will take your life!"

I, of course, didn't realize it, but as Jubelum readied himself to deliver the death blow, several of the brothers moved into position behind me, holding a large canvas, stretched out so as to catch me when I fell.

With that, Jubelum shouted, "If you will not give me the secret word of a Master Mason, then ... DIE!"

As he shouted the word, "DIE," he hit me right in the middle of my forehead with a setting maul! I saw stars. They were brilliant and in colors, and I fell backward onto the canvas, unconscious.[21]

I wasn't out very long and I came to, head still ringing and aching, with the three "ruffians" standing around me, talking over the situation, and discussing how to dispose of the body. They decided to conceal the body "in the rubbish of the Temple" until low twelve" (midnight), when they would meet and decide what to do. So they carried me, on the canvas, a little distance and covered me with "rubbish," consisting of chairs and other objects in the Lodge Hall. There was silence, then I heard a bell strike 12 times and the "ruffians" returned. Jubela said, "This is the hour."

Jubelo said, "This is the place." Jubelum then said, "And there is the body. Assist me to carry it in a due west course from the temple to the brow of a hill where I have dug a grave, six feet due east and west, and six feet perpendicular, in which we shall bury it."

They removed the chairs and other "Temple rubbish" from me, picked me up on the canvas, carried me to the west side of the Lodge Room and laid me down between the stations of the Master and the Senior Warden, my feet to the east. They lowered me to the floor a little at a time, pausing three times, to simulate lowering me into a grave.

After I was "buried," Jubelum said, "I will set this sprig of Acacia at the head of the grave, that the place may be known should the occasion require it. And now let us make our escape out of the country by the way of Joppa. We should be able to get a ship to take us to a foreign port."

The "ruffians" then acted out a scene in which they talked with a sea captain and asked for passage on his ship which was to sail the next day. Learning they could not sail without a pass from King Solomon, they decided to flee into the mountains and hide.

Meanwhile, the Worshipful Master, acting the part of King Solomon, heard a lot of commotion made by other brothers acting as workmen in the Temple. Solomon asked what the noise was all about and was told that Grand Master Hiram Abiff was missing and could not be found.

King Solomon ordered that a search be made and the brothers then did a lot of talking back and forth while I lay there, saying such things as, "Have you seen him?" "Not since high twelve yesterday," and, "Where is our Grand Master?"

Then King Solomon ordered that a search be made with one party going west, one east, one north, and one south. At this point there were three loud raps on the door and when the "alarm was attended" there were found to be 12 "Fellowcrafts" who confessed to the King that they and three others had conspired to force Hiram to reveal the secret word. They said that they (the 12) had not been able to go through with their evil plan, having "reflected with horror on the atrocity of the crime," but reported that the other three had gone through with it.

The King then sent out those 12, three in each direction, to search for Jubela, Jubelo and Jubelum. One group of three spoke with the sea captain and, following the direction he gave them, followed the murderers' path and found the new grave, marked with the Acacia sprig. Digging down, they "discovered" my body.

Reporting to Solomon, they were sent back to identify the body and, if Hiram, to raise it with the grip of an Entered Apprentice.

As the drama continued, they returned to the "grave" and saw that I was indeed Hiram;[22] but they could not "raise" me, as the body was decomposing, so the "flesh left the bone." They reported the problem to Solomon, who sent them back to raise the body with the grip of a Fellowcraft. When "the skin (slipped) away" they reported this failure to Solomon.

Then the Master, playing King Solomon, came over to me and took my hand with the grip of a Master Mason, "the strong grip of the lion's paw"[23] and, with the other hand behind my back, assisted me to a standing position. I was fully recovered by this time, but still stiff and a little wobbly from the strain and from lying still for so long while the latter part of the drama was acted out.

The Master explained that while the secret word of the Master Mason had been lost when Hiram was killed, the first word he spoke when raised from the dead was the substitute for the "lost word." He then placed his right foot alongside mine, instep to instep, his knee against mine, his chest against mine and his mouth next to my right ear. With my hand placed on his back, we were "on the five points of fellowship: foot to foot, knee to knee, chest to chest, hand to back and mouth to ear." He whispered into my ear the Grand Masonic Word, "Mah-Hah-Bone," and instructed me that it must never be given to any but another Master Mason, only "on the five points of fellowship" as he had given it to me and never above a whisper, under penalty of death.

I was then instructed by the Worshipful Master in giving the "Grand Hailing Sign of Distress." The Grand Hailing Sign of Distress is given by raising the hands above the head and looking up, then lowering the hands in supplication, then dropping them to the side. The words accompanying the sign are, "Oh, Lord my God, is there no help for the widow's son?"

He explained to me that I was never to give this sign unless in the most extreme distress and that it is the most important Masonic secret. I was reminded of the part of my obligation relating to my responsibility should another Master Mason ever give this sign to me and, with this, my initiation as a Master Mason was really finished at last.

With the instruction finished I was seated and there followed a rather long and involved lecture on the meaning of the symbols of a Master Mason and the lengthy charge of a Master Mason. When the Master closed the Lodge, the brothers crowded around me with congratulations and then went home.

Bonnie was waiting up for me and we shared the sense of accomplishment together. She was pleased and proud of me. It was a really wonderful moment of fulfillment. If only mother could know; I had a good job, a wonderful wife, and I had finally caught up with Uncle Irvin. I was a Master Mason.

ENDNOTES

19   It is noteworthy when considering Masonic morality that the Master Mason swears that he will not have sexual intercourse with the wife, mother, daughter, or sister of another Master Mason, "knowing her to be such"; apparently this is alright with anyone else's wife, mother, daughter, or sister and is even all right with those of a Master Mason if unaware of the Masonic relationship. Concerning this see Appendix C, "Masonic Morality."

20   For the purpose and significance of this dramatization of the legend of Hiram Abiff, see Appendix D, "The Legend of Hiram Abiff."

21   The man portraying Jubelum isn't supposed to hit the candidate that hard, but Jim was really knocked unconscious. The man who hit him was an undertaker, and the members of the lodge had many laughs later about his trying to drum up business in the Lodge while acting the part of Jubelum.

22   In the drama, the junior warden's "jewel," (symbol of the junior warden's rank), which was still around Jim's neck, plays a significant role in the candidate's being recognized as Hiram by the searchers.

23   The Master's Grip, or the "Strong Grip of the Lion's Paw," was not explained to Jim; but he had felt it and. in watching subsequent initiations, learned it. Jim later had occasions to use it as a Master Mason's pass grip, an alternate means of recognition to the primary grip explained by the Master that night. This grip is given by grasping the other's hand in the normal way, except that the thumb and small finger are wrapped around the edges of the hand, just below the thumb, with the middle three fingertips dug into the inside of the other's wrist. As Worshipful Master himself later on, Jim, used it in "raising the candidate."

Going Higher

Before I was even through with the Master Mason degree, I had noticed something, and decided something—two things that would shape the rest of my Masonic life. I noticed that a great many Masons were not only satisfied to stop at the Third Degree, but they often came to Lodge and, after about 45 minutes, went to sleep and slept through the rest of the meeting. This greatly offended me. My decision was that I would not be that kind of Mason—*not ever!*

I was determined to learn and to grow, to keep moving on up in the fraternity, to climb the "Masonic mountain." At that early point in my Masonic career I really didn't know what there was to be accomplished. I didn't know what higher ground there was to be reached; but I knew that I didn't want to come to Lodge and sleep like those men did. Whatever there was to achieve, I wanted it. I was going higher!

From Candidate to Instructor—Immediately

Within a month after I was raised to the Third Degree there was a new class of candidates to be brought through the Blue Degrees. I was still a "courtesy candidate" (Bonnie and I were still expecting to go back to Indianapolis), and grateful to that Lodge for bringing me through the Second and Third Degrees.

I was never bashful about such things, so I said to the Worshipful Master, "Sir, I am grateful to this Lodge and to you, and feel that l owe you something for what you have done for me. If you will appoint me, I will be glad to be the Instructor for this new class of candidates. "

He thought a moment, looking at me intently, and then said that I had the job. I could hardly believe it. I had just been raised, a member of the most recent class, and now I was the Instructor! I thanked the Master and promised to do my very best. I could hardly wait to get started.

The next week we took the class through the Entered Apprentice initiation and they took their first obligation. The following week I arranged to meet with them for instruction and a month later they were ready to take their examination. They all passed, were then "passed" into the Fellowcraft Degree, and the week after that I began to instruct them in the memory work of that degree. At the end of that month they were ready for examination in the Fellowcraft Degree and again they all passed easily.

They were motivated and I had taught them well. Then, one each week, they were raised to the Master Mason degree and I had the satisfaction of knowing that I had brought the entire class through all three Blue Degrees. I was not only a Master Mason now, I was a *maker* of Master Masons! It really felt good.

Why Leave at All?

By this time I had gone to work for the city and had an excellent job. Bonnie was well established in her job and was enjoying it. I was accepted in the Lodge and had a real sense of belonging. The more we thought and talked about it, the less reason we saw in leaving to go back to Indianapolis. There had been no hurry about leaving Florida and what we had found there through the winter and spring; and now, as we considered the situation, we asked ourselves, "Why shouldn't we just stay here? Why leave at all?"

So we decided: we would just settle in and stay right there. Florida would be our home. I would no longer be just a "courtesy candidate" or a visitor in the Lodge; it would be *my* Lodge. I would really *belong* there. With the decision made, we began to settle in and "get permanent."

Roy and his family moved to the west coast of Florida and we missed them, but that didn't matter so much now. We were making new friends in the Lodge.

Moving Up Through the Chairs

Not long after, elections were held in our Lodge and a new Worshipful Master was elected. I had already found out that there was a normal progression through the offices in the Lodge, beginning with the lowest office (Junior Steward) and proceeding up to the top (Worshipful Master). Since each office has a position (or "chair") in the Lodge Hall, this progression upward through the offices in the Blue Lodge is often called "moving up through the chairs." The positions of Junior and Senior Steward and Junior and Senior Deacon are appointed positions and men are selected for them by the Worshipful Master. The three top offices, Junior and Senior Warden and Worshipful Master, are elected positions. But the normal situation is that, once elected Junior Warden, that man will "move up." He can expect to move up to Senior Warden the following year and to the chair of Worshipful Master the year after that. Barring something unusual, these elections are virtually automatic.

As soon as I had the opportunity, I went to see the newly elected Worshipful Master and told him that I didn't want to be an "ordinary Mason." I said that I never wanted to be like those brothers who slept through the meetings, and I asked him to consider appointing me to a chair (an office) in the Lodge. I must have made a positive impression on him for he appointed me Senior Deacon, the highest appointed office in the Lodge. I had bypassed the three lowest offices and was off to a *big* head start in moving up through the chairs.

Beyond the Blue Lodge

Blue Lodge Masonry is the heart of Masonry and the Third Degree is the heart of the Blue Lodge. If one is not a Master Mason in good standing in the Blue Lodge, he cannot "go on" into the York Rite or the Scottish Rite and thence to "the top of the Masonic mountain." And, once advanced in the York Rite or the Scottish Rite, he cannot remain in those bodies (or the Shrine) if he doesn't continue in good standing in the Blue Lodge. This is the general structure and the Blue Lodge is its foundation.

I had been in the Blue Lodge about four months, had taken a class of candidates through all three degrees, and was Senior Deacon, learning, growing and feeling good about it when one day I was talking with a brother who owned a lumber yard.

He said, "I thought you joined the Masonic Lodge."

I said that I had and that I was very active.

He said something about the Scottish Rite and wondered why he hadn't seen me there.

I didn't know what he was talking about, but sensed that it was something I would want to do.

He said, "Jim, you've just got to get into the Scottish Rite, because you really don't know what Masonry is all about until you do. The Scottish Rite and its 29 degrees will really open your eyes." He said that if I wanted him to, he would get me a petition and get things rolling.

I said that it sounded good to me and asked him to go ahead. Although I was eager to begin, I found out that I couldn't enter the Scottish Rite until I had been a Master Mason for six months. But he went ahead with the petition while I waited. I went right on with my work in the Blue Lodge, the most eager and zealous man they had.

Two Paths From Which to Choose

As I have already said, the Blue Lodge, with its three degrees, is the heart and foundation of Freemasonry. This is where the vast majority of Masons stop and go no farther, their local lodge being all they ever know of Masonry. However, for those who are not willing to stay at that level, there are two options for "going on higher," two paths to follow: they are the Scottish Rite and the York Rite.

The Scottish Rite includes 29 degrees beyond the master Mason (3rd) degree, culminating in the 32nd degree. The York Rite has the equivalent of the 29 degrees of the Scottish Rite and advancement along this path culminates in the degree "Knight Templar." In addition, the Shrine ("Ancient Arabic Order, Nobles of the Mystic Shrine") has been available to 32nd Degree Masons and Knights Templar who wish to participate. In recent years, due to flagging membership, the Shrine has lowered its standards for membership; men can now go from the Blue Lodge, directly into the Shrine. For more information on the Shrine and its requirements for membership, see "The Shrine: Islam in Masonry" in Part Two of this book.

Devoted to community service and fun (and with the emphasis definitely on "fun," the Shriners are looked upon as the "party boys" of Freemasonry, and are best known for their hospitals for crippled children, for light-hearted participation in parades, and for their riotous, drunken parties and conventions.

Although at the time I was not fully aware of these options and how it all goes together, my path was determined. I was going into the Scottish Rite.

Into the Scottish Rite

The more my friend talked to me about the Scottish Rite, the more eager I was to get started in it. In the Scottish Rite, initiations are conducted and degrees conferred during meetings called "reunions" which are normally held twice a year, Fall and Spring.

In addition to the initiations into the degrees, there is also recognition of those brothers who have died since the previous reunion. They are, in this sense, memorials to the departed brothers. I could hardly wait for the Fall Reunion to come. As the time approached, I was told to report to the Secretary of the Scottish Rite for a briefing. I was there early, waiting for my turn to be called into his office.

The Secretary greeted me and explained the nature and structure of the Scottish Rite. He explained that the 29 degrees are divided into four groups called the "Four Bodies" of the Rite and that each of these bodies is somewhat like a separate lodge within the system. He also explained to me that the Reunion would last for four Sundays and that it would be possible for me to take all 29 degrees in the one Reunion, or just go to the 14th Degree at this Reunion and then continue to the 32nd Degree in the spring. He said that some men could not afford to take all of the degrees at one Reunion because of the cost.[24] He told me that the first of the four "bodies" of the Scottish Rite is called "Lodge of Perfection" and is the one in which business meetings are held on meeting nights. The second body, he said, is the "Chapter of Rose Croix," the third is the "Council of Kodosh" and the fourth is "The Consistory."

It all sounded wonderful to me and I asked the Secretary if I could just pay for all 29 of the degrees right then! He gave me the figure, I wrote the check, and he told me to report on the next Sunday (the first day of the Fall Reunion). He told me that we would meet from 9 a.m. to 6 p.m. each Sunday for the next four Sundays to receive instruction, and that on the fourth Sunday I would be made a 32nd Degree Mason.

I asked him if I would have to memorize all the passwords, signs and grips and then pass examinations as we had to do in the Blue Lodge, and he *roared* with laughter!

He said, "Are you kidding? It would take you a whole *year* of Sundays to do that! You just be here Sunday and you will find out."

On the morning of the first Sunday of the Fall Reunion I arrived promptly and, as soon as all the rest arrived, we were ushered into a large classroom. There were about 250 of us and our class was given the name "George Washington Bicentennial Class" (each class is given a name, or title, which it retains as long as there are any of its members left alive).

Our instructor was an attorney, a man in his sixties. His age and knowledge made him seem a little "larger than life" to me, very impressive, and I listened carefully to all that he said. He also had a sense of humor, which made him even more effective. I was totally receptive.

We had to have an "opening ceremony" which gave our class official identity and status and then we had a class picture taken. We also had to elect class officers, but I didn't try for any of those offices as I was only interested in the degree work (the lessons in religion and morality). I wanted to *learn*.

Through the Degrees

With all the preliminaries completed, we were taken into the auditorium. It was like a large and very nice theater, with fully equipped stage, sophisticated lighting and theater seats. We were told to be seated and the presentation of the Fourth Degree began.

The Fourth Degree was put on just like a play, with one candidate chosen from the class to represent us all as he participated. The presentation went on until time to take the oath at the end. At this time we were told to stand, put our hands over our hearts and repeat the oath[25] of obligation with the representative candidate on the stage. After we finished the oath we were given the sign of that degree,[26] and the Fourth Degree was completed. When a degree is given in this way it is said to be "exemplified."

When a degree is not put on as a drama, but merely explained, it is said to be "communicated." Such was the case with the Fifth Degree. Back in the classroom the Degree Master explained the content and meaning of the degree, administered the oath, and gave us the sign.

Now we were Fifth Degree Masons, and ready for the Sixth Degree. And so we progressed, through the degrees. The relatively unimportant degrees, about one third of the total of 29, were "communicated" in this way. It is also true that some degrees which are merely "communicated" in one Reunion will be "exemplified" at the following Reunion. The degrees of the Four Bodies (the four degrees whose names identify the Four Bodies), however, are always put on in full and not merely "communicated." That Sunday we completed the Fourth through the Ninth Degrees and I went home feeling good about it all.

I was so interested in the degree work that I could hardly wait from one Sunday until the next. The "old religions" (the mystery religions of Egypt, Greece, Persia, etc.) were taught. And, as I had never had a religion, but had only heard passing references to the major ones, I was fascinated.

There was also a great deal said about the ancient philosophers and occultists and I felt that I was really growing in knowledge. Each week I would tell my brother Masons in the Blue Lodge how great it was and how much they were missing by not being in the Scottish Rite. But this was not always well-received; some were really offended and a few hurt, because they could not afford to go into the Rite. So, although my zeal didn't diminish any, I tried to be more careful about such enthusiastic talk.

On the second Sunday we completed the 14th degree, the Degree of Perfect Elu, generally considered the halfway mark in the Scottish Rite. With this attainment comes the 14th Degree ring. This flat gold band with the Hebrew letter "YOD" on it is the official Masonic ring.

Many kinds of rings with Masonic symbols may be purchased and worn; but, except for the Thirty-third Degree ring, this ring is the only official one. It is the patent and property of the Supreme Council of the Thirty-third Degree, and is only obtained when presented with the 14th degree. In our case the rings had not arrived so we had to wait to get them the final Sunday.

Anointed a Priest and a Prophet

Finally, the last Sunday of Reunion arrived and we progressed to the 32nd Degree. Upon completion of the degree work, climaxing with the 32nd Degree lecture, we stood and were brought forward. One by one, we were anointed with oil. As the man placed his hand on my head and applied the oil, he said to me, "I anoint thee a Priest and a Prophet, and a Sublime Prince of the Royal Secret."

This part was definitely a new experience for me and I certainly didn't understand the part about being a priest and a prophet, but it was impressive and I liked the sound and solemnity of it. For me, it was rather awesome and a little unreal.

Each of us was presented, along with the Scottish Rite ring, a copy of Albert Pike's book, *Morals and Dogma*.[27] We were told that it was *the* source book for Freemasonry and its meaning. We were also told that it must never leave our possession, and that arrangements must be made so that upon our deaths it would be returned to the Scottish Rite. It was clear that this book was not only a terribly important source but was, it seemed, almost sacred.

It had all been so very interesting to me and, in a way, the time had passed much too quickly. I felt that I had learned so much, yet felt that I had so much more to learn.

"Perhaps in the future I will get to *work* in these degrees," I thought. "Then I can *really* learn about religions."

It was only about 5 P.M. when we finished and, after a lot of exchanging congratulations, I hurried home to tell Bonnie all about it (at least the parts I was free to tell her). As I headed home I was thinking, "If only mother had lived to see this day—she would really be proud."

ENDNOTES

24 There is a price to be paid, in dollars, for all "earned" Masonic degrees, from Entered Apprentice to the 32nd Degree. Dollar values change with time and fees vary some from place to place, but the total cost of going all the way to the 32nd Degree can be very substantial, from hundreds to thousands of dollars.

25　There is a blood-oath of obligation for each degree, as in the Blue Lodge. Unlike the Blue Lodge, however, since there was no memorizing, and since they were not written down, the candidates normally remember nothing of these oaths once they are spoken.

26　In all Jim's years of Masonry that followed, he was never once asked to give this sign.

27　Albert Pike (1809-1891) is easily the preeminent figure in American Freemasonry. His many lofty titles included "Sovereign Grand Commander of the Supreme Council of the Thirty-third Degree (Mother Council of the World)"; and "Supreme Pontiff of Universal Freemasonry." A scholar, student of ancient languages, and occult philosopher, he completely rewrote the degrees of the Scottish Rite into their present form. This work is explained in his magnum opus, the book, *Morals and Dogma of the Ancient and Accepted Scottish Rite of Freemasonry*. His position in Masonry was, and is today, unparalleled, not only in the United States, but throughout the world

Branching Out

The Monday after my initiation into the 32nd Degree, I was congratulated by a number of my superiors at work whom I had not even realized had been there. The extent of Masonry and its influence was far greater than I had suspected. Realizing that there were so many men such as these, seemingly everywhere, who were part of the Masonic brotherhood, and that they knew who I was and what I was doing, was both comforting and vaguely disturbing. But it was mostly comforting. I was seeing that this Masonic family of which I had become a committed part reached much farther into every part of life than I had suspected, and much of this Masonic family was invisible to the rest of the world.

Suddenly a Promotion

A short while after, the director of my department called me in and asked me to take an examination for a higher position which was opening up. I felt that I was completely unqualified for this position and told him so, But he smiled reassuringly, said that he thought I was qualified and urged me not to fail to take the test. I was so convinced that I wasn't qualified for the job that I almost decided not to show up; but, because of his urging, I went.

Expecting a room full of men competing for so important a job, I was surprised when I arrived to find that only two others were taking the test with me. I was given the examination paper and told to turn it face down on my desk until time for the examination to begin. When we were told to begin and I looked over the test, I was *amazed* at the simplicity of the questions. I thought, "Is this all there is to it? I'm sure glad the boss insisted that I come!"

I finished my paper quickly and easily. The other two men continued to struggle with theirs and were still working when the examiner told them to stop. We were told to turn our papers face down on the desks and leave, for time had expired. He said we would be notified later as to how we had done. I left thinking about how easy the test had been and wondering why the other two had seemed to have such a difficult time with it.

I went directly to the office and the director was waiting for me. He met me at the door, stuck out his hand and said, "Congratulations, Jim, you got the promotion! You were the only one who knew all the answers. You will soon be called to take an 'on-the job' training course, and then you can start on your new job."

He shook my hand again and went back to his office. I was pleased but a little bewildered. I still could not understand how it had been so easy and *how* could he know so soon that I was selected? Why, the ink was barely dry on my paper!

With questions about this still whispering in my mind, but mostly just excited and happy, I hurried home at the end of the day to tell Bonnie. She was, of course, delighted too. In light of her good job, plus my promotion, we decided to move out of the duplex apartment and buy our own home. We were making progress!

But Uncle Irvin Wasn't Pleased

I called Uncle Irvin to tell him the good news about my being in the Scottish Rite. I thought he would be pleased and proud. But he didn't seem pleased or proud of me at all. He appeared to resent it, envious of my being a 32nd Degree Mason.

He said that he had never been allowed to enter the Rite, and went on to explain, "Even though I was Past Master of my Lodge, I couldn't go in because there was a man in the Scottish Rite who didn't like me. He said that if I ever tried to enter he would 'blackball' me."

I was amazed, and asked, "Whatever became of' 'Masonic brotherhood'?"

Uncle Irvin wouldn't answer my question, so I didn't tell him that he had been lied to by that brother Mason. As long as a man is a Master Mason in good standing in his Blue Lodge, he *cannot* be blackballed and kept out of the Scottish Rite.

The Raising of Mike and the "Honds-off Policy"

Working with me on the same shift was a man named Mike. He was a Scotsman with a wonderful accent, a warm heart and a somewhat quick temper. He was not very tall, but very solidly built and strong as a bull. He had been badly injured as a fireman in New York City and. after a long time in the hospital, had retired from the Fire Department. He had come to Florida, had found work with the civil service of our large city, was assigned to my department, and we had become friends. Mike knew that I was a Mason (I had spoken to him about it from time to time), and one day he told me that he would like to be a Mason too. I, of course, was pleased, and asked him if he would like to belong to my Lodge. He said that was exactly what he wanted, so I got a petition and had another man (who worked with us) to sign it with me. Mike was duly investigated, approved, and was soon ready to take the degrees.

As I was now Senior Deacon, I was the one to conduct candidates through the initiations. I was pleased that I was going to get to lead my friend through. It happened that Mike was the only man going through at that time so things moved along smoothly and quickly. I had a pretty easy time of it—until the latter part of the Third Degree.

Before we began that final night of Mike's Blue Lodge initiation, I spoke with the three men who were to portray the "three ruffians" Jubela, Jubelo, and Jubelum. I asked them to take it easy on Mike and explained why. They said they understood and would be gentle with him.

Everything went smoothly until we came to the part where I was leading Mike, as Hiram Abiff, to the "South Gate" where he was met by Jubela, the first "ruffian." As is always done, Jubela grabbed him and jerked him around a bit. It was gentle compared with what the candidate usually goes through, but it was too much for Mike, much too much, and he *erupted*! He pushed Jubela away, ripped off the hoodwink, roared like a mad bull and picked Jubela up! In one mighty motion, Mike threw him across the Lodge Hall. Jubela hit the black and white tiles and went sliding across the floor on his back, spinning slowly around and slid right up against the altar, which stopped him. He wasn't hurt badly, but lay there against the altar, not moving.

Mike had assumed a wrestler's stance, feet widespread, powerful arms at the ready, and bellowed out, "No mon puts his honds on me!" At first there was not a sound in the Lodge Hall, except for Mike. He stood there, looking slowly around the room, glaring at the brothers assembled, and continued to roar, "No mon puts his honds on me!"

Suddenly the Lodge was in an uproar. Some of the brothers convulsed with laughter, some were shouting excitedly at one another and some sat still in stunned silence. Mike was still standing there, challenging them all, and continuing to roar, "No mon puts his honds on me!" This scene in the sacred precincts of the Lodge Hall was unprecedented, unheard of, *unthinkable*!

Many of the brothers were looking at the Worshipful Master, expecting him to "do something"; but he wasn't any more ready to "do something" about Mike than was Jubela the ruffian, who was still lying quietly against the altar. The Master just sat there in stunned silence, still as a statue in his black top hat, looking straight ahead.

I tried to calm Mike down but had no effect at all on him. I then went over to consult with the Worshipful Master. I tried to explain and told him that if I could take Mike out to the Preparation Room I thought I could calm him down and we would be able to proceed, He nodded his head and continued to sit there, glassy eyed, staring straight ahead, not moving.

I went back to Mike, who was still turning slowly from side to side in the center of this sudden storm, and spoke again with him. He agreed to go out with me. We closed the Lodge Hall door behind us. In the Preparation Room Mike began to relax some and I told him I was really sorry about what had happened and would try to work it out so that we could proceed with his initiation. He just said, "All right Jim—but *no* mon puts his honds on me!"

I left Mike in the Preparation Room and went back out to consult again with the Worshipful Master. I told him I thought it would be best to leave out Jubelo and Jubelum and just have Mike lie down on the canvas and let them bury him. The Master looked at me strangely and then asked, "Forever?"

Since that was all the Master said, I took it that my compromise solution was acceptable, so I returned to the Preparation Room. I explained to Mike the whole scene and what was going to happen. I told him that if he would just let us do the rest of it, gently, it would soon be over and he would be a Master Mason. He agreed, but firmly repeated the admonition, "No mon puts his honds on me." So we went back into the Lodge Hall, let him lie down on the canvas and completed his initiation, albeit considerably modified. Mike never lived down that night and for years there were many jokes and much laughter concerning Mike and the "Honds-Off Policy."

I Become a Degree Master

The Master of the 25th Degree in the Scottish Rite moved to California, and I was appointed to replace him. I got from him the degree book and, although it was not required of me, I memorized the entire degree (the ritual and lesson to be taught or performed in that degree). It was to be exemplified (put on in full, as a dramatization) at the next Reunion. I was determined to do it better than it had ever been done before.

Mike and I not only continued to be friends, but became closer and closer. With my encouragement he soon came into the Scottish Rite with me; since it is the "Scottish" Rite it seemed to me that we should have at least one Scotsman. Since by that time I was Master of the 25th Degree, I appointed Mike Orator. With his heavy Scottish accent, he seemed the perfect choice. I gave him his part and had him memorize it. When I told him he would have to wear a pasted-on artificial beard he decided just to grow his own, and he did.

When Reunion came around we were ready. It all went perfectly. The Secretary was so pleased with the way we exemplified the degree that he thanked and congratulated us all, making all the hard work and rehearsing worth it. We had not just "gotten by"; rather, we had done it better than anyone could remember its ever having been done before.

Filling the Void: A Religion at Last

From the very beginning I had been troubled by the fact that so many of the men just came to Lodge and sat there. When the Master rapped, they stood up; when he rapped again, they sat down. When he said anything that called for a vote, they said "So mote it be," and when the meeting came to an end they got up and went home. Some had to be awakened and told it was time to leave. Many were members for many years, and always sat in the same seat. I was determined not to be such a "seat warmer"; I wanted to function, to learn all that there was to learn. I wanted to grow, and that was exactly what I was doing—at last.

I have vivid memories of sitting, as a boy, on our front porch steps in Indianapolis, looking to the west, watching the Sun go down and the stars appear, ever-brighter in the deepening darkness of evening twilight. I wondered about the meaning of it. Surely, I reasoned, all of that vastness and beauty didn't just happen; surely there must be a Creator, one Who made all of this and causes it to function so perfectly. Out there somewhere, far above and beyond what I could see, there must be God, and I longed to learn of Him. More than that, I longed to find Him and know Him. But, in our unhappy home, there was no God; and when I asked about Him, or asked to be allowed to go to a Sunday School to learn of Him, the result was ridicule, verbal abuse and, not infrequently, severe beatings. Eventually I stopped asking.

As I had said to the incoming Worshipful Master when asking him to consider me for "a chair" in the Blue Lodge; I had no intention of just settling down and getting comfortable as a Mason. Later, looking back on it all, I realized why I was so eager to get to the higher offices and to do it so soon. It was not just prideful ambition, or a desire for recognition. It was something much more valid and substantial, some deeply felt need down deep inside of me. Having grown up with no religious training, no church affiliation of any kind, and no spiritual identity, I really had no concept of the meaning of life. I had no philosophy, nor any basic worldview concerning life, death and eternity. And, without realizing it at first, this emptiness in my life began to be filled with what I was learning and doing in Masonry. In the Lodge I had at last found the family that I had never had; and now, increasingly, the Lodge was filling the spiritual void. There, in the Lodge, I had not only found a family; in addition, I was at last on a pathway that would take me to God. I was finding a religion.

A Chaplin Learns to Pray

In the Scottish Rite I became acquainted with the undertaker who had knocked me out with the setting maul when I was initiated into the Third Degree. He was to be the new Venerable Master of the Lodge of Perfection (one of the Four Bodies and the one in which all business meetings are held).

I hadn't seen him for a while and told him of my appointment as Senior Deacon in the Blue Lodge. I then told him that I would like to be an officer in the Lodge of Perfection, if he had room for me, and he said he would keep me in mind.

I realize that this may sound a little pushy, but actually it wasn't; it is not at all easy for incoming Masters to get men to volunteer for offices and they usually appreciate such willingness. As is the case in all walks of life, most want the "honor" of belonging, but do not want to do the work. I didn't know what to expect from him, but when he assumed office he appointed me Chaplain.

At last I was finding a place for myself; I was an officer in both the Blue Lodge and the Scottish Rite. But there was a problem, a big one; as Chaplain I was going to have to pray and I didn't know how. I had not been in church since the last time my grandmother had taken me and I knew nothing of prayer. I had heard the prayers from the ritual in the Lodge, but couldn't remember any of them. I asked the new Venerable Master about praying and he eased my mind some. He said that he would give me two cards with the opening and closing prayers printed on them and that I could simply read them out loud. But he also said that I would be expected to "give prayers" at banquets and at the assembling of the Scottish Rite Guard. So I would have to get an idea of how to pray and what prayers to use. There was no way around it. I was going to have to learn to pray.

We had a new man in the incoming class at the Blue Lodge who was pastor of the Methodist Church next door to the Lodge Hall. I called on him and told him I was the new Chaplain in the Lodge of Perfection and that I needed to know something about prayer. He said he would help me and the next day when I looked in my mail box I found a book called "The Prayers of John Wesley."

I studied the book and then wrote out several of the prayers, just as they were in the book, just as Wesley wrote them. I thought they were really good and felt that I was at last prepared for my new office. Whenever I was called upon to pray, I could just read one of those prayers out loud. I was ready—or so I thought.

At the next assembling of the Scottish Rite Guard (for the opening of the initiation of a new class at Reunion) I gave the prayer while the Guard of 25 men stood. It was one of the prayers of John Wesley I had taken from the book.

I thought the prayer was first rate and felt good about it; but when the opening ceremony was finished the Commander of the Guard called me aside and rebuked me sharply. He said, "You kept my men standing at attention for five whole minutes!" He also called me a "religious fanatic" and said that it was bad enough I kept the men standing five minutes, but *then* I had ended the prayer "in Christ's holy name." For *that,* he said, I would be *reported*! I was stung by his rebuke, especially since I had worked so hard to get it right and had no idea I was doing anything wrong.

I said since he was so rude to me I didn't care what he thought, that I didn't know anything about his 30-second prayers, and that from that time on he could say them himself!

As I walked away, I thought, "Some brother *he* is, to speak to me like that! At least he could have left out that part about 'religious fanatic' since I don't even know what prayers are except for the ones on the cards and in the book."

Very soon after, I was called in to see the Secretary of the Scottish Rite about my unsatisfactory performance. He was nice about it, but told me that I was *never* to end a prayer "in Jesus' name" or "in Christ's name." He said, "Make your prayers *universal.*"

I wondered about all this fuss over a prayer, especially one that came out of a book a preacher had lent me; but I just thanked him and left.

I was to learn the meaning and significance of this fuss over a prayer later on; but for the time being I just accepted it[28]. At least the Secretary was nice about it. Many years later, when he died, I learned that he was a Christian Scientist.

Into the Eastern Star

Bonnie had supported and encouraged me in Lodge work from the start. As already stated, she had been an inactive member of the Order of the Eastern Star when we were married, although I had not known it at the time. After my promotion, and as I became more and more active in Blue Lodge and the Scottish Rite, Bonnie told me one night that she intended to begin attending the Eastern Star and thought it would be good for me to join.

I agreed, submitted my application, and was soon approved and initiated. Many people believe that "The Star" is only for women, but it isn't.

The Order of the Eastern Star was conceived by a man, men organized it, men wrote the rituals, and no meeting can be held without at least three male officers present. Men, one might fairly say, control The Order of the Eastern Star, but only from the background.

The social life was pleasant, and now there was one meeting each week that Bonnie and I could attend together.

Although I could have been an officer in the Eastern Star, I had no desire to be. I had plenty to do already in the Blue Lodge and Scottish Rite and I was content just to enjoy going with Bonnie to the meetings and the social functions that went with them.

The Koran, Fez, and Fun: Becoming a Shriner

The Shrine (Ancient Arabic Order, Nobles of the Mystic Shrine) is easily the most conspicuous of all forms of

Freemasonry and the most far-removed from basic Masonic principles and traditions. Many who know nothing of Masonry in general who perhaps don't even recognize the word "Mason" except for thinking it means some kind of bricklayer, have at least a vague awareness of "The Shriners."

At the mention of the word "Shriner" most will think of men in red hats with tassels, perhaps in colorful costumes, parading, clowning and doing some kind of public service.

If they are a little more aware than that, they will think of them as men who have big conventions and drink a lot. Most of the general public will go through life with no knowledge of the existence of the Scottish Rite or the York Rite; the degrees of these Bodies and such titles as Prince Adept, Master of the Royal Secret or Knight Templar will have no meaning at all for them.

They may never even have heard of the Blue Lodge and the degree of Master Mason. But they will probably have heard of the Shriners and will have some knowledge of what they do. The Shrine, the "Show Army of Masonry," maintains a *very* high profile.

I had been aware of the Shrine for a long time when I had only the most vague knowledge of the rest of Freemasonry. From the time of my very first entrance into the Lodge, I had the thought of someday being a Shriner. It seems to me that this is true of most Masons who go on beyond the Blue Degrees.

For this reason, one of their practices always puzzled me: after each Reunion in the Scottish Rite, the Shriners would come around, recruiting the new 32nd Degree Masons for the Shrine and it seemed unnecessary. Such was the case with me. Shortly after receiving the 32nd Degree they began approaching me about joining. In my case they were wasting their time, for I had decided a long time before to join them.

It was, until very recent times, necessary to be a 32nd Degree Mason (or, its York Rite equivalent, Knight Templar) for six months before being eligible to join the Shrine. Unlike myself in a way, I didn't rush in as soon as the six months passed. I was fully involved in the Blue Lodge and already was an officer in the Scottish Rite; perhaps, also, I sensed that work in the Shrine wasn't as serious as in Blue Lodge and the Rite. I wanted to *learn* about religions and the meaning of life, and I had plenty to learn where I was. So I didn't enter the Shrine after the Spring Reunion when I became eligible.

I was Chaplain in the Scottish Rite and a Degree Master. In the Blue Lodge I was Senior Deacon and preparing to be the Junior Warden, only two chairs away from the office of Worshipful Master. I was very busy with all this responsibility.

The following fall however, after Reunion, I decided it was time to enter the Shrine. Mike had come into the Scottish Rite at Spring Reunion and was now eligible also. We went into the Shrine together. I knew that the Shrine initiations got really rambunctious and wondered what might happen when they laid hands roughly on Mike. The initiation was performed in the Coliseum before a very large crowd of Shriners who came to see the fun. One of the first things done was to identify the men with health problems that might make the initiation a risk.

There were physicians there to question and examine the candidates; those considered risky were separated out, had a white tape put around the left wrist, and they simply sat while the other candidates went through the rowdy part of it all. In this way, because of his previous back injury, Mike was spared the hazing and the Shrine was thus spared a demonstration of the "Honds-Off Policy."

We began the initiation about noon that Saturday. After the medical screening came the hazing, which was very childish. Some of it was not only childish, but downright vulgar. At one point we were placed in a large, mesh cage, and one of the Shriners climbed up on top of it. He exposed a very convincing rubber penis which was connected to a water bag concealed in his clothing and hosed down all of us in the cage to the delighted howls of the spectators.

After the hazing it was time for the serious part, the ritual, and then time to take the oath. We took the obligation, again with terrible bloody consequences if we revealed any of the "secrets" (one form of mayhem we promised to accept was to have our "eyeballs pierced to the center with a sharp, three-edged blade"). And, with the Koran on the altar, we sealed our solemn oath in the name of "Allah, the God of Arab. Moslem and Mohammedan, the God of our fathers."[29]

I had taken so many bloody oaths already (one for each degree) that I paid little attention to this one, except to notice that it, like the rest of the ritual, featured desert settings, Arabs and Allah, the Mohammedan god. I was disappointed and a little offended at the childish and vulgar nature of the initiation but not really surprised. This, after all, was the Shrine; and "fun" was the Shriners' trademark.

The initiation was completed by 4 P.M., so we could all be ready for the big celebration banquet that night. With still another initiation behind me, I headed home to share the moment with Bonnie and to get ready for the celebration. It was to be a BYOB ("bring your own bottle") affair, Mike was going with us, and we were looking forward to wearing our brand-new fezzes. We enjoyed the party, which lasted until 2 A.M.; we were Shriners at last, and it felt good.

There was no "degree work" in the Shrine for there is no actual degree, so it didn't look like I would be learning a great deal there. However, I looked forward to being a part of all their benevolent community services. I was proud of my new red fez with its gold trim and tassel.

I didn't see how my life could be much more full—except for one thing. I still had a spiritual emptiness; I was still in search of a religion.

ENDNOTES

28 In a well-ordered lodge, Jesus is never mentioned except in vague, philosophical terms. Prayers are never prayed in His name, and when scriptures are quoted in the ritual,

all references to Him are simply omitted. For example, II
Thessalonians 3:6 is used in the ritual, but not the way it is in
your Bible; the words "in the name of our Lord Jesus Christ"
are entirely omitted. Likewise, the ritual includes I Peter
2:5, but with the words "by Jesus Christ" omitted. Albert
Mackey, after Albert Pike the highest Masonic authority,
called this mutilation of the scriptures "a slight but necessary
modification" (*Masonic Ritualist*, pg. 272).

29 Every Shriner, kneeling before the Koran, takes this oath
in the name of Allah, and acknowledges this pagan god of
vengeance as his own ("the God of our fathers"). And, in the
ritual, he acknowledges Islam, the declared blood-enemy of
Christianity, as the one true path. ("Whoso seeketh Islam
earnestly seeks true direction.") How it must break the heart
of God to hear these words from the lips of His own children,
particularly the leaders of His church.

A Religion at Last

As I continued my progression "through the chairs," from office to higher office in the Blue Lodge, I also continued to work in more and more of the Scottish Rite degrees. As I continued to study in the degree rituals and lectures, I developed more and more of a clear understanding of religious beliefs and moved ever closer to a personal religious belief of my own.

"The Lodge is a Good Enough Religion"

Through the years I must have heard hundreds of men say, "I don't need to go to church — the Lodge is a good enough religion for me." Very many such men never attend a church except with the Lodge once a year to hear Masonry exalted. They trust Lodge membership and their own "virtuous life" to assure them acceptance in the "Celestial Lodge above."

In a sense I agreed with such men, in that I believed that the churches and synagogues knew and taught only imperfect remnants and perversions of the "old religions," the ancient mystery religions of the East. But I was not in agreement with them in another sense: I was not going to be satisfied with basing my life on anything so vague. I was going to continue the search until I had a specific, foundational religious belief. And I wasn't there yet.

The Ten Commandments

Still motivated in my search for religious understanding, I was happy when asked to become Master of the 18th Degree. In this degree, the Degree of the Rose Croix, I read that "The ceremonies of this degree are interpreted by each individual according to his own faith, for in no other way can Masonry retain its universal character."

The degree book went on to say that the symbolism for this degree comes from the "ankh," the Egyptian symbol for life, which comes from Deity (God), meaning that the Egyptian gods were at least the equal of the Christian God. It also said that "In all religions there is a basis of truth; in all there is pure morality."

As I read these words I thought they sounded wonderful. I didn't stop to realize that this endorsement of "all religions" included all cruel forms of paganism with mutilation and human sacrifices, voodoo, witchcraft (which often refers to itself as "The Old Religion") and all forms of Satanism. The degree book tied all this together by saying that Masonry has the mission of bringing together "all men of all religions" under the Masonic banner and around the Masonic altar.

The degree also features the Ten Commandments, which I thought particularly nice, and in performing this part of the ritual one day a very important insight came to me.

A Disturbing Thought

At the next Reunion this Degree of Rose Croix was exemplified. I had my team well prepared for the performance. I was feeling good about it — not only the "truth" I thought I was expressing, but also the effective way we were performing the ritual. One of the candidates in the class of initiates was the mayor of our large city, a very important man and, in a way, my boss. As usual, one of the men in the class was selected to actually participate, representing the rest; we chose, of course, His Honor, the mayor.

At the end of the oath I had him kneeling at the altar, I had the Book of the Law in my hand, and he was vowing to keep the Ten Commandments. As I read each one from the book, he repeated it after me and promised to keep it. About half way through the Commandments the thought occurred to me, "You cannot possibly do what you are promising to do. I know you, and know something of your life, and you cannot keep these Commandments. As a matter of fact, I don't think I know *anyone* who *could.*"

Nevertheless, the mayor promised with a terrible oath followed by "So mote it be." This interesting contradiction stayed with me, returning to my thoughts from time to time. The vast majority of men administering and taking the oath, however, seem only to say it, get it over, and promptly forget it.

I Become Worshipful Master

When my time came to be elected Worshipful Master of the Blue Lodge I had to stop taking on extra responsibilities in the Scottish Rite. I was already working in four degrees, plus my participation in the Eastern Star and Shrine. Serving as Worshipful Master takes most of the "spare time" one has, for the duties are demanding. Of course, I had the full cooperation of my superiors at my job, for they were Masons and were pleased with what I was doing. They gave me plenty of time off for Masonic funerals and other extra activities, and this was never a problem.

An Interesting Testimony

On the evening after my installation as Master we had a special dinner party for the outgoing Master. It was very nice, with a private party room in a large hotel, complete with its own bar. During the party we asked the outgoing Master to share with us the story of how he had entered Masonry and his progression in it. He had already had quite a bit to drink and was very frank in the relating of his "testimony" as a Mason.

We laughed as he told us that when he applied for membership he was amazed that the Investigating Committee approved him for membership. He said, "I could hardly believe that they were telling me I was approved, for I was so drunk when they arrived that I couldn't get up. My wife had to let them in, for even if I had been able to get up on my feet I could not have taken the chance of walking across the room and falling down."

I laughed with everyone else at first. Then I was troubled by the obvious contradiction there. One of the basic tenets of Masonry is *sobriety*. Yet this Past Master was accepted for membership when so drunk he couldn't stand up and walk. This troubling thought, like the one about the Ten Commandments, stayed with me.

A Strange and Interesting Theory

We had regular luncheons at the Acacia Club, for Masons only. We would usually have a drink at the bar, then go into the club room and have lunch. After lunch we always had a speaker.

One such speaker was a Methodist preacher, a dedicated Mason and a student of the Ancient Mysteries. He had a strange and interesting theory to the effect that Masonry was actually founded by Nimrod at the building of the Tower of Babel. Of course I knew nothing of the Bible, so accepted everything he said as truth.

Now that I have made a study of the Scriptures I know that they teach no such thing. However, having also learned much of the dark and shadowy origins of Masonry, I realize that the strange preacher may not have been so far from the truth.

I Wanted to Understand

My year as Worshipful Master of the Blue Lodge was a pleasant experience. I enjoyed the work in the weekly meetings and bringing classes through the first three degrees. It was also nice being treated with such respect and being called "Worshipful" and "Master."

Because the office required so much of my time and energy, my thoughts were once more really focused on the Blue Lodge (rather than on the Scottish Rite degrees and the Shrine work). I had questioned things almost from my beginnings in Masonry, not that I was skeptical, but because I wanted so much to learn and to understand. I wasn't satisfied just to sit through it, say it and get it over with; I wanted to *learn*, Masonry was giving meaning to my life, and I wanted to *grasp* it *all*.

What is a Cowan?

I remembered a question that occurred to me during one of the very first lectures I heard. It was about Masonic origins and the lecturer said that the name "Blue Lodge" came from "our ancient brethren who met on the high hills and low vales at night, meeting under the starry canopy of Heaven," the blue sky. The lecture went on to say that the ancient brethren set guards "to keep off cowans and eavesdroppers."

My mind grabbed onto the word "cowan," as I had never heard it before. After the meeting I asked the Tiler (the officer in the Lodge responsible for guarding the door and keeping cowans and other "profane" persons out of the hall) what a cowan is. Since it was his duty to keep them out, I assumed that he would know what they were.

He looked puzzled, and finally said, "I think it is a no-good bum." So I asked about a dozen other men (including all the officers) the same question that night and no one could tell me what a cowan is.

Many years later I finally learned that it is an old term for an untrained builder of walls who hadn't the knowledge of stone masonry and who in the middle ages could be found eavesdropping on meetings of builders' guilds, trying to learn their secrets.

This questioning became a pattern in my life as a Mason. It sometimes got me in trouble but it also made me a much better informed Mason than most. Had anyone asked me, when I was Worshipful Master, what a "cowan" was, I could have answered the question. But no one ever asked.

The Junior Warden Leaves the Lodge

While I was Worshipful Master the man who was Junior Warden asked me one day about the Bible. He pointed out that in the ritual we say that the Bible is a "rule and guide for faith and practice" and that it teaches that the Christian God is the only true one and that Jesus is the only means of salvation.

Yet, he reminded me, we teach in the Lodge that all religions are valid. He pointed out to me that there is a contradiction there and asked me to explain it to him. When I couldn't do it he left the Lodge and renounced Masonry. I thought he was a bit extreme but never forgot the question. This man had been a dedicated Mason and a hard worker in the Lodge, only two chairs away from being Worshipful Master. He left it all for Jesus and the Bible.

More Questions Without Answers

With the closing of my year as Worshipful Master I returned to the work in the Scottish Rite with all my might. I studied more of the degrees, studied the references in "Morals and Dogma" and other sources and continued to ask questions. As before, my questions continued to be met with annoyed silence or advice to "Stop asking questions that have no answer and just follow the Ritual." I asked so many questions the Secretary finally had a special meeting of the officers to deal with the "problem" I was creating.

When they told me that my questions had no answers and that I should be satisfied just to follow the books, I said my piece. I told that body of officers that I believed the answers *were* there but that no one *cared* enough to find them.

For example, I wanted to know why we were called "Scottish" Rite, when the degrees and the system originated in France. "Why not call it the French Rite?"! I asked. Again there was no answer, and the conference concluded with, "Just stick to the Ritual and stop trying to write your own opinions into the system. It *is* Scottish, no matter what anyone else may say."

In spite of the special meeting's conclusions, several of the officers approached me later and asked how I had learned these things that were so disturbing. I gladly shared with them my irrefutable Masonic sources and they seemed to be taking it all in. But it didn't change anything. Their interest was only mild and temporary. They had no real desire to know the truth.

I began to realize that there are two classes of Masons: one that just sits through the meetings; and the other that does the work, but just keeps to the Ritual and memorizes or reads it without understanding.

I really didn't fit into either category but was still blind to the Bible and its truth. So I kept on asking. I continued searching for answers in the degrees and other writings of the Masonic authorities.

A Knight Commander of the Court of Honor

In spite of the fact that I was "making waves" with all my questioning and seeking for understanding, I continued to make real progress in the Rite and to accumulate honors and recognition. There is a special honor, beyond the 32nd Degree, called "Knight Commander of the Court of Honor" (K.C.C.H.). With the lifetime title goes a special red cap with the K.C.C.H. emblem. It was a happy day when I was notified that I had been selected (by the 33rd Degree representatives) to receive this high honor.

In order to receive the K.C.C.H. it was necessary for me to travel to a distant city. Since Bonnie was working she was not able to go along, so Mike said he would go with me. We were given time off from our jobs to make the trip (our superiors were pleased about it all) even though it wasn't necessary for Mike to go. We took the train to the Conclave, and it was a pleasant trip. I was excited and Mike was happy for me.

There was a great deal of drinking at the Conclave and it bothered me. "Why must we *always* do so much drinking?" I asked myself, but had no answer. I enjoyed a little drinking and did it regularly. But it bothered me that there was always so *much* of it and that it played such a major role in the Masonic life. I was duly made a Knight Commander of the Court of Honor, and we enjoyed a banquet after the ceremony. The next morning there was a meeting in the Lodge Hall and a lecture was given by the Grand Master of the Grand Lodge of Florida, a very prominent Mason. I felt greatly honored by all of it.

That afternoon Mike and I took the train back home. As we reflected on it all, he said that he hoped he could become a K.C.C.H. someday and I said that was my hope also. Bonnie was glad to see me, was proud of the honor I had received, and thought I looked distinguished in my snappy new red cap.

A Religious Belief at Last

It was time again to be getting ready for Reunion and there was much to be prepared as I was now working in four degrees at once. As I studied more and more, I saw with increasing clarity that Masonry teaches that whatever a man sincerely and conscientiously believes is truth, and that all religions are of equal worth and validity. Thus, Jesus Christ is reduced to the level of the other "exemplars" such as Buddha, Mohammed, Confucius, Pythagoras and Emmanuel Swedenborg.

Albert Mackey wrote (in *The Masonic Ritualist*):

> Thus the trestleboard [blueprint for life] of the Jew is the Old Testament, of the Mohammedan the Koran; the Veda Scriptures of Hinduism and the writings of Baha-ullah are just as good as the Word of the Christians'

God, for the fact is that all religions are never as good as the pure teachings of Freemasonry.

Albert Mackey, that eminent Masonic leader and philosopher who believed that all the religions of man are of equal validity, but are inferior to the "pure teachings of Masonry," also believed in reincarnation. As a matter of fact, Mackey believed that in one of his previous lives on Earth he had been Jacques DeMolay, the medieval soldier crusader who was burned at the stake in France for betraying the faith and victimizing pilgrims, whom he was supposed to protect, in the Holy Land.[30]

A Serious Contradiction

Of course, there are immediate problems here because many of these religious systems that are "all correct" or of "equal validity" claim to be the *only* valid and correct one. So it becomes obvious that they cannot all be "right" or of equal validity. But my mind was not prepared to see this serious contradiction. I accepted this idea that it doesn't really matter what you believe as long as you are sincere. To undergird and hold together this unsubstantial assortment of contradictory beliefs, there was the theory of reincarnation.

As Mike and I finished up the degree work in still another Reunion, we discussed the lecture he gave in the 25th Degree and the one I gave in the 32nd Degree. Neither of us had ever studied the Bible. No one had ever witnessed to us plainly about Jesus as the Redeemer, and so we decided that we would find the truth about religion in the degrees. Mike had been a Catholic in Scotland, but had left all that behind when he came to America. He said, "I don't want any more to do with Christianity."

We Embrace Reincarnation

With the degree work and other Masonic writings as our source, we finally decided that the truth lay in reincarnation and that if we would try to live a good life now, be good to our brother Masons, help the sick and attend to good deeds in general, when we died we would enter the next life on a higher plane—just like going through a door. However, if we did not try to live right and do well in this life, then we could expect to go through that door into a lower form of life, perhaps as a barbarian in the Dark Ages, or a poor wretch living in ignorance and poverty in the Far East.

We remembered, for example, the exemplification of the 31st degree. In this degree the candidate, as a typical man who has just died, is defending his life before the gods and goddesses of Egypt. The candidate tells of his good works in his just -ended life and of his hope for a better incarnation in the next. As the candidate tells of each work he has done, one of the Egyptian deities drops a stone into the pan of a scale. As the last stone is dropped into the pan by the god Anubis (a man with a ram's head), the scale tips and Osiris and Isis, who are presiding, say, "Weighed in the balance and found wanting." The candidate listens then as the Soul of Cheres, symbol of immortality, is brought before the Chamber of the Dead and he learns that he must improve in his next life in order to advance in the cycle of reincarnation.

A Duel Commitment

So we decided to accept the doctrine of reincarnation and made a dual commitment. We made a commitment to the concept as a religious belief. We also made a commitment to one another to do the best we could in this life so as to be together on a higher plane in the next. We examined all the evidence at our disposal, made a decision, and then a sincere commitment to try to live up to it.

Mike and I thought that somehow, by accepting reincarnation and doing the best we could, we would someday find ourselves together in that "Grand Lodge on High."

Bonnie really didn't agree with us concerning reincarnation but didn't say much about it. She seemed to know something, way down deep, that we didn't know. But she didn't object to our decision and commitment and we pressed on.

At last, I had a religion of my own! I had the religion of Masonry (the Egyptian Mystery Religion of Isis and Osiris) with its undergirding doctrine of reincarnation and the Lodge really was "a good enough religion for me."

ENDNOTES

30 The Order of DeMolay, Masonic organization for boys too young to enter the Lodge, is named for Jaques DeMolay, regarded in Masonic tradition as a hero. According to his detractors, DeMolay was a faithful Christian knight who led his order of Christian knights to Jerusalem to fight the Muslim invaders, defend the Temple of Solomon, and protect Christian pilgrims from thieves and murderers. Although pure and faithful at the beginning, they believe that DeMolay became apostate, worshiping Satan and pagan gods, and victimizing the Christian pilgrims he was supposed to protect. For more on Jacques DeMolay and his Knights of the Temple, see Part Two of this book, Chapter 4, "Freemasonry's 'Christian' Degrees."

The Gathering Storm

With a religion of my own, at last, I entered into a period of four satisfying years. It was a time of steady, single-minded work and accomplishment, a stable period of progress. In my work in the Scottish Rite, especially, they were years of fulfillment. But with the satisfaction of the work and the learning, there were some disappointments and a measure of disillusionment.

Disappointment in the Shrine

Soon after becoming a K.C.C.H., I spoke to the Illustrious Potentate of the Shrine about the possibility of my "moving up" to the office of Illustrious Potentate. I was working in the Shrine as much as my responsibilities in the Scottish Rite and Blue Lodge would allow. As a matter of fact, I was one of the hardest workers in our Shrine Lodge. I had become one of that committed few upon whom the Potentate depended to keep things going. Every organization, it seems, has such people—a committed few who do most of the work.

You Don't Qualify

When I told him I was interested in becoming "Illustrious Potentate" someday (this office, like that of Worshipful Master in the Blue Lodge, is held for only one year), I thought he would be pleased - that he would encourage me to seek it.

Instead, he looked at me a moment and then said, "Jim, you can never expect to be Illustrious Potentate in the Shrine. The office requires someone with more money and a nicer house than you have. This office requires entertaining visiting Potentates and other important people and you would not be able to do that properly. You may as well forget it."

This really took me by surprise and it hurt my feelings. Once again, I saw a sharp contrast between the seriousness and depth of the Blue Lodge and Scottish Rite and the shallow, social and public relations emphases of the Shrine.

The All-Star Football Game

Another disappointment came as I continued to work hard in the Shrine. I was appointed to a demanding and responsible job in connection with the All-Star Football Game we sponsored in order to raise money to build and operate our burn centers and hospitals for children. I was responsible for all arrangements for lodging, feeding and entertaining the coaches, players and others involved in putting on the game itself.

I was saddened and disillusioned by the vast amount of money that was spent on accommodations and entertainment for all these people, rather than going into the hospitals themselves. It really troubled me. But I soon learned that there was nothing I could do about it. So I just did my job and took comfort in the money that *did* go into the building and operation of the hospitals. But I couldn't forget it and it continued to trouble me.

Master of All Scottish Rite Bodies

I went on working diligently in the Scottish Rite degrees, learning more and more about the "Old Religion" that had become my own, and believing that I was growing spiritually. During the next four years I continued to work in still more degrees, to make occasional waves by asking questions (which still went largely unanswered) and to gather recognition and honors.

By the end of this time I had become, in succession, Master of all four of the Scottish Rite Bodies and served as such with success and satisfaction. I had become, without seeking to be, the man generally looked upon as the outstanding leader in the Rite - the one most likely to "really amount to something."

Except for all my questioning and seeking for knowledge and understanding, I maintained harmonious and friendly relationships with all in the system. I was a little "hard-nosed" in my insistence on getting the job done, maintained a no-nonsense attitude about the work and demanded excellence of those working with me. But it was all positive, except for a few lazy ones I wouldn't tolerate, and the results were consistently good.

By becoming Master of all four Bodies I had accomplished something seldom done. I felt good thinking of how much I had learned in the process and had satisfaction, both in the sense of jobs well done and of growing in my religion. I had my roots down deep in the "Ancient Mystery Religions," was depending upon reincarnation and my good works to eventually get me into that "Celestial Lodge on High" and I was growing rapidly in terms of responsibility and accomplishment in the Lodge. I felt good about it all, and wondered how it could be any better. I soon found out.

Good News and Bad News

Fall Reunion was a hard but good one with a large class of candidates coming through. At the end of Reunion I was told that I was being considered for the 33rd Degree.

The 33rd Degree! This was almost too good to be real! I was K.C.C.H. and Past Master of all Scottish Rite Bodies and that was a lot of success and honor for one who had been an abandoned little boy. The thought that I might also be given the 33rd Degree made my head swim.

The 33rd Degree cannot be earned or bought. As a matter of fact, it cannot even be sought, for to ask for or seek it means automatic and permanent disqualification for the honor.

The Supreme Council of the 33rd Degree, seated in Washington, D.C. at the House of the Temple, reaches down and selects those it chooses. Except for a seat on the Supreme Council itself, this honor is the end of the line - there is none higher. Not only that, I had been a K.C.C.H. for only four years. A man cannot even be considered for the 33rd Degree until he has been a KC.C.H. four years. I was being *considered* for the 33rd in the minimum time!

I was told that in about six months I would be notified as to whether I would actually be granted the 33rd. I thought, even if I were not selected, what an honor it was even to be considered!

Along with this almost unbelievably good news I began to notice a problem in my work and increasing difficulty on the job. In my work with the Port Authority I needed to be able to see names and numbers of ships and boats at a distance. Rather quickly, this became a problem. No matter how hard I tried, I noticed I could not read the names and numbers clearly from a distance as I had always been able to do.

Thinking I only needed to get some glasses that would solve the problem, I went to see an optician. He examined me and said he had bad news for me. He couldn't help me with the problem by prescribing glasses for distant vision. As a matter of fact, he said that he couldn't help me at all. He said that I had a progressive cataract developing on my left eye and would need to see a physician.

A Doctor With Simple Good News

I went home and told Bonnie what had happened. She said she knew of an ophthalmologist she could recommend. This doctor had helped a lady she knew and she felt that he was the one I should see. This recommendation of Bonnie's was perhaps the most important turning point in my life. Of course I had no way of knowing it at the time. Simply doing what seemed the logical thing at the time, and with not the slightest inkling of the importance of what I was doing, I called his office and made an appointment.

A Bold Diagnosis

When the day arrived I went to the doctor's office. My time came and I went into the examining room to wait for my pupils to dilate. The doctor came in, spoke with me briefly and began to examine my eyes. In what seemed to be a very short time, he completed his examination and then proceeded to give me a bold and startling diagnosis.

This man looked as if he were looking right through me for a moment and then said, "Mr. Shaw, it is true. You do have a developing cataract on your left eye, and there is one coming on your right eye also; but while your physical vision is bad, that isn't your real problem. Your real problem is with your spiritual vision."

I sat there feeling a strange kind of emotional impact, wondering what he meant.

Before I could ask, he spoke again with the same powerful simplicity and asked, "Mr. Shaw, are you saved?"

This time I did reply, and I asked him, "Saved from what?"

He said, "I mean, have you ever received the Lord Jesus Christ as your Savior and made Him the Lord of your life?"

By this time I was regaining my usual ability to carry on such verbal exchanges and, with a religious haughtiness rising up within me, I said to him, "Sir, I know more about religion than you do—as a matter of fact I know more about religion than most people will *ever* know!"

But he was neither impressed nor taken aback by my proud declaration. Without taking his eyes from mine, or changing his expression, he asked me, "But what do you know about *salvation?*"

Suddenly I had no more spirit for this exchange. I sensed that I was up against something very powerful, and said quietly, "I will think it over and let you know" and left as quickly as I could.

"He is a Religious Fanatic"

I left the doctor's office and went to my boss's office. I knew that I had a serious problem with my eyes and thought that I may have another problem of a different kind — one that I definitely didn't understand.

I asked my boss if I could take a two-week leave. He said, "Sure, Jim" and I went home to call my half-brother in Indianapolis. He was a Mason also, and I thought he might give me some advice. I told him what had happened, what the doctor had said, and he quickly gave me his opinion.

"That man is a religious fanatic," he told me. "You take the next plane here and I will meet you at the airport. Then I'll take you to see *my* ophthalmologist." The next plane left at 9 o'clock the following morning and I was on it.

"Go Back Home and Do Whatever He Tells You"

When I arrived in Indianapolis my half-brother was waiting. He told me that I had an appointment with his doctor for the next day and took me to his home to rest and wait. The following day the doctor there examined me and then asked me where I lived. I told him where I lived, and also what the other doctor had said about my eyes (I didn't mention what the other man had said about my *spiritual* vision).

He replied, "I will look the man up in our Register."

When he came back into the examining room he said to me, "Mr. Shaw, you have the very best medical facilities available to you in Florida, and the doctor who examined you there is one of the very best. My advice to you is to go straight home and do *whatever he says.*"

My brother wasn't at all pleased. I was feeling a strange combination of dread and excited anticipation. There seemed to be no alternative except to do as he said. But *what*, I wondered, would that strange and intense doctor in Florida tell me to do?

Increasing Knowledge and Growing Discomfort

Back home, I made another appointment and went to see the doctor. There was an unexpected complication: I had an infection in my eyelids. He said that he would not be able to operate for at least six weeks. So I returned to work and went each week for the next six weeks to be treated for the infection. Each time when I went to see the doctor for examination and treatment, he spoke to me about God's plan of salvation and my need of Jesus as my personal redeemer. He spoke to me about the Lord and quoted verses of Scripture.

Searching the Scriptures

His speaking to me this way no longer offended me. The verses of Scripture he quoted seemed to go way down inside of me. Some of them seemed to explode down there, stirring things I could neither describe nor understand. I decided that I would look up the verses he spoke of and read them for myself. The more I thought of it the more strongly I wanted to do it.

I had no Bible to read except for the big one on the coffee table. Bonnie had bought it when we were married and said that it would be our "family Bible." But it had lain there all those years without being read. At last it was opened and I began to look up the verses the doctor quoted and read them in their context. They sounded good as I read them. I would go back and read some of them again and again.

As the weeks passed I would sometimes wake up in the night thinking about one of the verses, get up and go into the living room to read it from that big Bible. The Scriptures definitely spoke to me—to needs deep within me. I noticed that they continued to speak to me, reverberating with meaning, no matter how many times I had read them. Those Bible verses were different from anything I had ever read before. They seemed *alive*.

There was a definite conflict going on within me as the Scriptures collided in my understanding with the teachings of the Masonic authorities and philosophers. I could feel the clouds swirling in my mind and was vaguely troubled, but didn't try to understand it. I just continued to read the big Bible in the living room, listen to the doctor as he witnessed to me, and do my Lodge work as well as I possibly could.

The Scriptures Were So Simple!

I didn't try to sort it all out or understand it. But I did notice something that became clearer and clearer. In addition to the strange "life" I sensed in the Scriptures, I noticed how *simple* their message was compared with the complexity of the Masonic writings.

The Conflict Comes into Focus

I had the surgery on my left eye and it was successful. With new glasses I could see well with that eye and after two weeks I went back to work. The operation on the right eye was scheduled to be done in six months. As surely as my vision was coming into clearer focus after the surgery, so was the conflict between the teachings of the Bible and the teachings of Masonry. I was increasingly aware of this in general terms, but it became clear in specifics when I gave the 32nd Degree Lecture at the next Coronation.

One or the Other Was Wrong

I had been understudy for some time to the judge who gave the Lecture of the 32nd Degree before I began to give it myself. I had heard it or given it many, many times and knew it well. Reunion was coming up, and Mike and I were making preparations. I studied all of my work thoroughly—the 32nd

Degree Lecture with particular care. As I studied the lecture, and when I delivered it to the new class of 32nd Degree Masons, I saw that there was a significant difference here. I saw for the first time how different from the teachings of the Bible was the lecture, this summing up of all the Masonic teachings the men had gone through in working up to this climactic degree. There was a difference there—one that could not be reconciled and I saw it clearly.

Either the "Old Religions" and the teachings of Masonry are right and the Bible is wrong, or the Bible is right and the "Old Religions" and Masonic teachings are wrong. Both could not be right. It was, I now saw clearly, that simple.

On a Collision Course With a Choice

With this fundamental conflict now clearly in focus in my understanding, I saw the long-range implications of it all. Masonry taught salvation by works, depending on one's own "virtuous life" to redeem him. The Bible teaches salvation by grace, depending on the perfect life of Jesus and His atoning death for us. Masonry teaches that Jesus is no greater than the other "exemplars" of history (such as Mohammed, Buddha, Aristotle or Joseph Smith), and was neither divine nor inspired. The Bible teaches that Jesus is God the Son, that He has always existed, and that no man can be reconciled to God the Father except through Him.[31] There is a choice to be made here—I saw this clearly—and I was on a collision course with that choice.

Seeking the Counsel of Others

Seeing clearly the conflict and the choice it demanded, I began, discreetly, to seek the counsel of others. I spoke with Bonnie and Mike about it, and with a few other close friends. I even went to see the Methodist preacher who had lent me the book of John Wesley's prayers when I was made Chaplain of the Lodge of Perfection. He really wasn't much help. He was not a zealous Mason and seldom attended Lodge meetings, but had no intention of leaving the Lodge altogether. He wasn't going to make that kind of trouble for himself! No one seemed to understand as clearly as I did. Bonnie came close, but none of them really saw the conflict and the choice it demanded, probably because they had not been reading the Scriptures as I had.

The Light Breaks Through

During one of my regular visits to the doctor after the operation on my left eye, I was sitting in one of his examination rooms, waiting for him to come to check me. I am very much inclined to read whenever I must wait, no matter how brief the waiting period, so I looked around to see what was in there that I might read until he came. There was not a thing in that room to read, except a Bible.

I picked it up, opened it to John's Gospel, and began to read again some of the verses I had read so many times in chapters one, three and four. Then, turning over to chapter six, I began to read verses I had not read before.

My eyes seemed to move quickly over the words of Jesus: "I am the bread of life; he that cometh to me shall never hunger; and he that believeth on me shall never thirst...him that cometh to me I will in no wise cast out...and this is the will of him that sent me, that everyone which seeth the Son, and believeth on him, may have everlasting life: and I will raise him up at the last day."

"Hey, Doc, Is This Really True?"

Then my eyes beheld verse 47, "Verily, verily, I say unto you, he that believeth on me hath everlasting life."

In spite of all the verses and passages of Scripture I had already read, and for reasons probably known only to God, this verse reached down inside me and grabbed my heart. I was staggered with the simplicity of what it said and the power of what it did to me. Trumpet fanfares inside my head could not have more effectively locked my attention on that simple verse, or more clearly shown its importance to me. It was doing powerful things, both in my heart and in my understanding.

"Could it really be true," I wondered, "that it could *all* be so *simple*? Could this really be *true?*"

Without thinking about courtesy or propriety in a large doctor's office, I called out loudly, "Hey, Doc!"

When, after a few seconds, he looked into the room where I was sitting, I pointed to that verse and asked, "Is this really true?"

He looked at the page, read the verse my finger was on and said, "Sure. Yes, Jim, of course it's true."

This Time It Was Real

When one has been exposed to Masonic religion and philosophy, with all its confusion, doubt and doubletalk, for as long as I had been, it is hard to believe the simple truth when finally confronted with it—even the living truth of the Bible.

After being really convinced of the truth of the "Old Religion" and the doctrine of reincarnation, after believing and teaching others that Jesus was neither divine nor unique, it is not at all simple or easy to accept the truth that He *is* divine *and* unique.

Even though the doctor had been quoting Scriptures to me for nearly six months, and I had been studying them myself, there had been much confusion within me about it all.

But the supernatural power of the words of God had been doing their work within me and the simple truth of this verse suddenly broke through the clutter of tangled concepts in my mind.

The light of Truth suddenly broke through the fog of confusion and doubt.

It was TRUE! It was really that simple and it was TRUE! I had told Doc on occasion before that I believed the verses he spoke of, but I really hadn't. Much of that time I had been playing mind games with him. Now I did—I really did! This time I wasn't playing any mind games; this time it was *real*.

Something Inside Me Changed

With the realization that the simple message of John 6:47 is true, a dark power within me was broken, a door in my heart opened and light came flooding into me. I felt an overwhelming sense of gladness and sadness—a rush of mixed emotions swirling within me.

I didn't try to interpret what I was feeling, but it was definitely a breakthrough of truth. I really *knew* it was truth and I was never the same again. Something inside me had changed, something that opened my eyes to truth and error, and the change was permanent. I would see things differently from that day on.

An Operation, a Prayer and a Hurricane

The time came for me to have the second operation, the one to remove the cataract on my right eye, and I went back into the hospital confident that it would turn out as well as the first one. I wasn't worried at all. When the operation was over and I was back in my room, someone came in and took me by the hand.

I couldn't see, for both eyes were bandaged. When I asked him who he was, he said that he was the doctor's pastor.

He said, "Mr. Shaw, I just came from the operating room. The doctor always prays for his patients, and he and I prayed for you—before and after the surgery."

His words penetrated clear to the center of me and shook my emotions loose. I had never before, to my knowledge, had anyone really pray for me—*never*—and I choked on the significance of it. When I regained my ability to speak I said to him, "Sir, as soon as I get out of the hospital and am able, I will be at your church."

He squeezed my hand and left me to think about it all. It was an overwhelming experience, but definitely a good one.

Before my recuperation was complete a hurricane approached and the hospital authorities were asking all patients who were able to leave to do so. I was making much more rapid recovery than had been expected, so I called Bonnie and asked her to come get me. As she drove me home, I told her that although people from the doctor's church had visited me and had prayed for me, not one person from the Lodge had been there to see me. She told me that she had announced to the Eastern Star members that I was having the surgery. But not a one of them had come. The contrast was clear and unmistakable.

The physical hurricane that was approaching was paralleled, if not exceeded, by the spiritual and emotional one building up inside of me.

ENDNOTES

31 See Appendix A, "Masonic Doctrine Versus Christian Doctrine."

Into the Light

The hurricane came and went without any harm to us. But the one within me continued to gather force. It seemed strange, from my point of view, for all the people around me seemed calm. Even the doctor was no longer speaking much to me about the Lord, for I wasn't seeing him regularly. Bonnie was quietly supportive, but we really didn't say much about it. Mike and my other friends went on with life. It was "business as usual" around me, but definitely not that way inside of me.

The Highest Masonic Degree

Easter was approaching and one quiet morning I was at home recuperating from the second operation when the doorbell rang. It was a special delivery letter from the Supreme Council in Washington, notifying me that I had been selected for the 33rd Degree.

I could hardly believe it was true! This honor is one most Masons never even think of receiving. It was just too much, too far out of reach, beyond limits of reality. It was unreal to think I had actually been selected. It was an honor just to be considered for this ultimate degree and I had actually been *selected,* chosen by that small and powerful group, the Supreme Council of the 33rd Degree.

I called Bonnie to share the good news with her. In talking with her, I surprised myself by asking her if she thought I should accept it.

"What a strange thing to ask her," I thought. But before I could contemplate it she said, "Why, *sure* you should accept it. You have worked so hard for so long to get there—by all means you should accept it."

So I returned my acceptance immediately and began making plans for the trip.

I Made It on My Own

With plenty of time to reflect, I thought about my long climb up the mountain of Masonry in search of light. I thought about the odds against anyone's ever making it to the 33rd Degree. I realized that in my case the odds had been even greater. I had made it by hard work and dedication alone. Some men have an edge on selection because of their wealth, political power or prominence. I had none of these.

Like the day I had carried the man all the way to the top of "Shaw Hill" between Camp Butner and Raleigh, I had made it to the top of the Masonic mountain because I was willing to make the effort required and refused to quit. Thinking of this, I felt particularly good about it and wished my mother could know.

I had come a long way since leaving the front gate that terrible day so many years ago. I had come the distance with no help from Uncle Irvin. Who would have thought that the lonely walk, begun so many years ago by that frightened little 13-year-old boy, would have led to this point? I had reached the pinnacle; I had made it all the way to the top.

Some of the most prominent and influential men in the world would undoubtedly be there to participate when I was given this ultimate degree—for me—little Jimmy Shaw, who had gone to work at age five and made it alone since age thirteen. They would be there to give the 33rd Degree to *me*. It was really a bit difficult to take it all in.

Three Days at the Mountain Top

In order to receive the 33rd Degree it was necessary to go to Washington, D.C. The initiation and related functions were to last three days.

Since Bonnie could participate in practically none of the things I would be doing each day, she decided not to go along. We were both excited as I made preparations to leave. But I was not as excited as I expected to be. The edge was taken off the excitement because, in me, it was mixed with a considerable amount of conviction. Way down deep there was a growing restlessness, an increasing conflict, produced by the things the doctor had been sharing and by all the Scripture I had been reading. Preparing to receive this "ultimate honor" was not as thrilling as it might otherwise have been.

Arriving at the House of the Temple

I flew into Washington National Airport and took a taxi to the House of the Temple on Northwest 16th Street. Upon arriving at the Temple I was met by a receptionist who asked if I were there to receive the 33rd Degree. I was surprised to find a woman in those sacred Masonic precincts, but said that I was and showed her my letter from the Supreme Council. She then told me that in order to receive the degree, I would be expected to make a "minimum donation" of a very large amount of money (at least it was a *very large* amount for me). This took me completely by surprise for there had not been a word about any such "minimum donation" in the letter sent me by the Supreme Council. I didn't carry that much money with me and had left my checkbook at home but was able to borrow the money from one of the other men and gave it to her. We candidates were all unhappy about this unpleasant surprise and grumbled to one another about it, but were not unhappy enough to forsake the degree over it. We were too close to the "top of the mountain" to turn back at that point.

The Temple Itself

The House of the Temple is quite impressive—a bit awesome, really. Standing large, grey and silent on the east side of Northwest 16th Street, between "R" and "S" Streets, it looms very wide and tall from the curb. There is a huge expanse of granite pavement in front of it, including three levels of narrowing steps as the entrance is approached. Flanking the entrance are two Sphinx-like granite lions with women's heads, the neck of one entwined by a cobra and decorated with the "ankh" (the Egyptian symbol of life and deity).

Adorning the neck and breast of the other is an image of a woman, symbolic of fertility and procreation. In the pavement, just in front of the tall bronze doors, are two Egyptian swords with curved, serpentine blades and, between the two swords, brass letters, set into stone, saying, "The Temple of the Supreme Council of the Thirty-third and Last Degree of the Ancient and Accepted Scottish Rite."

Over the tall, bronze doors, cut into the stone, is the statement, "Freemasonry Builds Its Temples in the Hearts of Men and Among Nations."[32]

High above the entrance, partially concealed by stone columns, is an elaborate image of the Egyptian sun god, backed with radiating sun and flanked by six large, golden snakes.

Inside, all is elegance: polished marble, exotic wood, gold and statuary. There are offices, a library, dining room, kitchen, Council Room, "Temple Room" and a large meeting room. This room is like a luxurious theater, rather elegantly furnished and decorated.

The ceiling is dark blue, with lights set into it to give the appearance of stars. These lights can even be made to "twinkle" like stars in the sky. There is a stage, well-equipped, and it is all very nicely done. But the thing that is most noticeable is the way the walls are decorated with serpents. There are all kinds; some very long and large. Many of the Scottish Rite degrees include the representation of serpents and I recognized them among those decorating the walls.

It was all most impressive and gave me a strange mixture of the sensations of being in a temple and in a tomb—something sacred, but also threatening. I saw busts of outstanding men of the Rite including two of Albert Pike, who is buried in the wall there.

Interviewed by the Supreme Council

The first day was devoted to registration, briefings and interviews. We were called into one of the offices, one at a time, and interviewed by three members of the Supreme Council.

When my turn came 1 was ushered into the office and seated. The very first question 1 was asked was, "Of what religion are you?" Not long before this I would have answered with something like, "I believe the Ancient Mysteries, the 'Old Religion,' and I believe in reincarnation." However; without thinking at all about how to answer, I found myself saying, "I am a Christian."

Then, to my surprise and theirs, I asked of them, "Are you men born again?" The man in charge quickly stopped me by saying, "We're not here to talk about that — we are here to ask *you* questions."

After they sent me back out I sat down and thought about it. When the next man came out, I asked him, "Did they ask you if you are a Christian?" He said, "Yes, they did."

"What did you tell them?" I asked, and he replied, "1 told them 'Hell no, and I never intend to be!'" Then he said a strange thing to me, "They said I'm going higher," and he left through a different door, looking pleased.

Becoming a Sovereign Grand Inspector General

The second day was the day of the actual initiation, held in the theater-like meeting room. Those of us who were receiving the degree were seated and the ceremony was "exemplified" (acted out in full costume) before us, in the same way that we had performed the lesser degrees of the Scottish Rite all those years. The parts in the exemplification were played by men of the 33rd Degree.

The representative candidate was dressed in black trousers, barefooted, bareheaded and draped in a long, black robe that reminded me of a very long, black raincoat. He had a black cabletow around his neck but was not hoodwinked. During the initiation he was led around the stage, conducted by two men with swords, as the degree was performed for us.

Instructions and signs were given. Upon the altar were four "holy books" (the Bible, the Koran, the Book of the Law and the Hindu Scriptures). At one point the "candidate" was told to kiss the book "of your religion" and, representing us all, he leaned forward and did so. I remembered the First Degree initiation, when I was told to kiss the Bible, and at that moment something came full cycle. It was the final such kiss to be a part of my life.

Wine in a Human Skull

When it was time for the final obligation we all stood and repeated the oath with the representative candidate, administered by the Sovereign Grand Inspector General. We then swore true allegiance to the Supreme Council of the 33rd Degree, above all other allegiances, and swore never to recognize any other brother as being a member of the Scottish Rite of Freemasonry unless he also recognizes the supreme authority of "this Supreme Council."

One of the Conductors then handed the "candidate" a human skull, upside down, with wine in it.

With all of us candidates repeating after him, he sealed the oath, "May this wine I now drink become a deadly poison to me, as the Hemlock juice drunk by Socrates, should I ever knowingly or willfully violate the same" (the oath).

He then drank the wine. A skeleton (one of the brothers dressed like one—he looked very convincing) then stepped out of the shadows and threw his arms around the "candidate." Then he (and we) continued the sealing of the obligation by saying, "And may these cold arms forever encircle me should I ever knowingly or willfully violate the same."

The Sovereign Grand Commander closed the meeting of the Supreme Council "with the Mystic Number," striking with his sword five, three, one and then two times. After the closing prayer, we all said "amen, amen, amen," and it was over.

Prominent Men Took Part

There were some extremely prominent men there that day, including a Scandinavian King, two former presidents of the United States, an internationally prominent evangelist, two other internationally prominent clergymen, and a very high official of the federal government, the one who actually presented me with the certificate of the 33rd Degree. Some made only brief appearances; others stayed much longer. However, they didn't do much mixing or socializing with us, except for those whom they already knew. Even though these celebrities weren't extremely "brotherly," it was still quite an experience for me just to be associated with them. It was easily the largest gathering of such prominent and influential men of which I have ever been a part.

The third day there was a banquet to celebrate our becoming "Grand Inspectors General, 33rd Degree." The banquet was a little anticlimactic, at least for me, and I was anxious to get it over with so I could return home. It was good to be a 33rd at last. But it wasn't as exciting or fulfilling as I had thought it would be during all those years in the Craft. I guess this was because of the profound changes going on down deep within me.

I returned home as soon as the 33rd Degree award and related social functions were finished, for it was time for my next appointment with the doctor. After he had examined my eyes he said that they were healing fine, that he felt good about the way they were looking, and as usual he spoke with me about the Lord. I told him that I planned to come to his church the next Sunday and that I had been reading the Bible. Obviously pleased, he said, "Good. Keep studying and your sight will soon be much better." By this time I knew what he meant — he was speaking of my spiritual sight.

Maundy Thursday
In the Scottish Rite the Thursday before Easter, "Maundy Thursday," is an important day. On this day we always performed a special service of Communion in the local Scottish Rite Temple. At this time I was Wise Master in the Chapter of Rose Croix, and it was my job to preside over the exemplification (dramatization) of the ceremony. I had done this many times and was known for my knowledge of the service and for "doing a good job" of putting it on.

The Words Had Meaning Now
On Thursday evening we gathered at our home Temple and dressed for the ceremony. It was always a most solemn occasion and seemed a little awesome, even to those of us who had done it many times. Dressed in long, black, hooded robes, we marched in, single file, with only our faces partly showing, and took our seats.

There was something very tomb-like about the setting. The silence was broken only by the organ, playing mournfully in the background, and there was no light except for the little that came through the windows. After the opening prayer (from which the name of Jesus Christ was conspicuously excluded), I stood and opened the service.

As I had done so many times before, I said, "We meet this day to commemorate the death of our 'Most Wise and Perfect Master,' not as inspired or divine, for this is not for us to decide, but as at least the greatest of the apostles of mankind."

As I spoke these words that I had spoken so many times
before I had a strange and powerful experience. It was as if I
were standing apart, listening to myself as I spoke, and the
words echoed deep within me, shouting their significance. They
were the same words I had spoken so many times before; but
they had meaning for me now. They made me sick, literally ill,
and I stopped.

The realization of what I had just said grew within me like
the rising of a crescendo. *I had just called Jesus an "apostle of
mankind" who was "neither inspired nor divine"!* There was a
silent pause that seemed to last a very long time as I struggled
with a sick smothering within.

When I was finally able, I continued with the service and
we gathered around a large table across the room in marching
order. The table was long, shaped like a cross, and covered with
a red cloth which was decorated down the center with roses.

A Black Communion

Once we were assembled at the table, I elevated (lifted high)
the plate of bread, took a piece, put my hand on the shoulder
of the man in front of me, gave him the plate and said, "Take,
eat, and give to the hungry."

This continued until all had partaken of the bread.

Then I lifted up the goblet of wine, took a sip, and said,
"Take, drink, and give to the thirsty."

Again, this continued until all had partaken of the wine.

Then I took the bread, walked over to the first row of
spectators and served it to the man previously chosen for the
honor of representing the rest of the Lodge. As I handed it to
him I again said, "Take, eat, and give to the hungry." In like
manner I served the wine to him saying, "Take, drink, and give
to the thirsty," and he sat down.

After this we took our places at the table shaped like a cross
and sat down. The setting was dark, our long, sweeping robes
were solid black, our faces nearly concealed in the hoods, and

the mood was one of heavy gloom. The Christ-less prayers and the hymns we sang fit right in. The one word that would describe the entire event would be "black." It was, indeed, a Black Communion—a strange, Black Mass.

Extinguishing the Candle

There was a large Menorah (candlestick with seven candleholders) in the center of the room, with seven candles now burning.

Standing again, I said, "This is indeed a sad day, for we have lost our Master. We may never see him again. He is dead! Mourn, weep and cry, for he is gone."

Then I asked the officers to extinguish the candles in the large Menorah. One by one they rose, walked to the center of the room, extinguished a selected candle and left the room.

Finally, with only the center candle still burning, I arose, walked sadly to the Menorah and extinguished the last candle— the candle representing the life of Jesus, our "Most Wise and Perfect Master." We had dramatized and commemorated the snuffing out of the life of Jesus, **without once mentioning his name,** and the scene ended with the room in deep, silent darkness. I walked out of the room, leaving only the darkness and the stillness of death.

Once again, the single word best to describe it would be "black"

All through the service I was shaking and sick. I have never felt so sad. I had stumbled over the words but, somehow, I made it to the completion of the ceremony and went back to the dressing room. I still didn't know much about praying but felt that I had been sustained by the Lord through it all.

The Final Parting

Back in the dressing room we hung up our black, hooded robes, put our street clothes back on and prepared to leave.

Less than two hours had passed since I arrived. But what had happened in that period of time had changed my life forever.

Still sick in my heart, I changed clothes without a word to anyone. The others asked me what was wrong. But I couldn't reply.

They reminded me that I had acted as Wise Master so many times before, that I was known for my smooth performance of it, and they asked what had gone wrong.

I was choking on the awful reality of what we had said and done, the way we had blasphemed the Lord, and the evil, black mockery we had made of His pure and selfless death. With weeping welling up within me, I could only shake my head in silence and walk out.

Mike was waiting for me at the door, expecting to get a ride home, and he asked, "What's the matter, Jim? Are you sick?"

Finally able to speak, I quietly replied, "No, Mike, I'm just sick of all *this.*"

"It Isn't Right"

I started down the wide steps in front of the large Scottish Rite Temple, realization and conviction growing within me, reached the bottom step and stopped. Turning around, I looked back at the huge, granite building and slowly studied the words, carved in the stone across the top of the entrance: "ANCIENT AND ACCEPTED SCOTTISH RITE OF FREEMASONRY."

Something came clearly into focus in my understanding and I made a decision. This crisis point in my life, one which had required so many years for me to reach, passed in seconds. The truth was revealed and the choice was made — a choice that would be the difference between darkness and light, death and life, one that would last for eternity. Looking up at those words I had walked under so many times, words of which I had been so proud, I spoke to myself out loud. It was as if I were the only man in the world as I heard myself say, slowly and deliberately, "It *isn't* ancient, it *isn't* Scottish, it *isn't* free, and it *isn't right!*"

Into the Light

I turned away and walked into the parking lot, knowing that I would never return. As I walked into the deepening darkness of that springtime night, I was walking into the growing light of the living God. As the natural darkness closed around me, the supernatural light welled up within me. With every step I took, as the Temple receded behind me, I was more free.

"I will never return," I thought with each step. "I will never return, I will never return ... ."

The decision was made, the die was cast. From that night onward I would serve the true and living God, not the Great Architect of the Universe. I would exalt and learn of Him, not Osiris, Krishna or Demeter. I would seek and follow Jesus, not the will-o'-the-wisp of "hidden wisdom."

I was walking, after such a long time, out of the darkness and into the light.

ENDNOTES

32 This statement is an interesting contradiction of the Temple it adorns, as well as with the thousands of other such Masonic temples built around the World at a total cost of many billions of dollars.

PART ONE — CHAPTER ELEVEN

Walking in the Light

I tried to explain to Mike that Thursday night, and told him quietly but forcefully that I was *never* going to return to the Lodge. He looked at me for a few seconds, trying to understand, but unable to do so.

Then he said, "Alright, Jim, but what you need is a drink. Let's go get one."

"Alright, Mike," I replied, "but just one." As we started for the bar near where he lived, I said, "I don't think I'll have a drink, Mike. I think I'll just have a soda with you."

A Friend Loveth at All Times

As we sat in the bar Mike continued to ask questions, trying to understand what was happening. I answered him as well as I could. He knew that I had dedicated my life to Masonry and how hard I had worked in it. He had been there with me for many years, working beside me when others were not willing to work. Since his first moment as a Masonic candidate, we had been together. I had urged him to join, had given him his petition, sponsored him and, as Senior Deacon, I was escorting him through the Blue Degrees when he threw Jubela across the Lodge Hall and established the "Honds-Off Policy."

We had worked together in the Scottish Rite Degrees so many times, working harder than all the rest. He had even

121

taken time off and gone with me when I received the K.C.C.H. If anyone on earth knew how truly I had loved and served Masonry, and how hard I had worked in and for it, it was Mike.

Now he was mystified, trying to understand why I was leaving it, but unable to do so.

The supernatural battle that had been going on within me was one of which Mike had not been a part. The truth of Scripture that had been lodged inside me from the doctor's witnessing and my Bible study was something in which he had not participated. He could not understand the things of the Spirit of God. At that point even I didn't fully understand it all. I just knew it was real—I just knew it was true.

But Mike was a friend—a true friend—and even though he couldn't understand this outrageous thing I was doing, he was still sticking by me. Like the friend of Proverbs 17:17, he was going to love me "at all times," and was going to stick with me through adversity. Sad to relate, the others would not feel that way about it. Finally Mike said, "Jim, I don't understand why you are leaving the Lodge, but I hope you won't be angry with me if I *don't* leave."

I assured him that I *did* understand his position and that neither his staying nor anything else would ever cause me to stop being his friend.

Making It Official

The next day I went to work. During my lunch period I wrote four letters of resignation: to the Blue Lodge, the Scottish rite, the Eastern Star and the Shrine. I sealed, stamped, and dropped them into the mailbox in front of the office. I have never forgotten the "clang" of the mailbox lid when it fell shut. It seemed as though that sharp and sudden sound had severed something and set me free; I felt as if that "clang" sent a new life surging through me. However, that was not to be the end of Freemasonry in my life—not by any means. It was not going to be that easy.

My Last Masonic Funeral

The next day was my day off from work and I was at home when the phone rang. It was the Worshipful Master of the Blue Lodge and he said, "Jim, we are having the funeral for George (the Tiler[33] of the Lodge) this afternoon. Be at the Lodge Hall at 1 p.m. for the Lodge of Sorrows (the Masonic funeral is always begun and ended at the Lodge Hall).

Before I could reply, he hung up. I had only put my letters of resignation in the mailbox after noon the day before. Yet, somehow, they *already knew*! "How could they know *already*?" I wondered. It was obvious that they were not going to let me go so easily.

I had no intention of going to that funeral and it never occurred to me that they might come to get me. But that is exactly what they did. About an hour after the phone call, they drove up to the front of my house and the Worshipful Master came to the door.

He said, "Jim, I thought you would be at the Lodge of Sorrows; are you ready to go?"

I just looked at him for a moment or two and then said, "I'm not going."

"Jim, You Had Better Go"

"WHAT DO YOU MEAN, YOU ARE NOT GOING?" he burst out angrily. "OF COURSE YOU ARE GOING!" Then, more quietly, he said, "Come on, let's go."

I didn't move, and said, "I have just put in for a *demit*."[34]

He wasn't at all surprised, but said, "Jim, you must be out of your mind! As long as you have served the Lodge, have served as Worshipful Master, and all the honors you have received, how can you do this?"

The tension was very great, and at that point Bonnie spoke up and said, "Jim, you had better go."

By this time I was beginning to wonder if they were planning to take me out and dispose of me, or perhaps keep me a prisoner until I "regained my sanity." But I said no more, kissed Bonnie goodbye and went out the door. At the car I stopped. I only had on trousers and a shirt. It is necessary in a Masonic funeral that participants wear a coat and tie. Without a word, the Master opened the trunk, took out a coat and tie and handed them to me. He had anticipated this also.

"Here," he said. "I know you think you won't have to take part in the funeral because you are not properly dressed but I brought these for you. Put them on."

I put them on, he ushered me into the car, and we drove away. At the funeral home there was a brief service conducted by the dead man's church. Although we took no part in it, I noticed how *very* similar it was to Masonic services. It could almost have been lifted right out of Masonic rituals. There was no mention of Jesus at all. The man was a Christian Scientist.

My Last Masonic Prayer

We left the funeral home and followed the hearse to the cemetery. In the graveside service I was "Great Lights Bearer;" I had a wooden tray, supported by a strap around my neck, and on the tray were the Book of the Law (Old Testament Scriptures), Square and Compass, the "Great Lights" of Masonry.

The Master, who was Priest, stood at the head of the grave. I stood at the foot and the others lined up on either side. The Master did all the talking until time for the prayer. Then it was my turn. I had the "official" prayer card on the tray before me. I looked at that card, decided not to follow it, and then prayed my own prayer which I ended "in the name of Jesus Christ our Savior."

I had come a long way from that day when I had been made Chaplain in the Lodge of Perfection and didn't know how to pray; this too had come full cycle. The prayer was greatly offensive to the Master and the other Masons who were there, of course, but because of the setting not a word could be said to me about it.

"Alas, My Brother"

We all had a sprig of Acacia which we dropped, in turn, into the grave and said, "Alas, my brother."

I dropped my sprig into the grave, said, "Alas, my brother," and it was as if I were looking down through the grave, into a dark eternity.

I said, "George, I wish you could have known Jesus as your personal Savior but, alas, my brother, it cannot be so. It is now too late."

"I Will Be Glad to Have You Gone"

We got back into the car and drove to the Lodge Hall where we completed the service by closing the Lodge of Sorrows. I started to leave when the Senior Warden came up to me and wanted to know what had happened to me to make me think of leaving the Lodge.

I told him as plainly as I could that I had been saved, I now belonged to the Lord Jesus Christ, and I could no longer belong to the Masonic Lodge, or any other lodge, which denied Him as Lord.

He immediately became very angry and shouted, "I WILL BE GLAD TO HAVE YOU GONE!"

I then insisted that I go to the office of the Secretary and talk with him and was allowed to do so.

Once a Mason, Always a Mason

The Secretary had just received my letter.

"Jim," he said, "I can hardly believe you would leave the Lodge after all these years and after the hard work you have done and the honors you have received. I just can't believe it." I knew that he could not understand, but tried to explain that I was now indwelt by the Holy Spirit and that He would be grieved if I went back into a Lodge Hall.

At least the Secretary was not hostile and, with that, I left. Of course, in the eyes of Masonry I would never leave—not really. The obligations (oaths) are considered unbreakable.

As a matter of fact, the "demit," the Masonic form for withdrawing from the Lodge, is looked upon by the Lodge only as a document which keeps you in good standing for the day when you will return. They do not look upon it as anything like a final resignation. From the Masonic point of view, the only way one can actually stop being a Mason is to die; and that, because of the general Masonic belief in reincarnation and the Masonic concept of Heaven, is not even the end of it in their eyes.

After I got back home I called Mike at work and told him all that had happened. He said that he wished he could have been at the service for the Tiler, for he had been a nice guy. Beyond that he made no reply. Mike was doing a lot of thinking.

Beginning a New Life

Jesus was now in my heart and everything was changing. I was seeing things in a different light, things I had never before seen at all. The Spirit of God was living in my human spirit at long last. A truly new life had begun.

There was still so much to learn, so much clutter in my mind that needed to be cleared out and thrown away. But I was on my way. I was learning to walk in the light and the Light of the World was my constant companion and guide. It was wonderful.

Bonnie and I began attending the doctor's church regularly. After a lifetime outside of church, a lifetime filled with pagan religion and occult philosophy, it should have seemed strange to begin suddenly to attend church regularly. It should have been a cultural, emotional and spiritual shock for us - especially in *that* church (where the Gospel was plainly declared and Jesus exalted). But it seemed natural to be there. It was where we belonged.

Drinking in a New Life

We also began to attend night classes at the Bible College associated with the church. It was a totally positive experience. From the very beginning everything we learned was a blessing— so positive, so "right"—that we wanted to learn more. What we were learning was not just interesting. It was like drinking in new life. We had, at last, found the real source of truth. We were taking in all that we could get.

Learning to Lead Someone to the Lord

After a few weeks of classes in the Bible College I had learned enough to realize that I really didn't know very much. Most importantly, I didn't know how to lead someone else to the Lord—that is, to help someone have the personal relationship with Him that I had found.

Except for the doctor's witnessing to me and the Scriptures he had shared, my being saved had been a thing entirely between the Lord and me. I wasn't even certain as to just how or when it had happened. I was learning that there are effective ways to witness, to approach people with the Good News, and that it is important to be able to show them the basis for it in the Bible.

But I also realized the importance of knowing how actually to lead someone to the Lord and I knew that I didn't know how to do it.

So I asked one of the teachers at the college, a man who had been a missionary to Cuba, to teach me.

He told me that there are many ways to approach it, taught me his method, and then gave me some tracts he had written. He advised me to memorize the verses of Scripture (such as John 1:12, John 3:3, John 3:16, Romans 3:23, Romans 6:23, Romans 5:8 and Romans 10:9, 10, 13) and the basic outlines of the tracts. I did just that and soon I was ready.

The Winning of Mike

Vacation time was coming soon and I asked Mike if he could get his at the same time as mine. I told him that the house needed painting and, since we had done it together in the past, I hoped he could help me with the job again. He agreed, our vacations were arranged for the same period of time, and when the day arrived we went to work. We would work for about two hours, then stop for a coffee break at the kitchen table.

I had made plans to witness to Mike during the painting project and, at the first break, on the first day, I began.

"Mike, do you ever worry about what would happen if you should die?"

He said, "I worry about it sometimes but you and I decided to believe in reincarnation. Also, as a Catholic I was taught to believe in Purgatory, a place where I could spend time to pay for my sins."

I said, "Mike, I was wrong about reincarnation. The Bible says (in Hebrews 9:27) that 'it is appointed unto men once to die, but after this the judgment.' If reincarnation is true, the death of Jesus was for nothing because we would eventually save ourselves. And as for Purgatory, there is no Scripture for that idea, not even in Catholic Bibles."

I could tell that Mike didn't want to hear any more just then, so I let the subject drop; but I could also tell he was really thinking. He was very quiet and ordinarily he would have been doing a lot of laughing and joking.

"I Have Led a Very Wicked Life"

At the next break I asked Mike if he would like to go to Heaven when he died.

He said, "I have thought about it and, of course, I would; but I have led a very wicked life. I believe the Masonic Lodge has helped me, because I have a purpose now and things are much more regular. I don't know as much about the Bible as you do but if you want to talk about it I will listen."

So I said to him, "Mike, I am asking you the most important question of your life—your joy and peace for all eternity depend on your answer. Are you willing to receive the Lord Jesus Christ as your personal Savior?"

Without waiting for his answer, I went on. "You say that you have led a wicked life but if you are willing to confess your sins to Him and receive Him as Savior and Lord, all your sins will be forgiven and forgotten, washed away in His blood, and your life will have a new beginning. There is no other way to have all this; Jesus said, 'no man cometh to the Father but by me.' He also said, 'ye must be born again.'"

Mike just lowered his head and quietly said, "I don't know how to be born again."

I said, "Mike, would you be willing to try if I show you how?" With his head still down as if already in prayer, he quietly said, "Yes."

In Moments It Was Done

We got down on our knees, right there in the kitchen, and prayed. First I prayed for him and then I led him in a simple prayer, asking Jesus to forgive him, save him and to come into his heart to live. In moments it was done—a thing that would last for eternity .

Now Mike and I would no longer have to work and wonder, trying to be good enough to make it into "that Celestial Lodge above." Now we would be together, in the presence of our wonderful Savior, for all eternity. Mike was a child of God.

I told him to get up. He looked up at me, his eyes full of tears, and tried to thank me. But I told him only to thank the One who had died for him. Then I gave him some very simple instructions about reading the Bible and praying.

I asked him, "Mike, are you saved?" and he replied, very positively, "Yes, I *am!*"

We went back to work, were nearly finished when Bonnie came home, and we all had dinner together.

When I prayed over the food, Bonnie said, "Amen" and then Mike chimed in with a big "AMEN!" He was learning fast.

Later he asked me, "Jim do I now have t' give up smokin' me pipe?"

I said, "No, Mike—just let the Lord speak to you about it. But as you learn to stay close to Him, don't be surprised if He changes the way you feel about a lot of things."

I didn't ask Mike to leave the Lodge. But he immediately gave up all the degrees he was working in. He gave up the Shrine and seldom attended the Blue Lodge.

Because so many of the men kept asking him why he continued to speak to me after I had left the Lodge, he soon left the Scottish Rite altogether. For all practical purposes he was out of it all, although I had said nothing to him about it.

Shunned by the Brothers

The change in our social life after I resigned from the Lodge was immediate and absolute. Bonnie and I were cut off. For all those years we had been so busy with social functions and most of it was pleasant. Suddenly we were shunned by our friends. It was as if we had leprosy.

Not only had we been busy with parties, banquets and receptions associated with the Lodges, we had enjoyed so many good times in one another's homes. Never did I enjoy being a Mason more than at these informal parties in the homes. In our home we had entertained as many as 20 guests at a time—complete with music—and there was never a guest who left unhappy. We met so many friendly people at these parties that it was seldom we went anywhere in the city that we didn't see someone we knew.

Now, not a one of them would even speak to us when we chanced to meet, with the single exception of Mike. He stuck by us from the start and it was the hostility with which the rest treated us that hastened his decision to leave the Lodge. I never had a better friend, nor a more stubborn one, than Mike.

Now, however, we were making new friends in the church and in the Bible College classes. The social functions that we were beginning to enjoy with our new friends were a lot healthier than the ones we had known before.

Persecution on the Job Brings Blessing

On my job, I was almost immediately changed to the night shift. There was no attempt to conceal the fact that it was because of my leaving the Lodge.

At first I was stung by it. But the Lord quickly showed me that it was a blessing. As was the case with Joseph of old, what was intended for evil, the Lord had used for good. Now I was able to enroll in the daytime program in the Bible College. Because the work wasn't so demanding on the job at night, I could do my studying at work and still do my job well.

Uncle Irvin's Parting Words

My half-sister in Indianapolis called me one day to tell me that Uncle Irvin was in failing health and that she thought I should see him. I returned to Indianapolis and the two of us drove out to his house.

Uncle Irvin did look ill, as if he might not live much longer.

I wanted to know that he would be with the Lord when he died, but I didn't get to speak with him about his salvation. He had already found out about my leaving the Lodge and was not at all open to hearing my reasons. He was already upset when I got there and went immediately on the attack.

Quickly becoming very angry, he shouted at me, "Don't you ever THINK? Don't you realize that Masonry is the SAME as JESUS CHRIST?"

I made no reply, for he expected none, nor would he listen to me. So, with this ultimate deception of the Masonic philosophy expressed in a few angry words ringing in our ears, we left.

I never saw Uncle Irvin again. In a matter of weeks he was dead.

The Past Is Prologue

I returned home, heavy in heart for Uncle Irvin, and went back to work. I had my job to do and my studies at the Bible College to pursue. There was so much to learn and I was hungry to learn it all.

Like my days in the Army in World War II, I was much older than the rest of the students. It didn't bother me at all. As a matter of fact, in some ways it was an advantage, for I had seen a lot of life and death that they hadn't seen.

There were many of them, for example, who were timid about speaking before a group. For me this was not a problem. My many years as a leader in the Lodge had provided rich experience in public speaking. When I went regularly to minister in one of the nursing homes, two or three of them would often go with me. They would help me with the music. I helped them to overcome the fear of public speaking. My Masonic years definitely paid off in this way.

So Many Men Like Me

There were many times when I would think about all those years I walked in darkness and wondered what I might have been able to do had I used all of that time for the Lord. I felt that, somehow, it was not all wasted. As He promised in Romans 8:28, God could work it all together for good. He could convert those "wasted" years into something useful. If nothing else, those years in Masonry had equipped me to reach out to other Masons with the truth, the simple truth that can set them free.

"There are so many men like me out there," I thought, "so many Mikes, so many Uncle Irvins, deceived and being destroyed by a deadly deception. Some of them might listen to me."

At the End of a Long Night

Very early one morning, as a long, dark night was giving way to the growing light of a bright new day, I stood on the

132

pier, thinking. I looked back over all those years that seemed to have been wasted and tried to look into the years of my life that still lay ahead. I thought of how far I had traveled, searching for truth, seeking light, only to be led ever more deeply into the darkness by men who meant to do right. I thought of mother— looking so helpless as she sent me up the street and out of her life, with nothing to give me but her pitiful legacy of advice to try to be like Uncle Irvin.

I thought of all the men to whom I had passed on that deadly inheritance; and I thought of the long suffering of God as He had pursued me through the years with His love.

"Maybe," I thought, "just maybe all this was preparation for serving Him. Maybe, with His Spirit to guide and strengthen me, I can lead some of those men out of the deadly deception of Masonry and into the truth and light of Jesus." A ship was underway outbound, growing smaller as it followed the channel lights toward the open sea. Seagulls wheeled and circled overhead, squawking and seeking.

"Maybe that could be His plan," I thought. "Perhaps the Lord could use me to help them find their way. Maybe I can lead some of those sincere, deceived, victimized men out of the pagan darkness of the Lodge and into the Light!"

With hope rising in my heart, with answers beginning to take shape in my understanding, and with a vision for the future finding form, I turned back toward the office. There was work to do.

ENDNOTES

33 The Tiler (the spelling varies) is the officer in a Lodge responsible for keeping all "profane persons" (non-Masons) from entering the Lodge Hall. He is usually armed with a sword and guards the door during meetings.

34 A "demit" is the Masonic form for withdrawal (becoming inactive) from the Lodge. For a more complete explanation of the demit see Part Two, Chapter 10, Question 3.

A Personal Word From Jim

As this true story is closed, I would be greatly remiss if I did not make it clear that in my pre-Christian life I truly loved Freemasonry. I loved the men with whom I was associated in the Lodge and the men with whom I worked so hard in the degrees and bodies of the Scottish Rite. Most of all, I was so very sure that I was doing what was right and pleasing in the sight of the Great Architect of the Universe.

Never in all my years of dedicated service to Masonry did anyone in the Lodge witness to me about the love and saving grace of Jesus. The Lodge attended a church once each year as a group. Each time the pastor (who was himself a Mason) would introduce us to the congregation and then exalt the Craft, telling them about all our wonderful works. We usually left the church thinking of how wonderful we were and feeling sorry for all those in the church who were not Masons, participating in all our good deeds.

After having been witnessed to by my ophthalmologist for some time I read those simple, wonderful words of Jesus, "Verily, verily, I say unto you, he that believeth on me hath everlasting life." These words, so short and so sweet, went right through my heart. I looked in the Bible for more and I found blessed assurance everywhere I looked. Jesus the Christ, the Son of God, really loved me. That truth set me free. I received the One who loved me as a real Brother! He will do the same for you.

Jim Shaw
Ocala, Florida

Part One – Epilogue
In the Years That Followed

Jim and Bonnie attended classes at the Bible College together and Jim continued his work with the Port Authority. Not long after leaving the Lodge, Jim suffered the first of two detached retinas. Laser surgery to restore his vision did so, but left him with sufficient visual handicap to eventually force his retirement after a bad fall on the job did additional, permanent damage to one of his eyes.

Two years after being born again, Mike began to have increasing pain and limitation in his back where he had been injured fighting the fire in New York so many years before. He also began to suffer a dramatic weight loss, and his once-powerful body became steadily weaker.

He was found to have cancer of the spine and was treated in the hospital where Jim had had his eye surgeries. During his last hospitalization, one of his old girlfriends came to see him. She asked Jim where the nearest Catholic church was, and said she would like to go there to light a candle for Mike. Jim said, "He doesn't need a candle lit for him. Mike has Jesus in his heart now and his sins are all washed away."

Wearily, but gladly, Mike said, "Yes, that is true." It was the last time Jim saw him alive; in less than two days Mike was dead.

Two years after retiring from the Port Authority, Jim graduated from Florida Bible College. Following graduation and ordination, for the rest of his life, he traveled, preached, and produced tracts, pamphlets and teaching tapes which were published and widely distributed in the US and in other countries. Jim dedicated the rest of his life to reaching others, especially Masons, with the simple good news of Jesus— the truth which had made him free. He carried on a steady correspondence with all who contacted him for information, and he did it all from a tiny "office" (it was actually a walk-in closet, smaller than most modern bathrooms) in the house trailer where he and Bonnie lived out the rest of their lives. He never had a staff to assist him—not even a secretary; and he never owned a computer or a copy machine. His office equipment consisted of a desk, a chair and a small, portable electric typewriter.

Jim and Bonnie lived simply; in fact, they lived in what is today classified as "poverty." But I never once heard them complain. They lived quietly, simply and pleasantly with what they had. They traveled together to preaching and speaking engagements until both were seriously injured when their old sedan was sabotaged. Jim recovered from his injuries, but Bonnie never fully recovered from hers; she was bed-ridden for the last years of her life.

Jim died in April 1995, at age 83; Bonnie died nearly four years later, in December 1998 at age 90. They had no children.

My Memories of Jim and Bonnie

My memories of Jim and Bonnie are pleasant. Bonnie was quiet and rather private. I remember that she didn't want the book to be written, for she was in fear for their lives. Southern people take their history and their heritage very seriously, and this includes their commitment to the Lodge; and she and Jim had already suffered much from Masonic anger. Jim recognized the elevated danger that would result from the book's publication; but he was willing to accept it for the benefit of reaching a much wider audience. Bonnie never changed her mind, but she accepted his decision with little complaint.

Jim was extremely intelligent, and had a great, droll sense of humor; he was much like a godly W.C. Fields. I called him one day, and without his expecting the call. Without even identifying myself, and with no warning, I said, "Oh Lord my God, is there no help for the widow's son?" This is the "grand hailing sign of distress," an important Masonic "secret" to which other Masons are supposed to respond and come to the rescue. Without a half-second's hesitation he replied, in his dry, witty way, "Not unless he gets saved." I could never catch him off-balance on anything like that.

Jim was the favorite of the window clerks at the post office, where he went daily to mail out his letters, publications and tapes. He knew them all by name, joked with them, and they lit up with smiles when they saw him come in. I know, because I went with him to the Post Office more than once.

As I am writing this I am, in a sense, reliving those years of vicious attacks on Jim and on me, following publication of "Deadly Deception." They ranged from very personal attacks, from sincere, furious, Blue Lodge Masons who threatened to kill us, to the more restrained pronouncements of Scottish Rite officials, speaking ex cathedra from the House of the Temple. At first Jim and I appeared together on talk shows (usually by telephone, because Jim could not afford the expense of so much travel). However, the response from Masonic listeners quickly became verbally violent, and Bonnie feared for their lives. From that time on, I did most of the talk shows alone.

In one memorable example of the furious rank-and-file response, I was interviewed, live, on a large TV station in Mississippi. Callers threatened to blow up the TV station for having trash like me on the air. I have been in two wars, and I have never seen such panic and confusion as took place in that TV station! No bomb was exploded. The angry Masons really didn't have time to arrange for it before I was gone from the station; but it was fun to watch all those previously cool and self-confident, perfectly dressed, blow-dried, "beautiful people" running frantically around the TV station like a Chinese fire drill. Such Masonic denunciations, from all levels of enlightenment, civility and positions in the Craft, usually took the form of, "They concocted these vicious lies to write a book and get rich," and/or "Jim Shaw is a liar and Tom McKenney is a fool."

Jim's Troubled Conscience

With this in my mind, I will share with the reader a vignette—one small memory from my years of knowing Jim Shaw—one that may shed some light on his character. Jim confided in me one day that he was troubled by his conscience, and he wanted my advice. What troubled him, he said, was the fact that in all his ministry of speaking and writing he was identified as "The Reverend" James D. Shaw. He was a graduate of Florida Bible College, and he had been ordained to the Christian ministry. Yet, he told me, he had never been pastor of a local congregation. Because of this, he said, he wondered if he should cease to identify himself as "The Rev. James D. Shaw."

I assured him that since he had been ordained by an accredited institution, it was indeed correct and proper for him to be identified in this way. I didn't tell him this part (because of his theological fundamentalism), but every Roman Catholic seminarian who is ordained to the priesthood is ever afterward properly addressed as "The Reverend so and so," and this appellation is valid and proper even if that priest never in his life serves as a parish pastor. In fact, many who are so ordained to the priesthood are never parish pastors; instead they devote their lives to academics, bureaucratic service in the Vatican, or some other non-pastoral vocation within the Church. The same may be said of Anglican, Episcopal and Eastern Orthodox priests. Although I didn't mention this fact about Roman Catholic, Eastern Orthodox and liturgical Protestant denominations, my reply seemed to satisfy him and we never spoke of it again.

Was Money Our Motive?

After appearing on (literally) hundreds of radio and television talk shows, discussing "The Deadly Deception" and "Please Tell Me," the hostile callers became so predictable that I could have done the programs all by myself, both asking the hostile questions, and answering them. And, by far the most common attack made by the callers was to accuse me (and Jim) of "writing a bunch of lies" just to make money.

I have been personally accused of this by Masons, from nameless (and countless) Blue Lodge Masons, all the way to the Sovereign Grand Commander himself, C. Fred Kleinknecht. I always reply by stating a very simple fact, and that fact is that neither Jim nor I ever received so much as one copper penny from the sale of the book(s). Both books (*Deadly Deception* and *Please Tell Me*) were then, and are today, the intellectual property of my teaching ministry, Words for Living Ministries, Inc. Publication rights to both books belonged to Huntington House Publishing Company, of Lafayette, Louisiana, until that company declared bankruptcy and closed its doors. During the years of publication, all proceeds from sales of the book went to the publisher. From those proceeds, the publisher paid royalties directly to my ministry—not to me or to Jim Shaw. The same is true of this new book; Bridge-Logos Foundation owns the publication rights, and all royalties will belong to Words for Living—not me.

The difference between being insulted by the Blue Lodge Masons, and by the Sovereign Grand Commander, C. Fred Kleinknecht, is that the Blue Lodge Masons sincerely believed what they were saying. Grand Commander Kleinknecht had to know that he was not speaking the truth.

But What About My Income From the Ministry?

But, the thinking person will surely ask, what about my salary, and other personal income from the ministry? If the proceeds from book sales went into the ministry's account, and the ministry pays me (salary, bonuses, etc), some of that money paid to me must come from sales of the book. Right? Nope. Wrong—and wrong for the simple reason that I have never received pay, in any form, from the ministry. *None—not one farthing!* In fact, I spent a great deal of my own money on the expenses of travel and research necessary for the production of both books. In a material sense, the books cost me a lot of money that will never be repaid; in a spiritual sense, however, I believe that the money, time, and strength that I spent on the books represent treasures laid up for me in Heaven. The books have brought liberating truth to a great many people who are precious in the sight of God, and they will go on doing so.

I learned much from Jim and Bonnie about selfless service in the Kingdom, as I watched them serving God daily, in that hot little house trailer in a dusty trailer park on the edge of Ocala, Florida. They accomplished much, with so little in the way of resources. They both died poor. Avaricious greed, calculated dishonesty, and the writing of malicious propaganda, of which they are still accused, should be made of sterner stuff.

I am blessed to have known them.

Tom C. McKenney
Ocean Springs, Mississippi
2010

Masonic Doctrine Versus Christian Doctrine

The following is a brief comparison of the doctrines and practices of Freemasonry with the fundamental doctrines of the Christian faith and its foundational source, the Bible.

Masonic doctrines summarized here are, in every case, based upon the consensus of the most revered and widely accepted Masonic philosophers, writers and sourcebooks. Any knowledgeable Mason will know at a glance that this is true. He has taken oaths to lie if necessary in order to conceal such things, and so will probably deny some things, and try to justify others. But the Masonic writers, and common practices in the Lodge, will verify it all.

Although most Masons have never read some of the sourcebooks cited, and have been deliberately deceived as to some of the facts in them, they could read them if they would. All these Masonic sourcebooks are in the libraries of most local Lodges and the libraries of all the Grand Lodges of the states. In addition, they can be purchased from Masonic publishing companies or in bookstores. In spite of their availability, however, most Masons have never read them.

Many, many more similar references could be cited in addition to the ones included here but these will suffice.

Capitalization and other means of emphasis are as in the Masonic originals; nothing has been added or changed.

1. JESUS CHRIST

MASONIC DOCTRINE

Jesus was just a man. He was one of the "exemplars," one of the great men of the past, but not divine and certainly not the only means of redemption for lost mankind. He was on a level with other great men of the past like Aristotle, Plato, Pythagoras and Mohammed. His life and legend were no different from that of Krishna, the Hindu god. He is "the son of Joseph," not the Son of God.

(1) "Nor can he [the Christian Mason] object if others see[in Jesus] only the Logos of Plato, and the Word or Uttered Thought or first Emanation of Light, or the Perfect Reason of the Great, Silent Supreme, Uncreated Deity, believed in and adored by all" (Albert Pike, *Morals and Dogma*, 26th Degree, p. 524).

(2) "And the Divine Wise Intellect sent teachers unto men ... Enoch, and Noah, and Abraham, and Moses the son of Imram, and the Prophets, and Pythagoras, and Plato, and Yesus the son of Joseph, the Lord, the Messiah, and his Apostles, and after these Mohammed the son of Abdulla, with his law, which is the law of Islam, and the disciples of truth followed the law of Islam" (Albert Pike, *Morals and Dogma*, 25th Degree, p. 34).

(3) "In his private petitions a man may petition God or Jehovah, Allah or Buddha, Mohammed or Jesus, he may call upon the God of Israel or the First Great Cause. In the Masonic Lodge he hears petition to the Great Architect of the Universe, finding his own deity under that name. A hundred paths may wind upward around a mountain; at the top they meet" (Carl H. Claudy, *Introduction to Freemasonry*, p. 38).

(4) "It has been found that every act in the drama of the life of Jesus, and every quality assigned to Christ, is to be found

in the life of Krishna [Sun god of India]" (J.D. Buck, *Mystic Masonry*, pp. 119, 138).

(5) "We meet this day to commemorate the death [of Jesus], not as inspired or divine, for this is not for us to decide" (Maundy Thursday Ritual, Chapter of Rose Croix).

CHRISTIAN DOCTRINE

Jesus Christ is divine, eternal and the second Person of the Godhead. When He was living on earth as a man, the only begotten Son of the Father, He was God incarnate, truly God and truly man. He was and is the only means of redemption for fallen mankind. Anyone who denies or rejects Him or His preeminent position as sole Redeemer also denies and separates himself from God the Father.

(1) "In the beginning was the Word [Jesus] and the Word was with God, and the Word was God. The same was in the beginning with God. All things were made by Him; and without Him was not anything made that was made. In Him was life; and the life was the light of men" (John 1:1-4).

(2) "Jesus said unto them, 'Verily, verily I say unto you, before Abraham was, I am'" (John 8:58).

(3) "And now, O Father, glorify thou me with thine own self with the glory which I [Jesus] had with thee before the world was" (John 17:5).

(4) "Jesus saith unto him, 'I am the way, the truth, and the life; no man cometh unto the Father, but by me'" (John 14:6).

(5) "Neither is there salvation in any other; for there is none other name [but Jesus] under Heaven given among men, whereby ye must be saved" (Acts 4:12).

(6) "He that hath the Son hath life; and he that hath not the Son of God hath not life" (1 John 5:12).

(7) "Who is a liar but he that denieth that Jesus is the Christ? He is antichrist, that denieth the Father and the Son. Whosoever denieth the Son, the same hath not the Father" (1 John 2:22, 23).

(8) "For there is one God, and one mediator between God and men, the man Christ Jesus" (1 Timothy 2:5).

(9) "I and my Father are one" (John 10:30).

(10) "... he that hath seen me hath seen the Father...." (John 14:9).

2. THE BIBLE

MASONIC DOCTRINE

The Bible of the Christian is merely one of the "holy books" of man, no better than the Koran, the Hindu scriptures or the books of the Chinese and Greek philosophers. It is not to be taken literally, for its true meaning is esoteric (hidden from all but a small number of "enlightened," elite leaders); the literal, obvious meaning is only for the ignorant masses. It is right to remove references to Jesus in passages used in the ritual. Masonry, contrary to popular belief, is **NOT** based upon the Bible. Masonry is actually based on the Kabala (Cabala), a medieval book of magic and mysticism.

(1) "Masonically, the Book of the Law is that sacred book which is believed by the Mason of any particular religion to contain the revealed will of God... thus to the Christian Mason [it is] the Old and New Testament; to the Jew the Old Testament;, to the Musselman [Muslim], the Koran; to the Brahman the Vedas; and to the parsee the Zendavesta" (*Masonry Defined*, a compilation of the writings of Albert Pike and Albert Mackey, pp 78, 79).

(2) "Masonry makes no profession of Christianity ... but looks forward to the time when the labor of our ancient brethren shall be symbolized by the erection of a spiritual temple... in which there shall be but one altar and one worship; one common altar of Masonry on which the Veda, Shastra, Sade, lend-Avesta, Koran and Holy Bible shall lie ... and at whose shrine the Hindoo [sic], the Persian, the Assyrian, the Chaldean, the Egyptian, the Chinese, the Mohammedan, the Jew and the

Christian may kneel...." (*The Kentucky Monitor*, Fellowcraft Degree, p 95).

(3) "What is Truth to the philosopher would not be truth, nor have the effect of truth, to the peasant. The religion of many must necessarily be more incorrect than that of the refined and reflective few.... The truest religion would, in many points, not be comprehended by the ignorant.... The doctrines of the Bible are often not clothed in the language of strict truth, but in that which was fittest to convey to a rude and ignorant people, the doctrine" (Albert Pike, *Morals and Dogma*, 14th Degree, p, 224).

(4) "... the literal meaning [of the Bible] is for the vulgar only" (Albert Pike, *Digest of Morals and Dogma*, p. 166).

(5) "To all this [error of stupidity] the absurd reading of the established Church, taking literally the figurative, allegorical, and mythical language of a collection of Oriental books of different ages, directly and inevitably led" (Albert Pike, *Morals and Dogma*, 30th Degree, p. 818).

(6) "The Jews, the Chinese, the Turks, each reject either the New Testament, or the Old, or both, and yet we see no good reason why they should not be made Masons. In fact Blue Lodge Masonry has nothing whatever to do with the Bible. It is not founded on the Bible; if it was it would not be Masonry; it would be something else" (*Chase's Digest of Masonic Law*, pp, 207-209).

(7) "Beautiful around stretches off every way the Universe, the Great Bible of God. Material nature is its Old Testament ... and Human Nature is the New Testament from the Infinite God" (Albert Pike, *Morals and Dogma*, 28th Degree, p, 715).

(8) "Masonry is a search after Light. That search leads us back, as you see, to the Kabalah. In that ancient and little understood [source-book] the Initiate will find the source of many doctrines; and [he] may in time come to understand the Hermetic philosophers, the Alchemists, all the Antipapal

Thinkers of the Middle Ages, and Emanuel Swedenborg"
(Albert Pike, *Morals and Dogma*, 28th Degree, p. 741).

(9) "All truly dogmatic religions have issued from the
Kabalah and return to it; everything scientific and grand in the
religious dreams of the Illuminati, Jacob Boeheme, Swedenborg,
Saint Martin, and others is borrowed from the Kabalah: all
Masonic associations owe to it their secrets and their symbols"
(Albert Pike, *Morals and Dogma*, 28th Degree, p. 744).

(10) "The removal of the name of Jesus and references to
Him in Bible verses used in the ritual are slight but necessary
modifications" (Albert Mackey, *Masonic Ritualist*, p. 272).

CHRISTIAN DOCTRINE

The Bible is the *only* written revelation of, and from, the
only true God. The Bible, as contained in the Old and New
Testaments, is the Word of God, inspired and preserved by Him,
and is the only valid rule of faith and practice for His people,
the church. No part shall be added to, or taken from the Bible
as delivered to us in the Old and New Testaments.

(1) "If they speak not according to this Word, it is because
there is no light in them" (Isaiah 8:20).

(2) "All Scripture is given by inspiration of God"
(2 Timothy 3:16)

(3) "The Words of the Lord are pure words, as silver tried
in a furnace of earth, purified seven times. Thou shalt keep
them, O Lord, thou shalt preserve them from this generation
forever" (Psalm 12:6, 7).

(4) "... whose hope is in the Lord his God, which made
heaven, and earth, the sea, and all that therein is: which keepeth
truth forever" (Psalm 146:5, 6).

(5) "Every word of God is pure: He is a shield unto them
that put their trust in Him. Add thou not unto His words, lest
He reprove thee, and thou be found a liar" (Proverbs 30:5, 6).

(6) "Heaven and earth shall pass away, but my words shall
not pass away" (Matthew 24:35).

(7) "Being born again, not of corruptible seed, but of incorruptible, by the word of God, which liveth and abideth forever.... But the word of the Lord endureth forever. And this is the word which by the gospel is preached unto you" (1 Peter 1:23, 25).

(8) "For we have not followed cunningly devised fables, when we declared unto you the power and coming of our Lord Jesus Christ, but were eyewitnesses of his majesty.... Knowing this first, that no prophecy of the scripture is of any private interpretation. For the prophecy came not in old time by the will of man: but holy men of God spake as they were moved by the Holy Ghost" (2 Peter 1:16-21).

(9) "Ye shall not add unto the word which I command you, neither shall ye diminish aught from it...." (Deuteronomy 4:2).

(10) "... If any man shall add unto these things, God shall add unto him the plagues that are written in this book: And if any man shall take away from the words of the book of this prophecy, God shall take away his part out of the book of life...." (Revelation 22:18, 19).

3. GOD

MASONIC DOCTRINE

God is, basically, whatever we perceive Him to be; our idea or concept of God becomes our God. Usually referred to with the vague and general term, "Deity," the god of Masonry can be the one of our choosing, spoken of generically as "The Great Architect of the Universe." However, those who pursue the higher studies in Masonry learn that God is the force of nature, specifically the Sun with its life-giving powers. To the "advanced, enlightened ones," the adepts at the top, this nature worship is understood as the worship of the generative principles (i.e. the sex organs), particularly the phallus. Human Nature is also worshipped by some as "Deity," as are Knowledge and Reason. Since Masonry is a revival of the ancient pagan mystery religions, its god can also be said to be Nature, with its fertility (sex) gods and goddesses representing the Sun and Moon (in Egypt, Osiris and Isis).

(1) "... Since every man's conception of God must be proportioned to his mental cultivation, and intellectual powers, and moral excellence, God is, as man conceives Him, the reflected image of man himself" (Albert Pike, *Morals and Dogma*, 14th Degree, p. 223).

(2) "... every religion and every conception of God is idolatrous, in so far as it is imperfect, and as it substitutes a feeble and temporary idea...of that Undiscoverable Being who can be known only in part, and who can therefore be honored, even by the most enlightened among His worshippers, only in proportion to their limited powers of understanding and imagining to themselves ..." (Albert Pike, *Morals and Dogma*, 25th Degree, p. 516).

(3) "The only personal God Freemasonry accepts is humanity in toto.... Humanity therefore is the only personal God that there is" (J.D. Buck, *Mystic Masonry*, p. 216).

(4) "Phallus: a representation of the virile member [male sex organ] which was venerated as a religious symbol very universally ... by the ancients. It was one of the modifications of Sun worship, and was a symbol of the fecundating [impregnating] power of the luminaries. The Masonic point within a circle [important Masonic symbol] is undoubtedly of phallic origin" (Albert Mackey, *Symbolism of Freemasonry*, p. 352).

(5) "These two divinities [the Sun and the Moon, Osiris and Isis, etc] were commonly symbolized by the generative parts of man and woman; to which in remote ages no idea of indecency was attached; the Phallus [penis] and Cites [vagina], emblems of generation and production, and which, as such, appeared in the Mysteries [the ancient religions of which Masonry is a revival]. The Indian Lingam was the union of both, as were the boat and mast and the point within the circle [important

Masonic symbols]" (Albert Pike, *Morals and Dogma,* 24th Degree, p. 401).

(6) "Masonry, successor to the Mysteries [the pagan religions of Isis, Osiris, Baal, Mythras, Tammuz, etc.], still follows the ancient manner of teaching" (Albert Pike, *Morals and Dogma,* Fellowcraft Degree, p 22).

(7) "Though Masonry is identical with the ancient Mysteries, it is so only in this qualified sense: that it presents but an imperfect image of their brilliancy, the ruins of their grandeur ..." (Albert Pike, *Morals and Dogma,* Fellowcraft Degree p. 23).

(8) "The Absolute is Reason. Reason IS, by means of Itself. It IS because IT IS ... If God IS, HE IS by Reason" (Albert Pike, *Morals and Dogma,* 28th Degree, p. 737).

(9) "This is the immutable law of Nature, the Eternal Will of the Justice which is God" (Albert Pike, *Morals and Dogma,* 32nd Degree, p. 847).

CHRISTIAN DOCTRINE

God is a Spirit, eternal, self-existent, unchanging, almighty, all-knowing and sovereign. There is one God who created all things, existing in three Persons: Father, Son and Holy Spirit. God the Father is revealed in His Son, Jesus Christ, and is perfect. He is holy, and requires holiness of His people.

(1) "In the beginning God created the Heaven and the Earth" (Genesis 1:1).

(2) "God is a Spirit: and they that worship Him must worship Him in spirit and truth" (John 4:4).

(3) "Hear, O Israel: the Lord our God is one Lord" (Deuteronomy 6:4).

(4) "Before the mountains were brought forth, or even thou hadst formed the earth and the world, even from everlasting to everlasting, thou art God" (Psalm 90:2).

(5) "For I am the Lord, I change not ..." (Malachi 3:6).

(6) "There is none other God but one ... the Father, of whom are all things" (1 Corinthians 8:4, 6).

(7) "But the Lord is the true God, he is the everlasting God, and an everlasting king" (Jeremiah 10:10).

(8) "Thy throne, O God, is forever and ever" (Psalm 45:6).

(9) "For there are three that bear record in Heaven, the Father, the Word [Jesus], and the Holy Ghost: and these three are one" (I John 5:7).

(10) "... Ye shall be holy: for I the Lord your God am holy" (Leviticus 19:2).

(11) "God said unto Moses, 'I am that I am ...'" (Exodus 3:14).

4. REDEMPTION

MASONIC DOCTRINE

Redemption is a matter of self-improvement, morality, and good works, including obedience to the Mason's obligations (death oaths) and all higher Masonic authorities.

Faith in the atonement of Jesus has nothing to do with it; it is rather a matter of enlightenment, step by step, which comes with initiation into the Masonic degrees and their mysteries.

(1) "By the lambskin the Mason is reminded of that purity of life and rectitude of conduct which are so essentially necessary to his gaining admission into the Celestial Lodge above, where the Supreme Architect of the Universe presides" (Albert Mackey, *Encyclopedia of Freemasonry*, "Apron").

(2) "... and in Thy favor, may we be received into Thine everlasting kingdom, to enjoy, in union with the souls of our departed friends, the just reward of a pious and virtuous life. Amen. So Mote it Be" (*Texas Monitor*, Masonic Burial Service, p. 10).

(3) "In Egypt, Greece and among other ancient nations, Freemasonry was one of the earliest agencies employed to effect improvement and enlightenment of man ... and make them comprehend the true principles of morality, which initiate

men into a new order of life" (Daniel Sickles, *Ahimon Rezon or Freemason's Guide*, p. 57).

(4) "The rite of induction signifies the end of a profane and vicious life, the palingenesis [new birth] of corrupt human nature, the death of vice and all bad passions and the introductions to the new life of purity and virtue" (Daniel Sickles, *Ahimon Rezon or Freemason's Guide*, p. 54).

(5) These three degrees [1st, 2nd, 3rd] thus form a perfect and harmonious whole, nor can it be conceived that anything can be suggested more, which the soul of man requires" (Daniel Sickles, *Ahimon Rezon or Freemason's Guide*, p. 196).

(6) "If we with suitable true devotion maintain our Masonic profession, our faith will become a beam of light and bring us to those blessed mansions where we shall be eternally happy with God, the Great Architect of the Universe" (Daniel Sickles, *Ahimon Rezon or Freemason's Guide*, p. 79).

(7) "Acacian: a term signifying a Mason who by living in strict obedience to obligations and precepts of the fraternity is free from sin" (A. Mackey, *Lexicon of Freemasonry*, p. 16).

(8) "When you shall have become imbued with the morality of Masonry ... when you shall have learned to practice all the virtues which it inculcates; when they become familiar to you as your Household God; then will you be prepared to receive its lofty philosophical instruction, and to scale the heights upon whose summit Light and Truth sit enthroned. Step by step men must advance towards Perfection; and each Masonic Degree is meant to be one of those steps" (Albert Pike, *Morals and Dogma*, 8th Degree, p, 136).

(9) "The dunces who led primitive Christianity astray, by submitting faith for science ... have succeeded in shrouding in darkness the ancient discoveries of the human mind; so that now we grope in the dark to find again the key..." (Albert Pike, *Morals and Dogma*, 28th Degree, p. 732).

(10) "... salvation by faith and the vicarious atonement were not taught as now interpreted, by Jesus, nor are these

doctrines taught in the esoteric scriptures. They are later and ignorant perversions of the original doctrines" (J.D. Buck, *Mystic Masonry*, p. 51).

CHRISTIAN DOCTRINE

All have sinned and fallen short of the perfection God requires; none is righteous in his own virtue and our own righteousness is as filthy rags compared with the righteousness of God. However, Jesus, God's only begotten Son, lived a sinless life for us, and laid down His life a perfect sacrifice to make atonement for our sins.

By faith in Him, and His provisions for us, we can be made the righteousness of God and be born of the Spirit of God into everlasting life, becoming a part of the family of God. There is no other way to be reconciled to God and live in His presence forever. We cannot, by our own efforts, redeem or perfect ourselves.

(1) "As it is written, There is none righteous, no, not one" (Romans 3:10).

(2) "For all have sinned and come short of the glory of God" (Romans 3:23.)

(3) "But we are all as an unclean thing, and all our righteousnesses are as filthy rags" (Isaiah 64:6).

(4) "For He hath made Him to be sin for us, who knew no sin, that we might be made the righteousness of God in Him" (2 Corinthians 5:21).

(5) "For ye [Christians] are all the children of God by faith in Christ Jesus" (Galatians 3:26).

(6) "For God so loved the world, that he gave his only begotten Son, that whosoever believeth in him should not perish, but have everlasting life" (John 3:16).

(7) "For by grace are ye saved through faith; and that not of yourselves: it is the gift of God. Not of works, lest any man should boast" (Ephesians 2:8, 9).

(8) "Neither is there salvation in any other [than Jesus]. For there is none other name under heaven, given among men, whereby we must be saved" (Acts 4:12).

(9) "And this is the record, that God hath given to us eternal life, and this life is in his Son. He that hath the Son hath life, and he that hath not the Son of God hath not life" (1 John 5:11, 12).

5. SATAN

MASONIC DOCTRINE

Satan, as an enemy of God and his Kingdom, as an evil power seeking to tempt, deceive and destroy, does not exist. Mankind has merely "supposed" this. The usual Christian perception of Satan is merely a distortion of the truth about Lucifer, the "Light Bearer," who is actually good and the instrument of liberty, but generally misunderstood and maligned.

(1) "The true name of Satan, the Kabalists say, is that of Yahveh reversed; for Satan is not a black god.... For the initiates this is not a Person, but a Force, created for good, but which may serve for evil. It is the instrument of Liberty or Free Will" (Albert Pike, *Morals and Dogma,* Master Mason /3rd Degree. P. 102).

(2) "Lucifer, the Light-Bearer! Strange and mysterious name to give to the Spirit of Darkness! Lucifer, the Son of the Morning! Is it he who bears the Light, and with all its splendors intolerable blinds feeble, sensual, or selfish Souls? Doubt it not!" (Albert Pike, *Morals and Dogma,* 19th Degree, p. 321).

(3) "The conviction of all men that God is good led to a belief in a devil ..." (Albert Pike, *Morals and Dogma,* 19th Degree, p. 324).

(4) "All antiquity solved the enigma of the existence of evil by supposing the existence of a Principle of Evil, of demons, fallen angels ... a Satan ..." (*Kentucky Monitor,* "The Spirit of Masonry," p. xiv).

(5) "... there is no rebellious demon of Evil, or Principle of Darkness coexistent and in eternal controversy with God,

or the Principal of Light ..." (Albert Pike, *Morals and Dogma*, 32nd Degree, p. 859).

CHRISTIAN DOCTRINE

Satan is a proud, rebellious angel, created by God but fallen, the father of lies, accuser of the brethren, deceiver, tempter and ruler of the Kingdom of Darkness. He blinds the lost to the glorious light of the gospel, and seeks to be worshipped as he also works to steal, kill and destroy. He is the enemy we are to resist and the one whose works Jesus came to destroy.

(1) "How art thou fallen, O Lucifer, son of the morning! How art thou cut down to the ground, which did weaken the nations! For thou hast said in thine heart, I will ascend into heaven, I will exalt my throne above the stars of God: I will sit also upon the mount of the congregation, in the sides of the north: I will ascend above the heights of the clouds; I will be like the most High. Yet thou shalt be brought down to Hell..." (Isaiah 14:12-15).

(2) "... Thou art the anointed cherub that covereth; and I have set thee so: thou wast upon the holy mountain of God; thou hast walked up and down in the midst of the stones of fire... Thine heart was lifted up because of thy beauty, thou hast corrupted thy wisdom by reason of thy brightness: I will cast thee to the ground ..." (Ezekiel 28:13-19).

(3) "Ye are of your father, the devil ... he is a liar, and the father of it" (John 8:44).

(4) "And the great dragon was cast out, that old serpent, called the Devil, and Satan, which deceiveth the whole world: he was cast out into the earth, and his angels were cast out with him...the accuser of our brethren is cast down ..." (Revelation 12:9, 10).

(5) "And Jesus being full of the Holy Ghost returned from Jordan, and was led by the Spirit into the wilderness, being forty days tempted of the devil ..." (Luke 4:1, 2).

(6) "And if Satan cast out Satan ... how shall then his kingdom stand?" (Matthew 12:26).

(7) "Put on the whole armor of God, that ye may be able to stand against the wiles of the devil.... For we wrestle ... against the rulers of the darkness ..." (Ephesians 6:11, 12).

(8) "... the god of this world hath blinded the minds of them which believe not, lest the light of the glorious gospel of Christ... should shine unto them" (2 Corinthians 4:4).

(9) "The thief [Satan] cometh not, but for to steal, and to kill, and to destroy" (John 10:10).

(10) "Resist the devil, and he will flee from you" (James 4:7).

(11) "For this purpose the Son of God was manifested, that he might destroy the works of the devil" (1 John 3:8).

(12) "... Your adversary, the devil, as a roaring lion, walketh about, seeking whom he may devour" (1 Peter 5:8).

6. SPIRITUAL LIGHT AND DARKNESS

MASONIC DOCTRINE

All "profane" people (non-Masons), including godly, genuine Christians, are wretched, blind and lost in complete spiritual darkness. Only initiation into the degrees and mysteries of Masonry will bring them out of darkness and "into the light," cleansing them and imparting new life.

(1) "In Masonry, the darkness, which envelops the mind of the uninitiated [non-Mason] is removed by the effulgence of Masonic Light. Masons are appropriately called the 'Sons of Light'" (*Lightfoot's Manual of the Lodge,* p. 175).

(2) "Freemasons are emphatically called 'Sons of Light' ... while the profane or uninitiated [non-Masons] who have not received this knowledge ... are said to be in darkness." (*Masonic Dictionary,* "Light," Chicago, Consolidated Book Pub., 1963).

(3) Blindfolded ("hoodwinked") and kneeling, half naked and bound by a rope ("cabletow"), the candidate for initiation into the Blue Degrees is asked, by the Worshipful Master, "In your present, blind condition, what do you most desire?" His

reply, according to the ritual, must be "Light" (1st Degree), "Further Light" (2nd Degree) and "More Light" (3rd Degree) (Verbal Masonic Ritual, 1st, 2nd, 3rd Degrees).

(4) "There he [the man to be initiated] stands, without our portals, on the threshold of his new Masonic life, in darkness, helplessness and ignorance. Having been wandering amid the errors, and covered over with the pollutions of the outer and profane world, he comes inquiringly to our doors, seeking the new birth, and asking a withdrawal of the veil ..." (Albert Mackey, *Manual of the Lodge*, p. 20).

(5) "Applied to Masonic symbolism, it [the darkness] is intended to remind the candidate of his ignorance, which Masonry is to enlighten; of his evil nature, which Masonry is to purify; of the world in whose obscurity he has been wandering and from which Masonry is to rescue him" (Albert Mackey, *Manual of the Lodge*, p. 39).

CHRISTIAN DOCTRINE

Jesus is the Light of the World; those who follow Him shall not be in darkness. He, and He alone, is the source of spiritual enlightenment. If we are "in Him" we are not in darkness, for in Him is no darkness at all. The life that He alone gives is the light of men.

(1) "I am the Light of the World: He that followeth me shall not walk in darkness, but shall have the light of life" (John 8:12).

(2)"But ye are a chosen generation, a royal priesthood, an holy nation, a peculiar people; that ye should show forth the praises of him who hath called you out of darkness into his marvelous light" (1 Peter 2:9).

(3) "For ye were sometimes darkness, but now are ye light in the Lord" (Ephesians 5:8).

(4) "This then is the message which we have heard of him [Jesus], and declare unto you, that God is light, and in him is no darkness at all" (1 John 1:5).

(5) "In him [Jesus] was life; and the life was the light of men" (John 1:4).

7. PRAYER

MASONIC DOCTRINE

Prayers are to be offered to "Deity," to "The Great Architect of the Universe" (GAOTU), and are to be "universal" in nature, so as not to offend anyone and so as to apply to everyone. Prayer is NEVER to be made "in Jesus' name," or "in Christ's name"; to do so would offend a Muslim, Hindu, Buddhist, etc. If a Worshipful Master allows prayers to be made in Jesus' name, his lodge can be closed and its charter revoked by the Grand Lodge of his state.[35]

Masonic prayers are usually ended with "So mote it be" rather than "Amen." It is interesting to note that in Satanism, witchcraft, sorcery, and similar abominations to God, prayers and declarations are closed with "So mote it be."

(1) "All sectarian tenets must be carefully excluded from the [Masonic] system" (Morris, *Webb's Monitor*, p. 285).

(2) "Prayer in Masonic lodges should be of a general character, containing nothing offensive to any class of conscientious brethren" (Ibid).

(3) "The religion then, of Masonry is pure Theism on which its different members engraft their own peculiar opinions; but they are not permitted to introduce them into the lodge ..." (Albert Mackey, *Lexicon of Freemasonry*, Religion).

(4) "Every important undertaking in Masonry is both begun and completed with prayer. The prayers given in the handbooks of the Blue Lodge are such as all Masons, whatever their religious faith, may unite in ... (Morris's *Dictionary*, Prayer).

CHRISTIAN DOCTRINE

Prayer is to be made to God the Heavenly Father, in the name of (through) God the Son, in the power of, and inspired by, God the Holy Spirit. Only through the mediatory office of Jesus can we approach the throne of God in prayer.

(1) "For there is one God, and one mediator between God and men, the man Christ Jesus" (1 Timothy 2:5).

(2) "... whatsoever you shall ask of the Father in my [Jesus] name, he may give it to you" (John. 15:16).

(3) "Giving thanks always for all things unto God and the Father in the name of our Lord Jesus Christ" (Ephesians 5:20).

(4) "And whatsoever ye do in word or deed, do all in the name of the Lord Jesus, giving thanks to God and the Father by him" (Colossians 3: 17) .

(5) "I will therefore that men pray everywhere, lifting up holy hands..." (1 Timothy 2:8).

(6) "Pray without ceasing (1 Thessalonians 5:17).

(7) "The effectual fervent prayer of a righteous man availeth much" (James 5:16).

8. TRUTHFULNESS

MASONIC DOCTRINE

It is right to lie, if necessary, to protect the "secrets" of the Lodge, or to protect another Mason by concealing his wrongdoing. It can even be "right" to deliberately deceive sincere Masons seeking to learn the lessons and "secrets" of Masonry.

(1) "The Blue Degrees are but the portico [porch] of the Temple. Part of the symbols are displayed there to the initiate, but he is intentionally misled by false interpretations. It is not intended that he shall understand them; but it is intended that he shall imagine that he understands them ... their true explication [explanation/understanding] is reserved for the Adepts, the Princes of Masonry" (Albert Pike, *Morals and Dogma,* 30th Degree, p. 819).

(2) "Furthermore do I promise and swear that a Master Mason's secrets, given to me in charge as such, and I knowing

them to be such, shall remain as secure and inviolable in my breast as in his own, when communicated to me, murder and treason excepted; and they left to my own election" (Master Mason's / 3rd Degree Oath of Obligation).

(3) "A companion Royal Arch Mason's secrets given to me in charge as such, and I knowing them to be such, shall remain as secure and inviolable in my breast as in his own, without exception" (Royal Arch Mason's Oath of Obligation).

(4) "You must conceal all the crimes of your brother Masons ... and should you be summoned as a witness against a brother Mason be always sure to shield him.... It may be perjury to do this, it is true, but you're keeping your obligations" (Ronayne, *Handbook of Masonry*, p. 183).

(5) "If your wife, or child, or friend, should ask you anything about your initiation—as for instance, if your clothes were taken off, if you were blindfolded, if you had a rope around your neck, etc, you must conceal ... hence of course, you must deliberately lie about it. It is part of your obligation ..." (Ibid, p. 74).

CHRISTIAN DOCTRINE

We must speak the truth at all times,

(1) "Thou shalt not bear false witness against thy neighbor" (Exodus 20:16).

(2) "Ye shall not steal, neither deal falsely, neither lie one to another" (Leviticus 19:11).

(3) "Lie not to one another" (Colossians 3:9).

(4) "... all liars, shall have their part in the lake which burneth with fire and brimstone; which is the second death" (Revelation 21:8).

(5) "But speaking the truth in love, may grow up into Him in all things, which is the Head, *even* Christ" (Ephesians 4:15).

9. SECRECY

a. MASONIC DOCTRINE

Secrecy is the essence of Masonry, necessary for its very existence, and protected by blood oaths of mayhem and murder.

(1) "Secrecy is indispensable in a Mason of whatever degree" (Albert Pike, *Morals and Dogma*, 4th Degree, p. 109).

(2) "The secrecy of this institution is another and most important landmark.... If divested of its secret character, it would lose its identity, and would cease to be Freemasonry ... death of the Order would follow its legalized exposure. Freemasonry, as a secret association, has lived unchanged for centuries; as an open society it would not last for as many years" (Albert Mackey, *Textbook of Masonic Jurisprudence,* 23rd Landmark, "Secrecy").

(3) "I ... do hereby and hereon most solemnly and sincerely promise and swear that I will always hail, ever conceal and never reveal any of the arts, parts or points of the secret arts and mysteries of ancient Freemasonry which I have received, am about to receive, or may hereafter be instructed in ..." (Oath of Obligation, Entered Apprentice/1st Degree, and included in all subsequent degrees, always on penalty of mayhem and violent death).

CHRISTIAN DOCTRINE

There are no secrets in the Kingdom of God; there are mysteries, but no secrets. The truth of God that sets men free is for all who will hear it, and we are to shout it from the housetops and tell it to all the world!

(1) "I [Jesus] spake openly to the world; I ever taught in the synagogue, and in the temple ... and in secret have I said nothing" (John 18:20).

(2) "What I tell you in darkness, that speak ye in light; and what ye hear in the ear, that preach ye upon the housetops" (Matthew 10:27).

(3) "Go ye into all the world, and preach the gospel [good news] to every creature" (Mark 16:15).

(4) "Provide things honest in the sight of all men" (Romans 12:17).

10. BLOOD OATHS

MASONIC DOCTRINE

Blood Oaths, on penalty of mayhem and violent death, are administered at the end of initiation into all Masonic degrees, binding the initiate to protect the "secrets" of the degrees. These oaths of obligation (usually called just "obligations") are considered unbreakable, and are (collectively) the thing that makes a man a Mason. In this way, these oaths are the cornerstone of Freemasonry.

(1) Question: "What makes you a Mason?" Answer: "My obligation" (Question and answer from the Entered Apprentice / First Degree).

(2) "... binding myself under no less a penalty than that of having my throat cut from ear to ear, my tongue torn out by its roots, and with my body buried in the rough sands of the sea, a cable's length from the shore, where the tide ebbs and flows twice in twenty-four hours ..." (from the oath of obligation, entered Apprentice / First Degree).

(3) "... binding myself under no less a penalty than that of having my left breast torn open, my heart plucked out, and given to the beasts of the field and fowls of the air as a prey ..." (from the oath of obligation, Fellowcraft / Second Degree).

(4) "... binding myself under no less a penalty than that of having my body severed in twain, my bowels taken out and burned to ashes, the ashes scattered to the four winds of heaven ..." (from the oath of obligation, Master Mason / Third Degree).

(5) "... In willful violation whereof may I incur the fearful penalty of having my eyeballs pierced to the center with a three-edged blade, my feet flayed and I be forced to walk the hot

sands upon the sterile shores of the Red Sea until the flaming Sun shall strike me with a livid plague, and may Allah, the god of Arab, Moslem, and Mohammedan, the god of our fathers, support me to the entire fulfillment of the same" (from the Oath of Obligation, Ancient Arabic Order of Nobles of the Mystic Shrine ["Shriners"]).

CHRISTIAN DOCTRINE

A Christian is enjoined not to take oaths at all, especially oaths of mayhem and murder. It is particularly offensive to God for a Christian to take such an oath, swearing on the pagan Koran, calling upon Allah to sustain and make possible his faithfulness to the terrible oath, confessing that Allah is "the god of our fathers," A Christian (or Jew) is not even to speak the name of a pagan god in a way that expresses respect or honor.

(1) "Thou shalt not kill [do no murder]" (Exodus 20:13).

(2) "But I say unto you, swear not at all ... but let your communications be, Yea, Yea; Nay, Nay; for whatsoever is more than these cometh of evil" (Matthew 5:34-37).

(3) "But above all things, my brethren, swear not, neither by heaven, neither by the earth, neither by any other oath; but let your yea be yea; and your nay, nay; lest ye fall into condemnation" (James 5:12).

(4) "... and make no mention of the name of other gods, neither let it be heard out of thy mouth" (Exodus 23:13).

(5) "Their sorrows shall be multiplied that hasten after another god; their drink offerings of blood will I not offer, nor take up their names into my lips" (Psalm 16:4).

(6) "That ye come not among these [pagan] nations...neither make mention of the name of their gods, nor cause to swear by them..." (Joshua 23:7).

11. SEEKING AND FINDING

MASONIC DOCTRINE

Masonry is a never-ending search for "light," always promised but never quite realized.

(1) "It is one of the most beautiful, but at the same time one of the most abstruse doctrines of the science of Masonic symbolism that the Mason is ever to be in search of truth, but is never to find it"(Albert Mackey, *Manual of the Lodge*, p. 93; Daniel Sickles, *Ahimon Rezon or Freemason's Guide*, p. 169).

(2) "You have reached the mountain peak of Masonic instruction, a peak covered with mist, which YOU in search for further light can penetrate only by your own efforts" (Lecture of the 32nd Degree, final earned degree, Scottish Rite).

CHRISTIAN DOCTRINE

If we sincerely seek truth (light) in Jesus, who declared Himself to be Truth and Light, we are promised that we will find it. Jesus is the beginning and the ending of our search. Coming unto Him we find life, meaning and understanding; for all that we need and desire, He provides. We are guaranteed, by God who cannot lie, that if we call upon Him we will not be disappointed or ashamed.

(1) "And I say unto you ... seek and ye shall find" (Luke 11:9).

(2) "... he that seeketh findeth" (Luke 11:10).

(3) "... and him that cometh to me [Jesus] I will in no wise cast out" (John 6:31).

(4) "For Christ is the end [fulfillment] of the law for righteousness to everyone that believeth" (Romans 10:4).

(5) "And ye shall seek me, and find me, when ye shall search for me with all your heart" (Jeremiah 29:13).

12. EXCLUSIVENESS

MASONIC DOCTRINE

The "light" of Freemasonry, its "secrets" and its pathway to "perfection" are only for the elite, enlightened few who are initiated into its knowledge and wisdom. Excluded are women, blacks, the poor (who haven't the money with which to pay), the crippled, blind and deaf who can't perform the recognition signs (or see and hear them), and the feeble-minded who can't receive the teachings or be trusted to protect them. All such people, including the wives, the daughters and the non-Mason fathers, brothers and sons of Masons, are considered "profane" (unclean, unworthy) and can never be anything else. No references are required here for it is common knowledge and all of the above confirms and establishes it.

CHRISTIAN DOCTRINE

The life, knowledge, wisdom and freedom offered by God in Jesus are for "whosoever will"; anyone can come to Him and receive these priceless blessings, free, just by asking. Everyone who asks, sincerely, receives; none is turned away and none is disappointed or ashamed. God is not willing that anyone should perish; rather, He wants all to come to Him and receive the life that He alone can give.

(1) "The Lord is ... not willing that any should perish but that all should come to repentance" (2 Peter 3:9).

(2) "Come unto me all ye that labour and are heavy laden, and I will give you rest. Take my yoke upon you and learn of me; for I am meek and lowly of heart: and ye shall find rest unto your souls" (Matthew 11:28, 29).

(3) "If any man thirst, let him come unto me [Jesus] and drink ..." (John 7:37).

(4) "And let him that is athirst come. And whosoever will, let him take the water of life freely" (Revelation 22:17).

ENDNOTES

35 (a) It is true that in some local lodges, in small communities
where all churches are Christian, prayers are made in Jesus'
name. This is particularly true in small towns in the South and
lower Midwest; for in this region God and his Word are more
widely believed and honored than in the rest of the nation.
However, if this were to be reported to the Grand Lodge of
that state, the local lodge so praying would be required to stop
it immediately or have its charter revoked. Jack Harris, past
Worshipful Master of a Baltimore, Maryland lodge, was told
just this. (Harris, Jack. *Freemasonry—The Invisible Cult in
Our Midst,* Daniels Pub Co. 1983, pp ix, x, 121, 122)
(b) Harmon Taylor, former Grand Chaplain of the Grand
Lodge of New York, says, "The only instruction I was given as
New York State Grand Chaplain, and I was given it repeatedly,
was not to end a prayer in Jesus' name ("Attention Masons,"
HRT Ministries, Box 12, Newtonville, NY 12128).
(c) It is a fact, known to every Mason who cares to know, that
in all the prayers printed in his monitors, handbooks and other
guides to rituals there is NOT ONE which closes in Jesus'
name. The same is true of the auxiliaries, such as the Order of
the Eastern Star, Rainbow Girls, and the Order of DeMolay.

Masonic Symbolism

1. THE ULTIMATE DECEPTION

Masonry is, according to its own philosophers, a system of pure religion expressed in symbols, one which cannot be understood without a knowledge of the true meaning of them. This makes a proper understanding of those symbols terribly important. For the Christian Mason, accepting and guarding those symbols and their "secrets" with his physical life at stake, he must understand them to know that he is doing right.

For the many zealous Masons, trusting their obedience to their obligations to gain them entrance into that "Celestial Lodge Above," those for whom "the Lodge is a good enough religion," the correct understanding of these symbols is the key (they believe) to their eternal destiny. They are trusting in the teachings of the Lodge concerning these symbols with their eternal redemption, or damnation, at stake.

Herein lies the most terrible manifestation of Masonic morality, that philosophy of the elite, which makes whatever they do "right" because it is they (the elite) who do it. Having established and taught the sincere but deceived masses of Masons (the Blue Lodge Masons plus the vast majority of 32nd Degree Masons and Knights Templar) that everything depends upon their proper understanding of the symbols of

Masonry, they have then deliberately deceived them as to the true meaning of those symbols. Hear the arrogant words of Albert Pike, Supreme Pontiff of Universal Freemasonry, that preeminent Masonic authority: 'The Blue Degrees are but the court or portico [porch] of the Temple. Part of the symbols are displayed there to the initiate, but he is intentionally misled by false interpretations. It is not intended that he shall understand them; but it is intended that he shall imagine that he understands them...their true explication [explanation and understanding] is reserved for the Adepts, the Princes of Masonry [those of the 32nd and 33rd Degrees]." (*Morals and Dogma*, page 819).

2. THE FOUNDATION OF MASONIC SYMBOLISM: PHALLIC WORSHIP

Since the true meaning of Masonic symbols (and, thus, the true meaning of Masonry itself) is to be known only by the Prince Adepts of Masonry, we must hear what they say concerning them. They (Albert Pike, Albert Mackey, J.D, Buck, Daniel Sickles and others) teach us that Masonry is but a revival of the Ancient Mysteries (the pagan mystery religions of Babylon, Egypt, Persia, Rome and Greece).

These ancient religions had two meanings, or interpretations. One was the apparent (exoteric) meaning, known to the uninitiated, ignorant masses; the other (esoteric) meaning was the true meaning, entirely different, and known only by a small, elite group, initiated into their secrets and secret rituals of worship. These mystery religions were forms of nature-worship, more specifically and most commonly the worship of the Sun as source and giver of life to the Earth. Since ancient times, this worship of the Sun (and of the Moon, stars and of nature in general) has been sexual in its out-workings and rituals. Since the Sun's rays, penetrating the Earth and bringing about new life, have been central to such worship, the phallus, the male "generative principle," has been worshipped as representing the Sun's rays. In this way, the phallus has been worshipped and the rituals climaxed with sexual union in the mystery religions of Isis and Osiris, Tammuz, Baal, etc.[36] In summary, then, since the Ancient Mysteries (especially those of Egypt) are in fact the "Old Religion" of which Freemasonry is so proud to be a revival, the symbols of Masonry should be expected to be phallic in true meaning. This, in very fact, is the case, A thorough treatment of this unpleasant reality is beyond the scope of this brief summary; however, some examples, with references to the Masonic authorities, will suffice to illustrate this astonishing fact.

a. THE SQUARE AND COMPASS

Blue Lodge Masons are taught that the Square is to remind them that they must be "square" in their dealings with all men, i.e. to be honest. The Compass, they are taught, is to teach them to "circumscribe their passions," i.e., to control their desires and to be temperate. The real meaning of these "great lights," however, is sexual. The Square represents the female (passive) generative principle, the earth, and the baser, sensual nature; and the Compass represents the male (active) generative principle, the sun/heavens, and the higher, spiritual nature. The Compass, arranged above the Square, symbolizes the (male) Sun, impregnating the passive (female) Earth with its life-producing rays. The true meanings, then, are two-fold: the earthly (human) representations are of the man and his phallus, and the woman with her receptive eteis (vagina). The cosmic meaning is that of the active Sun (deity, the Sun-god) from above, imparting life into the passive Earth (deity, the earth/fertility goddess) below and producing new life.[37]

b. THE LETTER "G"

The Blue Lodge Mason is taught that the "G" in the basic Masonic symbol represents God. Later on, he is told that it also represents "deity." Later still, he is told that it represents "geometry." In reality, this letter represents the "generative principle," the Sun god and, thus, the worshipped phallus, the male "generative principle...." In its position (along with the Square and Compass) on the east wall over the chair (throne) of the Worshipful Master, it is the representation of the Sun, thus of the Sun-god, Osiris. Its earthly meaning, then, is of the sacred phallus; its cosmic meaning is of the Sun, worshipped since antiquity by pagans while facing the East. (See c. below.)

c. THE "G" AND THE "YOD"

The English letter "G" in Masonic symbolism is inseparable from, and identical with, the Hebrew letter "YOD." This "YOD" is the symbol on the Scottish Rite ring. "YOD" represents deity in general (its cosmic meaning), and the worshipped phallus in particular (its earthly meaning). Albert Pike wrote that the "G" displayed in English speaking lodges is merely a corruption of the "YOD" (with which it should be replaced), and that "the mysterious YOD of the Kabalah" is the "image of the Kabalistic Phallus."[38] The "Kabalah" he refers to here is a medieval book of the occult, a highly mystical and magical interpretation of the Old Testament,[39] and an important sourcebook for sorcerers and magicians.[40]

d. THE POINT WITHIN A CIRCLE

The Masons of the Blue Lodge are taught that the Point within a Circle represents the individual Mason (the Point), contained and restricted by the boundary line of his duty (the Circle). Its real meaning, however, is that of the phallus, positioned within the female generative principle (sex organ) in sexual union, the climactic act of Sun-god worship.[41]

Dr. Albert Mackey, already quoted herein, also writes in his classic work *Symbolism of Freemasonry*, page 352, "Phallus, a representation of the virile member, which was venerated as a religious symbol.., It was one of the modifications of sun worship, and was a symbol of the fecundating power of that luminary. The Masonic point within a circle is undoubtedly of phallic origin."

The cosmic meaning of this symbol is that of the Sun, surrounded by the Universe; on the following page (353) he writes, "Point within a circle, It is derived from Sun-worship, and is in reality of phallic origin." In his *Manual of the Lodge*, page 156, Mackey writes, "The point within a circle is an interesting and important symbol in Freemasonry, but it has been debased in the interpretation of it in the modern lectures, and the sooner that interpretation is forgotten by the Masonic student, the better it will be. The symbol is really a beautiful but somewhat abstruse allusion to the old Sun-worship, and introduces us for the first time to that modification of it, known among the ancients as the worship of the phallus."

e. THE VERTICAL LINES

The two vertical lines touching the sides of the circle are represented to the Blue Lodge Mason as "the Holy Saints John." By this is meant John the Baptist and John the Apostle. In reality, the two vertical lines represent the Summer and Winter Solstices, the shortest and longest nights of the year, respectively. These nights are, and have been since antiquity, important periods for pagan worship,

Concerning these two lines, Albert Mackey has written (*Symbolism of Freemasonry*, page 352), "The lines touching the circle in the symbol of the point within a circle are said to represent St. John the Baptist and St. John the Evangelist, but they really refer to the solstitial points, Cancer and Capricorn, in the Zodiac."

f. THE BIBLE

The Bible, only one of the "Three Great Lights" of Masonry (along with the Square and Compass), is represented to Blue Lodge Masons as symbolizing truth. In reality, the Bible may be replaced with the Koran, the Book of the Law, the Hindu scriptures or any other "holy book," depending on the preferences of the men in the Lodge. In most American Lodges, the members are told that the entire Masonic system and its rituals are "based on the Bible." Such, however, is not the case. In Chase's *Digest of Masonic Law*, pages 207-209, it is clearly written that "Masonry has nothing whatever to do with the Bible," and that "it is not founded upon the Bible, for if it were it would not be Masonry, it would be something else."

Albert Pike, in writing on the subject of Masonry's source-book, said, "Masonry is a search after light. That search leads us directly back, as you see, to the Kabalah" (*Morals and Dogma*, page 741). The Kabalah, then, seems to be the actual sourcebook of Masonry and the Bible merely (as it is spoken of in the ritual) a piece of the "furniture" of the Lodge.

NOTE: For more information concerning Masonic symbols and their true meanings, see McQuaig, C.F., *The Masonic Report,* Answer Books and Tapes, Norcross, GA 1976; Storms, E.M., *Should a Christian Be a Mason?*, New Puritan Library, Fletcher, NC 1980; and Mackey, Albert G., *Symbolism of Freemasonry,* Charles T. Powner Co, Chicago 1975.

ENDNOTES

36   "Phallus: a representation of the virile member (male sex organ) which was venerated as a religious symbol very universally...by the ancients. It was one of the modifications of Sun-worship, and was a symbol of the fecundating (impregnating) power of that luminary. The Masonic point within a circle is undoubtedly of phallic origin." (Mackey, Albert G., "Symbolism of Freemasonry," p. 352)

37   Pike, Albert, *Morals and Dogma,* pp. 11, 839, 850, 851.

38   Pike, Albert, *Morals and Dogma,* pp. 5, 757, 758, 771, 772.

39 "Cabala (Kabalah) is a medieval and modern system of
    theosophy, mysticism, and thaumatology (magic)," Webster's
    New Collegiate Dictionary, p. 53.
40 Baskin, Wade, "The Sorcerer's Handbook," New York,
    Philosophical Library, 1974.
41 "These two divinities ... were commonly symbolized by the
    generative parts of man and woman...the Phallus and Cteis
    (vagina), emblems of generation and production, and which,
    as such, appeared in the Mysteries, The Indian Lingam was the
    union of both, as were the Boat and Mast, and the Point within
    the Circle." Pike, Albert, *Morals and Dogma*, p. 401.

PART ONE — APPENDIX C

Masonic Morality

1. Underlying Attitudes and Assumptions

There is, underlying all Masonic thinking and writing, an attitude and spirit of elitism which says, "Masonry is not for everyone, just for the select few." At the same time Masonry teaches it is the only true religion and that all other religions are but corrupted and perverted forms of Masonry. This is both elitist and contradictory, in that it leaves no hope for the non-elite to find the "true religion." Freemasonry proudly proclaims it makes good men better; but this makes no provision for bad men to become good.

a. No room in the Lodge for the blind, crippled, poor, etc.

It is significant, I think, that those whom Masonry rejects and excludes are the very ones Jesus sought out to accept and minister to.

The Lodge excludes and rejects the blind, for they cannot see to engage in the signs and due-guards; it rejects the crippled and maimed, for they cannot assume the body positions necessary for the signs and due-guards. The deaf are excluded because they cannot hear the "secret" words. The poor are excluded, for they cannot pay the fees and dues. The feeble-minded are rejected because they cannot learn and function in the Lodge.

The emotionally ill are rejected because they cannot be trusted with the "secrets." Blacks and women are excluded simply because they are considered inferior and unsuitable.

Jesus, on the other hand, proclaims that His gift of redemption is for "whosoever will," and that all may "take the water of life freely" (Revelation 22:17). He especially reached out to the blind, the crippled, the feeble-minded and mentally ill, the poor and the unwanted—the very ones Masonry excludes and rejects.

b. Even within the Lodge the elite spirit rules

Even within Masonry the spirit of elitism, the principle of the superiority of the "chosen few," prevails. Those Blue Lodge Masons who lack the money cannot pursue the higher degrees and the Shrine. And, even for those who can afford the higher degrees and the Shrine, there are offices and positions closed to some who haven't the wealth, nice home or social position required.

c. It can be "right" in Masonic morality to deceive sincere Masons

The deadly danger of this elitist attitude (in any organization or society) is that whatever the elite leadership decides is "right" is then right, regardless of external moral considerations. A significant case in point is the fact that the "ordinary" Masons of the Blue Lodge are deliberately deceived by the Masonic philosophers and writers of doctrine into believing they understand the meaning of Masonic symbols and rituals when they do not.

The masses of "ordinary" (Blue Lodge) Masons who pay the dues and work faithfully to make the entire system possible are deliberately deceived as to the true nature of what they are saying and doing. But this deliberate deception becomes "right" in Masonic morality, simply because the elite leadership decides that it is right. For documentation of this profound deception, see Appendix B, *Masonic Symbolism.*

2. Specific Examples of Masonic Morality

So much of the morality expressed in Masonic teachings, particularly the oaths of obligation, sound good on the surface but do not stand up under even casual scrutiny. Most Masons really believe they are binding themselves to moral standards of behavior, But this is because they have never really thought about what they have said. Their basic assumption—that it is all "good"—closes their eyes to the reality. Although volumes could be written concerning the flawed morality of Masonry, for the purposes of this brief summary a few examples will suffice. The following are selected examples of the moral standards of Masonry, compared with the teachings of the Bible.

a. Fornication and adultery

The Master Mason swears not to "violate the chastity" of the mother, wife, sister, or daughter of another Master Mason, "knowing her to be such." This may sound good superficially, but it permits intercourse with anyone else's mother, wife, sister, or daughter (even those female relatives of brother Masons of the First and Second Degrees), and permits intercourse with those relatives of a Master Mason, as long as one isn't aware of their Masonic relationship. It could even permit such illicit intercourse with female relatives of a Master Mason, knowingly, if they are not chaste and, therefore, have no chastity to be violated. The Bible, on the other hand, is very clear concerning the matter. We are told to flee fornication, and are forbidden to commit adultery with anyone (Exodus 20:14; Acts 15:20; 1 Corinthians 6:18; et al).

b. Cheating, wronging, defrauding

The Master Mason swears not to "cheat, wrong or defraud" another Master Mason or a Lodge of Master Masons, "I knowing them to be such." This may seem like lofty morals to the casual observer, but it will not bear scrutiny. This promise permits the cheating, wronging or defrauding of anyone not a Master Mason, or an organization other than a Lodge of Master Masons; and even they may be cheated, wronged or defrauded if the Mason doing it doesn't realize who or what they are. The Bible is likewise very clear concerning this class of behavior, stating plainly that we must not cheat, wrong or defraud anyone at any time (Exodus 20:15; Leviticus 19:13, 35; Proverbs 11:1; Ephesians 4:28; et al).

c. Lying and perjuring

The Mason swears to keep the secrets of another Mason, protecting him even if it requires withholding evidence of a crime. In some degrees treason and murder are excepted; in other, higher degrees, there are no exceptions to this promise to cover up the truth. The obligations, if the Masonic teachings are believed, may require a Mason to give false testimony, perjure himself or (in the case of a judge) render a false verdict in order to protect another Mason. Again, the Bible is quite clear in teaching that we must never lie or bear false witness, and states that liars will have their part in the Lake of Fire (Exodus 20:16; Proverbs 19:5, 9; Ephesians 4:15; Revelation 21:8; et al).

d. Falsifying records

Destroying, altering or otherwise falsifying records is a form of lying. A fascinating example of this is the case of Past Master Duane Washum, who was Master of Vegas Lodge Number 32 in Las Vegas, Nevada for the year 1983. Two months after his term as Worshipful Master ended, Duane was convicted of the sinfulness of remaining in Freemasonry; he resigned and left Masonry completely. As he became active in researching the truth concerning Freemasonry he affiliated with the organization, Ex Masons for Jesus, and became an embarrassment for his old Lodge. What could they do? Vegas

Lodge 32 has a web site and the web site has a section with the lodge's history. One page in the history, "Past Masters of Vegas 32," lists all past masters, with photographs, in decades, i.e. ten-year groups. If you go to the site and open the decade of the 1980s you will see a strange thing: there are only nine past masters there; and none of the nine served twice in that decade. What could explain this? You have probably guessed the answer by now: the record jumps from 1982 when John D. Clifton was Master to 1984 when Clarence C. Van Horn was Master. According to the "official" history of Vegas Lodge number 32, Duane Washum never existed and 1983 didn't happen. You can see this for yourself by going to www.vegas32.org/past_masters/history-past_masters-1980.html (if it hasn't been removed from the site by the time you are reading this).

e. Helping others

The Master Mason swears to assist widows, orphans and others in need of help, so long as it is not inconvenient or sacrificial for him to do so ("so far as … my abilities permit without material injury to myself"). He also swears to go to the aid of another Master Mason who gives the "Grand Hailing Sign of Distress," that most extreme call for help, given only when life is threatened. However, he agrees to help that distressed brother Master Mason only if he can do it without unduly risking his own life ("only if there is a greater probability of saving the other's life than of losing my own"). Given the wrong circumstances here, the Master Mason would apparently allow the other Master Mason to die, to say nothing of one in peril who is not a Master Mason, The most casual student of the Bible and its teachings knows that it teaches us to give to those in need, whether or not it is easy, and that we are to consider others' needs, comfort, lives, etc, more important than our own (Proverbs 3:27; Matthew 25:31-46; John 15:12, 13; James 2:15, 16; et al).

NOTE: For a more thorough study of Masonic morality and its flaws, see McQuaig, C.F., *The Masonic Report*, Answer Books and Tapes, Norcross, GA, 1976.

The Legend of Hiram Abiff
(The Egyptian Connection)

The heart of Freemasonry is the Blue Lodge with its three degrees. The climactic degree in the Blue Lodge (and the final degree for most Masons) is the Third, or Master Mason Degree. The heart of the Master Mason Degree, the thing that gives it both meaning and substance, is without any doubt the reenactment of the Legend of Hiram Abiff. It is this central figure in the legend, this Hiram "The Widow's Son," the "Tyrian Architect," this "First Grand Master," who is impersonated by every man who is initiated as a Master Mason. It is Hiram who is at the very heart of the foundation of all of Masonry. His true identity and nature become, then, matters of extreme significance. Just who—and what—was this man, Hiram Abiff?

1. THE MASONIC TRADITION

According to the Masonic legend, Hiram Abiff was a man of Tyre, the son of a widow, and the chief architect of the Temple built by King Solomon. He was the central character in the building of the Temple and one of three leading characters along with King Solomon and Hiram, King of Tyre. Hiram Abiff, Masonry teaches, was the only one on Earth who knew the "secrets of a Master Mason," including the most important secret of all, the "Grand Masonic Word," the name of God (the "ineffable name"). Since, in occult lore, knowing the name of a spirit is a key to having its power, there was very great power in knowing this word. Knowing the other "secrets of a Master Mason" would enable the masons/workmen working on the Temple project to go out on their own, working as Master Masons and earning "Master Mason's wages."

This Hiram had promised to reveal the "secrets of a Master Mason," including the name of God ("Grand Masonic Word"), upon completion of the Temple and to make the workmen Master Masons, able then to go out on their own as masters (they were, as yet, only "Fellowcraft" Masons). One day, as was his custom, Hiram went into the unfinished Holy of Holies at noon ("High Twelve") to worship and to draw up the work plans (on his "trestleboard") for the workmen to follow the next day. The workmen were outside the Temple for their lunch break ("... the craft were called from labor to refreshment ...").

As Hiram was leaving the Temple he was accosted by three "ruffians" in succession, who demanded that they be given the secrets immediately (without waiting for the Temple to be completed). He was handled roughly by the first ruffian (Jubela), but escaped. Accosted and handled roughly by the second ruffian (Jubelo), he again refused to divulge the secrets and again escaped. The third ruffian (Jubelum) then accosted him, and, when Hiram again refused to divulge the secrets, Jubelum killed Hiram with a blow to the forehead with a setting maul. The body was hastily concealed under some rubbish in the Temple until midnight ("low twelve") when it was taken out to the brow of a hill and buried. The grave was marked by a branch of Acacia (an evergreen tree common in the Middle East), and the three ruffians attempted to escape the country. Denied passage on a ship out of the country, they retreated into the hills to hide.

Meanwhile, back at the Temple, it was noticed that Hiram was missing, and King Solomon was notified. Solomon immediately ordered a search in and about the Temple with no success. At this point, twelve "Fellowcrafts" reported to the King that they and three others (the three "ruffians") had conspired to extort the secrets of Hiram Abiff, but they had repented and refused to go through with the murderous plan. They reported that it was those other three who had murdered Grand Master Hiram, and King Solomon then sent them out in groups of three to search in all directions.

After questioning the sea captain who had refused the murderers passage, three of the searchers then followed the murderers' path and discovered the grave with its Acacia at the head. Digging down and recognizing the body, they reported back to Solomon. Solomon sent them back to locate the grave, positively identify the body as Hiram, and attempt to raise it from the grave with the grip of an Entered Apprentice. They relocated the grave but were unable to raise the body because decomposition had caused the flesh to leave the bone.

Reporting back to Solomon, they were told to return to the grave and attempt to raise the body with the grip of a Fellowcraft. When this failed because the skin slipped away, they reported back to Solomon who, himself, went to the grave and raised the body up with the grip of a Master Mason—the "Strong Grip of a Lion's Paw." Hiram was not only brought up out of the grave, but restored to life. The first word he spoke was to be the replacement for the "Grand Masonic Word," lost at his death. That word, spoken to Solomon upon his restoration to life, is the one passed down to Master Masons to this day.[42] This, then, is the Masonic legend of Hiram Abiff, and most Blue Lodge Masons believe that it is a factual, scriptural, and historical account.

This is generally believed, in spite of the fact that the Masonic authorities and writers of Masonic doctrine agree that it is not only a myth, unsupported by facts, but acknowledge that it is but a retelling of the legend of Isis and Osiris.

2. THE BIBLE RECORD

Does the Bible record such a person as Hiram Abiff? Definitely not, although part of his identity is taken from the Bible. The Scriptures record two men named Hiram who were important in the building of Solomon's Temple. One is Hiram, King of Tyre, who was supportive of Solomon and who provided materials and workmen for the project. The other Hiram, called "a widow's son of the tribe of Naphtali," was a worker in brass, not the architect of the entire Temple. He made the brass pillars, the brass sea with its twelve oxen to support it, ten bases of brass with brass bowls, and all the brass lavers, shovels and basins. The Scriptures record that this Hiram, the widow's son, completed all the work that he had come to do on the Temple. Presumably, he then returned to his home in Tyre, safe and sound; there is no indication in the Bible of anything to the contrary, and he never appears again in the Bible.[43] Concerning the Masonic claim that Hiram, the widow's son, was chief architect of the Temple, the Bible is clear in establishing that he was no such thing. The Bible reveals that God, Himself, was the designer and architect of the Temple, that He gave the plans in minute detail to David and that David gave them to Solomon, along with most of the materials.[44] To claim that anyone but God was the Chief Architect of the Temple is unfounded and, I believe, blasphemous,

3. THE EGYPTIAN CONNECTION

It is the consensus of opinion among Masonic authorities, philosophers and writers of doctrine that the legend of Hiram Abiff is merely the Masonic version of a much older legend, that of Isis and Osiris, basis of the Egyptian mystery religions. The following is a brief summary of that legend, and a comparison with the Masonic legend of Hiram Abiff. This comparison is supported, beyond doubt, by the conclusions of the Masonic authorities.

a. The Legend of Isis and Osiris

Osiris, both King of the Egyptians and their god, went on a journey to bless neighboring nations with his knowledge of arts and sciences. His jealous brother, Typhon (god of Winter) conspired to murder him, steal his kingdom and did so. Isis, sister and wife of Osiris and his queen (as well as Egypt's Moon goddess) set out on a search for the body, making inquiries of all she met.

After certain adventures, she found the body with an Acacia tree at the head of the coffin. Returning home, she secretly buried the body, intending to give it a proper burial as soon as arrangements were made. Typhon, by treachery, stole the body, cut it up into fourteen pieces and hid them in as many places. Isis then made a second search and located all the pieces but one; the one missing and lost part was the phallus.

She made a substitute phallus, consecrated it, and it became a sacred substitute, an object of worship.

This, in extremely abbreviated form, is the Egyptian legend of Isis and Osiris. It is, without doubt, the basis for the Masonic legend of Hiram Abiff. To support this "Egyptian connection," let's consider two things: a brief comparison of key elements in both stories and the conclusions of the Masonic authorities in Masonic source-writings.

b. A Brief Comparison of the Legends of Hiram Abiff and Osiris

The fundamental similarity between the two stories may be seen in many respects; the following are some of the most important:

(1) Both men went to foreign lands to share their knowledge of arts and sciences.

(2) In both legends there is a precious thing possessed: Hiram has the secret word; Osiris has the kingdom.

(3) In both legends there is a wicked conspiracy by evil men to seize the precious thing.

(4) In both legends there is a struggle and a murder of the virtuous leader.

(5) Both are murdered by their brothers (Osiris by Typhon, Hiram by Jubelum, his brother Mason).

(6) Both bodies are buried hastily with the intention of a later, deliberate burial.

(7) Locations of the bodies are both marked by Acacia at the head.

(8) In both legends there are two separate searches for the bodies.

(9) In both legends there is a loss of something precious: in Hiram's death the secret word is lost; in Osiris' death the phallus is lost.

(10) In both there is a substitution for the precious thing that has been lost: concerning Hiram, it is the substitute for the secret word; concerning Osiris, it is the substitute phallus, made by Isis.

c. Conclusions of the Masonic Authorities

A few statements from the most authoritative Masonic scholars will suffice to express the doctrinal consensus:

(1) "The legend and traditions of Hiram Abiff form the consummation of the connecting link between Freemasonry and the Ancient Mysteries" (Pierson, *Traditions of Freemasonry*, p. 159).

(2) "We readily recognize in Hiram Abiff the Osiris of the Egyptians …" (Pierson, p. 240).

(3) "Osiris and the Tyrian Architect [Hiram Abiff] are one and the same" (Sickles, Daniel, *Freemason's Guide*, p. 236).

(4) "That part of the rite (Master Mason initiation) which is connected with the legend of the Tyrian Artist [Hiram Abiff] … should be studied as a myth and not as a fact.… Outside of Masonic tradition there is no proof that an event such as is related in connection with the "Temple Builder" ever transpired, and, besides, the ceremony is older by more than a thousand

years than the age of Solomon.... It is thoroughly Egyptian" (Sickles, Daniel, *The Ahiman Rezon*, p. 195).

(5) "It [the Legend of Hiram Abiff] is thoroughly Egyptian and is closely allied to the Supreme Rite [highest degree] of the Isianic Mysteries [Mystery religion of Isis and Osiris]" (Mackey, Albert, *Lexicon of Freemasonry*, p. 195).

CONCLUSION

Thus, it seems clear that the Hiram Abiff of Freemasonry is not an historical character and certainly not a biblical one. Rather, he actually represents Osiris, the Egyptian Sun god; and the reenactment of the Legend of Hiram Abiff is actually the reenactment of the legend of Isis and Osiris.

Thus, each sincere man who is initiated into the Third (Master Mason) Degree of Masonry impersonates Osiris, the Sun-god of Egypt, and enters into his life of good deeds, his death, his burial, and is "raised" in his resurrection from the dead. With this understood, it is then easy to understand the statement in the *Kentucky Monitor* (handbook for all Blue Lodge Masonry in the Grand Lodge of Kentucky) that, while the Christian's Messiah is called Jesus, the Mason's Messiah is called Hiram (*Kentucky Monitor*, "The Spirit of Masonry," xv).

ENDNOTES

42 It puzzles me that no one has questioned the necessity for a "substitute" for the lost Grand Masonic Word. If it was lost at the death of Hiram because only he knew it, then why, when Hiram was raised back to life, didn't Solomon just ask him what the real, original one was? All Solomon needed to do was to say something like, "Hiram, praise the Lord that you are no longer dead! Now, what was that word all this fuss has been about?"

43 I Kings 7:13-47

44 I Chronicles 17:1-15; 22:11-29:9 (especially 28:19)

The 32nd Degree Lecture

As the Masonic candidate comes into the Lodge for the first time he is told that he will be brought to the light. Then he is told that he has made a beginning toward the light but has not yet arrived. In the Second Degree light is again sought but not quite attained. He receives "additional light" but, again, it is only partial fulfillment. Then, in the Third (Master Mason) Degree, he is supposedly brought to final fulfillment. Again, he only receives "more light." Even in this climactic degree of the Master Mason where he goes through the death, burial and resurrection of Osiris the Sun-god, he is not fully enlightened. He has been given more teaching about the mysteries and their symbols, relating to the meaning of life, death and eternity. The "true light" of understanding and intellectual rebirth is still beyond his grasp … it is still up there somewhere, higher up the mountain and farther out ahead.

Then he is led to believe that the light—the real enlightenment—is to be found in the "higher degrees." In each one of these degrees beyond the Blue Lodge the seeker expects to finally reach and obtain the light. However, like the carrot on the stick, always out before the reluctant donkey to draw him onward, it remains, each time, beyond his reach. "Next time you'll reach it," the system implies each time; but the light still remains out of reach. Each time, in every higher degree, the seeking candidate doesn't quite get there. But there is always the next degree. "Surely," the candidate reasons, "... surely I will reach the light in the next degree." But he is disappointed each time.

Then comes the final degree, that terminal earned degree, the 32nd Degree. This is the top of the mountain, final fulfillment! From the very top of the Masonic Mountain one can surely see all things clearly. At the top of the mountain there should be pure air, full light and nothing hidden! It has been a long and expensive climb, one that not everyone makes. At least the light will be reached *there!* After all, that is the ultimate goal—the end of the line—and you can't go any higher than the top!

Alas, however, it is not to be. The candidate receiving the 32nd Degree is told that he has still not reached the light. He is told that he has, indeed, reached the top of the mountain, but that the mountaintop is covered with clouds and mists. The light is still obscured, still "out there somewhere" beyond him.

"Sorry, brother," the candidate is told in effect, "you will just have to press on and find the light for yourself." Here at the pinnacle of the earned degrees of Freemasonry the candidate is given his final teaching, the very last revelation in his quest for that light. Here is that lecture, verbatim, exactly as it is given to the candidates, just as Jim Shaw gave it so many times. Let's allow this final, ultimate revelation of hidden truth to speak for itself.

THE LECTURE OF THE 32ND DEGREE

"You are here to learn, if you can learn, and to remember what you have been taught. In the Scottish Rite you will be taught that our ancient ancestors who knew all the Mysteries left enough traces so that we today with diligent labor and teaching may renew them and bring them to light for your enlightenment. We now come to the great symbol of Pythagoras. Our symbols have descended to us from the Aryans, and many were invented by Pythagoras, who studied in Egypt and Babylon. In order to

192

preserve the great truths learned from the profane, there were invented some of our symbols that represent the profoundest of truths descended to us from our white ancestors. Many have been lost, lost as was the true word at the death of our Grand Master Hiram Abiff.

"The ancient Masters invented some of these symbols to express the result of deity. They did not attempt to name him, but rather tried to express their reverence by describing him as Ahura-Mazda, spirit of light. They conceived the idea that Ahura had seven potencies or emanations, four of these they thought of as Male and three Female. The four male potencies of Ahura by which he governed the universe were: the divine might; the divine wisdom; the divine word; and the divine sovereignty. The three female potencies were: productiveness; health; and vitality.

"Look to the East, my brothers ... and behold the seven-pointed star, the great symbol of this degree, with the seven colors of the rainbow. The seven colors and seven points represent the seven potencies of Ahura.

"Observe now the great Delta of Pythagoras consisting of 36 lights arranged in eight rows to form an equilateral triangle. The light at the apex of the Delta represents Ahura-Mazda, source of all light. This represents the seven remaining potencies of Ahura.

"The right angle triangle of three lights around the altar represents the famous 47th proposition of Euclid, or the Pythagorean theorem, which is used to conceal and reveal philosophical truths. The real significance of the cross is that of Ahura and his four male emanations, emanating from him. The four animals of the prophet Ezekiel represent these same four male emanations: Man, the divine word; the Eagle, divine wisdom; the Bull, divine might; and the Lion, divine sovereignty.

"Every equilateral triangle is a symbol of trinity, as are all groups of three in the Lodge, as the Sun, the Moon, and the Worshipful Master, in the sacred and mystic symbol AUM of the Hindus, whose origin and meaning no one here knows, the great trinity of the Aryans was symbolized by the Adepts. Among the Hindus it symbolized the supreme god of gods. The Brahmins, because of its awful and sacred meaning, hesitated to pronounce it aloud, and when doing so placed a hand in front of the mouth to deaden the sound. This triliteral name for god is composed of three Sanscrit letters. The first letter A stands for the creator (Brahma); the second letter U for (Vishnu) the preserver; the third letter M for (Siva) the destroyer. AUM it is, ineffable, not because it cannot be pronounced, but because it is pronounced A-A-A-U-U-U-M-M-M. All these things which you can learn by study, concentration, and contemplation, have come down to us from our ancient ancestors through Zaranthustra and Pythagoras.

"You have reached the mountain peak of Masonic instruction, a peak covered by a mist, which YOU in search for further light can penetrate only by your own efforts. Now we hope you will study diligently the lessons of all our degrees so that there will be nurtured within you a consuming desire to pierce the pure white light of Masonic wisdom. And before we let you go, let me give you a hint and that is all that the greatest Mystics ever give. The hint is in the Royal Secret, it is there that you may learn to find that light. Yes, brothers, the hint is in the Royal Secret. The true word-Man, born of a double nature (of what we call Good and what we call Evil; spiritual and earthly; mortal and immortal) finds the purpose of his being ONLY WHEN THESE TWO NATURES ARE IN PERFECT HARMONY.

"Harmony, my bretheren, Harmony, is the true word and the Royal Secret which makes possible the Empire of true Masonic Brotherhood!"

AND THAT'S IT! REALLY!

Well, there it is. This absurd, disarticulated mixture of silly contradiction, pagan blasphemy, and unfulfilled promise is all they get. They are now "Princes of the Royal Secret" and aren't even sure what the secret is! However, the most significant thing about it is, I believe, that the mountaintop they have *finally* reached is "a peak covered with mist" which they can penetrate only by their own efforts.

Here they are at the final destination, the 32nd Degree, and they find out that it isn't the final destination at all! In fact, they learn that not only must they press on and reach the final destination on their own, they don't even know what that destination is! After spending all this money and effort to reach "the Light," they are told they still are not there, that they must search farther and find it on their own. And they still don't really know what it is!

And these victimized men, "ever learning, and never able to come to the knowledge of the truth," don't even realize that they are victims. How very sad.

A Prayer For Freedom

The effects of involvement in such things as Freemasonry and its affiliates such as DeMolay, Rainbow Girls, and Eastern Star can cling to us—even to the sincere Christian—hindering, limiting and blinding. The seeds of spiritual confusion, having been sown, can put roots down deeply into our lives, bringing ongoing trouble. The resulting problems may be obvious and dramatic; or they may be so subtle as to be hardly noticed.

Whatever the situation, having once been exposed to this pagan poison with its sugar coating of "goodness," the remedy is the same: "Whosoever shall call on the name of the Lord shall be delivered" (Joel 2:32).

God will never override our wills and force us to be free. He waits, more than willing, to liberate us when we ask Him. It seems true that if we don't ask, we will go on indefinitely, carrying the doubts, fears and other problems that entered our lives through the open door of Masonic involvement. God grieves, and we suffer; yet the problems remain until we ask Him to free us.

So why not ask? Even if you're not sure you need to, what is there to lose? Just tell the Lord, out loud, that you renounce all involvement in Masonry, its branches and all other pagan, occult things, and ask Him to deliver you from all their effects and make you truly, fully and freely His child by faith in Christ

Jesus. If you mean it, He will do it—not because you deserve it, but because you need it. God is not legalistic; He is infinitely gracious. You have only to ask, and mean it; He will do the rest.

If you would like a model prayer to follow, just pray this prayer:

Heavenly Father, I want truly to be your child, and I want to be completely free. I confess that Jesus is Lord. I believe you raised Him from the dead, and I confess my need of the new birth and freedom that Jesus alone can give. I want this. I renounce Freemasonry and all its affiliated groups, forms and activities, with all the paganism they represent. I renounce all things occult and pagan that have touched my life directly or come into my life through my family. I renounce it all, turn from it and ask you to forgive me, free and deliver me from all its consequences. I ask you to fill me completely with your Holy Spirit and lead me in the way that I should go. I count this done, and thank you for it, in the mighty name of Jesus Christ my Lord. Amen.

Author's Note Concerning Jim Shaw and the 33rd Degree

A Private Meeting with a Prominent Christian

After the first publication of the Jim Shaw story in 1988, in my book "The Deadly Deception," I appeared on hundreds of radio and television talk shows, including the Moody Network and Dr. D.J. Kennedy's *Truths that Transform*. During that time there was a significant, closed-door meeting with Dr. D.J. Kennedy. There were only three of us present: Dr. Kennedy, the producer of "Truths that Transform", and I. Dr. Kennedy knew nothing of Freemasonry, and the producer and I gave him a brief but clear overview of the subject. He listened intently, asked incisive questions, and we answered them. His conclusion was, and this is a direct quotation as I remember it, "Then this is a cancer in the Church which must be removed."

I appeared on Dr. Kennedy's program, "Truths that Transform," to discuss the book. The tape of that program quickly became Dr. Kennedy's all-time best seller; and the book, *Deadly Deception,* quickly became his second-highest selling book at Coral Ridge. The program was re-broadcast, and interest in the book caught fire, from coast to coast. Jim's story was (and is still) a compelling human story; but what people were responding to was not Jim's story, per se. Rather, they were responding to a vast need, and a compelling desire, for the factual information which the book contained about Freemasonry itself.

The Attack on Jim Shaw Began

As a result of the demand for "Deadly Deception," and my ongoing appearances on radio and television to discuss the book, an attack on Jim, and his record, was mounted by the hierarchy of the Scottish Rite of Freemasonry, Southern Jurisdiction, with headquarters at the House of the Temple in Washington, DC. The situation, which had been simmering, exploded into open, public assault; and I have reason to believe that the spark which ignited the fuse on that Masonic bomb was a man in Dr. Kennedy's church who was a high-ranking Scottish Rite Mason.

Unable to dispute the content of the book concerning Freemasonry and its conflict with orthodox Christian doctrine and Holy Scripture (the heart of the book), Scottish Rite Masonry instead concentrated its big guns in an ad hominem attack on Jim, his record, and his character.

To state the conflict in the simplest terms, the Scottish Rite confirmed Jim's reaching the position of Knight Commander of the Court of Honor (KCCH), the doorstep to the 33rd Degree; but they denied that he had actually received the 33rd Degree. The compelling part of their position was that, when he had resigned from the Scottish Rite, he had not yet been KCCH long enough to be eligible to receive the 33rd Degree The waiting period for a KCCH before being eligible for consideration to receive the 33rd Degree was four years. And, according to their records, Jim had been KCCH for slightly less than one year when he resigned from the Scottish Rite.

I traveled to Ocala to see Jim about this, and showed him the correspondence between the Supreme Council and me, plus the things they were releasing to the news media. Although he didn't say so, Jim was obviously stung by what I told him; he was also offended, because it seemed to him that I was questioning his honesty. We had become good friends, and it was a decidedly uncomfortable moment for both of us. I explained to Jim the argument being set forth by the hierarchy at the House of the Temple, i.e. that sufficient time for him to be considered for the 33rd Degree had not yet passed when he resigned from the Scottish Rite. His reply (and it was immediate, with no hesitation—not even a moment's pause to think about what to say) was, "They [the Supreme Council of the 33rd Degree, the entity which confers the 33rd Degree] can do anything they wish to do in this way." I accepted his response; but when I left, the tension was still there, and I was still troubled.

This continued to trouble me until the truth of what Jim had said was unexpectedly played out before the eyes of the World, publicly and rather dramatically. It was the experience of an elderly man, John J. Robinson, of Cincinnati, Ohio.

The Case of John J. Robinson

John Robinson was a man of diverse interests, talents and accomplishments. Although he was not a Mason, he searched medieval history for a connection between the medieval Knights of the Temple in Jerusalem, and modern York Rite Masonry. His findings were published in a book, "Born in Blood," which became popular among Masons, particularly those who were Knights Templar of the York Rite. He traveled widely with the book, speaking mostly to Masonic groups. He became increasingly involved with modern Masonry, and eventually he petitioned a local lodge and became a Master Mason. He wrote of his own journey into Freemasonry in a second book, *A Pilgrim's Path.*

Mr. Robinson became a Master Mason in November 1992, and a Scottish Rite Mason of the 32nd Degree (Northern Jurisdiction) in late April 1993. Ten days later, in early May, he was made a 32nd Degree Mason (Southern Jurisdiction). Gravely ill and on his death bed, on September 3rd 1993, he received the Thirty-third Degree (Northern Jurisdiction). Three days later, September 6th, he died. He had gone from "profane" status to the Thirty-third Degree in ten months.

Obviously, Mr. Robinson's case was unusual—very different from Jim Shaw's case; but it does tell us that the four-year waiting period can be, and has been, waived. It appears that when Jim said that the Supreme Council can do anything it wishes to do (in terms of conferring honors and degrees), he was right.

The Position Paper

The attack on Jim's testimony became relentless, and it was greatly troubling for some of my Christian colleagues in the world of Masonic research and writing; today some of them are convinced that he had never received the 33rd Degree. As a result, in early 1995, I composed and circulated a position paper stating the case for Jim's full testimony, and my conclusion that his testimony was true. Unfortunately, I lost all copies of the paper, my computer, discs and other documents including my research notes, when Hurricane Katrina completely destroyed and removed my house in August 2005. Except for the pilings, which still stood, it was as if the house had never been there. Those documents are now somewhere at the bottom of the Gulf of Mexico. However, producing this new book and facing the issue anew, and after giving the matter much thought, I have reassembled as much of the rationale for my 1995 conclusion as I can recall; it is as follows.

The Basis for My 1995 Conclusion Concerning Jim Shaw and the 33rd Degree

The basis for my conclusion in 1995 included the following:

1. I have seen his certificate of membership in an international order of Masons which listed him as a 33rd Degree Mason. The Scottish Rite spokesman dismissed this document by declaring the issuing body to be "clandestine" (not worthy of recognition by the Scottish Rite).

2. I have seen a 33rd Degree medal in his study many times. As I recall there was a purple1ribbon attached. The Supreme Council's spokesman dismissed this fact by saying that the medal could have been purchased in a pawn shop. Those people have a way of talking down to those of us whom they see as being beneath their rank and station in life.

3. Jim published dozens of tracts and pamphlets, and circulated his teachings on cassette tape, for more than 25 years. He also traveled all over the nation, speaking in churches and other public venues. In every one of his publications, every cassette tape, and in every public appearance, he identified himself as "James D. Shaw, 33rd Degree." And yet neither the Supreme Council, nor any other voice for the Scottish Rite, *ever* objected, publicly or privately, to what he was doing; nor did they *ever* deny his testimony or challenge his Masonic credentials. This denial began—in fact, erupted—only after the publication of *The Deadly Deception* and my appearance on the radio and television programs.

Those 20-plus years of silence cry out for an explanation. Yet the Supreme Council's spokesman responded to this with sarcasm. He dismissed this fact simply by declaring it to be irrelevant and not worthy of his consideration.

4. Freemasonry is an occult, Christ-denying institution with its roots deeply imbedded in Egyptian paganism, and the entire system is demonstrably based upon deception and lies (as this book overwhelmingly demonstrates).

5. The Scottish Rite hierarchy holds and controls the records, with every opportunity to alter or destroy them if they should choose to do so. Am I accusing them of doing so? No. But they have certainly had the opportunity; and if they did, it wouldn't be the first time in human history that such a thing was done. In fact, it wouldn't be the first time in recent Masonic history.

Altered Records: The Mystery of the Missing Year.

Duane Washum, who wrote the Foreword to Part One of this book, was once an active member of Vegas Lodge number 32 in Las Vegas, Nevada. He served the lodge as Worshipful Master during the year 1983. After serving as Worshipful Master he became convicted that it was sinful to remain a Mason and he resigned from Masonry completely. Vegas Lodge 32 has a web site and the web site has a section with the lodge's history. One page on the site, "Past Masters of Vegas 32," lists all past masters, with photographs, in decades, i.e. ten-year groups. If you go to the site and open the decade of the 1980s you will see a strange thing: There are only nine Past Masters there; and none of the nine served twice in that decade. What could explain this? You have probably guessed the answer by now: the record jumps from 1982 when John D. Clifton was Master to 1984 when Clarence C. Van Horn was Master. According to the "official" history of Vegas Lodge number 32, Duane Washum never existed and 1983 didn't happen.

Does this "prove" anything, other than some petty misrepresentation in a Masonic lodge? No; but it does illustrate a fact: alteration of records does happen

Conclusion

With both Jim and Bonnie now deceased, their voices are silenced forever; and, regrettably, they had no children. I must choose whom to believe, and there are only two possible choices:

a. the Rev. Jim Shaw, who devoted the last 30 years of his life to proclaiming the Gospel of Christ and the verifiable truth about the Church and Freemasonry; or,

b. the spokesmen for the Scottish Rite of Freemasonry, and their records.

Today, only God and a few men at the House of the Temple know what actually happened concerning Jim Shaw in 1966. Doubts and unanswered questions remain, and will probably persist until the Lord returns to reveal all things. In the mean time, in the face of this obviously difficult and troubling dilemma, I really have only one valid option. I choose to believe Jim.

Postscript to the Shaw Controversy

I have had more than 20 years to think about the Jim Shaw dilemma; and, in the clarity of retrospect, I can see that the controversy over Jim's 33rd Degree became an enormous red herring, dragged across the pathway to truth. Whether or not this was the intention of the Supreme Council, it is what took place. In that ongoing vehement controversy concerning Jim and the 33rd Degree, we were almost completely diverted from what really matters: the truth about what Freemasonry is, and what it does. We could have taken the Jim Shaw story completely out of the book and it would not have changed the facts about the Masonic institution. The truth concerning Freemasonry would still stand, undiminished, even if Jim Shaw had never lived.

In creating this new book, I considered leaving some, or all, of Jim's story out of it. But I thought of the good that his story has done, and continues to do. Only God knows how many thousands of lives have been changed by *The Deadly Deception,* in spite of the controversy over Jim's record. While the spokesmen for the Scottish Rite and we "anti-Masonry" researchers were completely engrossed in the debate over Jim and the 33rd Degree, the book was spreading truth in all directions, changing lives. I *still* receive orders for that book, and receive letters from grateful ex-Masons whose lives the book changed. And this in spite of the attack on it by the Scottish Rite, and the fact that it has been out of print for many years. Somewhere out there, even as I am writing these words, someone may be praying the Prayer for Freedom on page 158 of *Deadly Deception* and finding liberation from Masonic darkness. And, as I place this new book entirely in

God's omnipotent hands, I pray that He will use it to reach still
more deceived multitudes, and that they will find the freedom
that only Jesus can give.

Tom C. McKenney
Ocean Springs, Mississippi
2011

Part Two

Please Tell Me

Questions People Ask About Freemasonry,
and the Answers

IF YE CONTINUE IN MY WORD, THEN ARE YE MY DISCIPLES
INDEED; AND YE SHALL KNOW THE TRUTH, AND
THE TRUTH SHALL MAKE YOU FREE.
JOHN 8:12

Foreword to Part Two

BY EVANS CRARY, JR., 33RD DEGREE, KNIGHT TEMPLAR, PAST GRAND MASTER OF THE GRAND LODGE OF FLORIDA

Dear Reader,

I labored diligently in the halls of Freemasonry for twenty years, attained its highest honors and enjoyed Masonic fellowship with men of the highest integrity and good morals; but, I did not find true peace and happiness until I met Jesus Christ as my personal savior and baptizer in the Holy Spirit in the spring of 1975. From the moment that I was "Born Again" until now, I have experienced the truth of Jesus' words, "I am the way, the truth and the life, no man comes unto the Father but by me" and have discovered that His truth and His word are indeed the liberating, empowering presence that men have sought since the beginning.

Tom C. McKenney has labored diligently to investigate and chronicle the foundations, teachings, and theological roots of Freemasonry and has presented them in this book in a thoughtful, powerful, and logical way to the consideration of those who are truly seeking further light for their lives and those of their loved ones. The inescapable conclusion is that Jesus is the only way to the Father and that all other ways lead to darkness and death.

Having walked the wrong way for so long a time, I know from personal experience that "there are none so blind as those who will not see." I commend this work to you, the reader, in the hope that your eyes will be opened to the truth and light of Jesus Christ as the only way to the abundant life both now and forever.

Your faithful servant in Jesus,
Evans Crary, Jr.

Introduction to Part Two

Over the five years of traveling, speaking, signing books and listening that followed the release of *The Deadly Deception,* I noticed two interesting things. First, there seemed to be no end to the interest in this subject. Although it seems to me that the nation should soon have been saturated with the truth about Freemasonry, the demand for my appearances on talk shows continued undiminished; and on each one the listeners reacted as if it were a brand new topic! Second, many of the same questions were asked repeatedly, often prefaced by the plea, "Please tell me...."

This book contains those most repeated, most important questions, and the answers, taken from the very best Masonic sources. Concerning Masonic philosophy, doctrine, rituals, and practices, except for news items and testimonies, not one "anti-Masonic" publication is referenced here; I have allowed the Masonic authorities to speak for themselves, without editing or tampering. There are also, in the back of the book, appendices containing more in-depth information about some of the most important (and most controversial) aspects of Masonry. These, like the answers in the book's main body, are carefully documented and based on the very best Masonic authorities and historical sources.

Here, in Part Two, are the questions and the answers, with citations to the most respected and authoritative Masonic sources.

PART TWO — CHAPTER ONE

The Nature and Origins of Freemasonry

FOR THEY HAVE SOWN THE WIND, AND THEY SHALL
REAP THE WHIRLWIND.
HOSEA 8:7

1. What is Freemasonry?
Freemasonry, according to the *Encyclopaedia Britannica*, is the world's largest secret society. It is a fraternal order, for "freeborn" white men, "sound of limb" (not blind, deaf, or crippled), of age twenty-one or older, binding its initiates to one another and to the institution, for life, by death oaths.[45]

2. Why the *free* in Freemasonry?
I have deliberately called the society *Freemasonry* here at the beginning because it is the correct term, and because many people, knowing little or nothing of the institution, when hearing just *Masonry*, may think we're speaking of bricklayers.

Different Masons may give you different answers here (and each will believe that he is right), but the most generally accepted answer is the following. The *free* part of the name comes from the symbolism of the medieval stonemasonry guilds in which,

213

once a man had advanced to the status of a master mason, he worked for himself and was "free" to travel over the land practicing his trade without supervision.

However, in Masonic speech the terms *Mason* and *Freemason* are synonymous and are used as such throughout this book.

3. In what way is it secret?

Although its existence is not a secret, its rituals, handshakes, passwords, recognition signs, penalty signs, and death oaths (what they call "the secret work") are supposedly secret. Their meetings are held behind guarded doors, in buildings with no windows (or with the windows painted over or heavily curtained). One condition of their binding death oaths is never to reveal any of the "secret work" to a non-Mason (or a Mason who has not been initiated into that particular degree).

4. Where and when did Freemasonry begin?

You will get different answers to this question from different Masonic sources. Most Masons will tell you that it had its beginnings in the building of the first temple in Jerusalem by King Solomon. Others will claim that its origins are even more ancient, with a few who will tell you that it goes clear back to Adam in the Garden of Eden. Serious Masonic scholars, however, laugh at such claims.[46]

The fact is that Freemasonry, as we know it, had its beginnings in eighteenth century England. The first recorded meeting was held in London in the Goose and Gridiron Tavern, 24 June 1717. Most early meetings of English lodges were held in taverns.

5. How did it happen?

It seems to have begun because wealthy, educated men with time on their hands were looking for a social and intellectual distraction, apparently never dreaming that it would eventually develop into what it has become. Although there seems to be no reliable record, Masonic tradition has it that two clergymen, James Anderson, D.D., and the Reverend John Desaguliers, scientist, philosopher, and third Grand Master, took the pagan mystery religions of Egypt, especially the worship of Isis and Osiris, reduced them to degree form, and created the first three degrees of Masonry. Much of their symbolism was borrowed from the medieval stonemason guilds and the biblical account of the building of Solomon's Temple. The work of Anderson and Desaguliers was subsequently improved upon, added to, and revised by others so that by the late eighteenth century these first three degrees were in final form, very much as they are today.

The secrecy and the exclusivity of the membership apparently appealed to British gentlemen of means. Prominent men were attracted, and the lodges duplicated rapidly, spreading first to the other British Isles, then to Europe and the American colonies.

This summary of Freemasonry's beginnings is necessarily abbreviated and, therefore, imperfect; but for our purposes it must suffice.[47]

6. But, why do they call themselves *Masons*, if they don't lay brick or stone?

They refer to what they do as "speculative" (symbolic) Masonry, as opposed to laboring as masons building things with bricks, blocks, or stone, which they call "operative" masonry. In the beginning, it was an organization for educated gentlemen of means, something of a philosophical society with the symbolism of a stonemason's trade. There were no "operative" masons in the order. Today, of course, there are some working (operative) masons who are also "speculative" Masons, members of the Masonic Lodge.

7. Do you mean that Masonry has something to do with Egyptian pagan religions?

Masonry has **everything** to do with Egyptian pagan religions. With no exception, the Masonic philosophers and writers of Masonic history trace Freemasonry directly back to the mystery religions of the East, especially those of Isis and Osiris of Egypt. Agreeing with Albert Pike and Joseph Fort Newton, two of Masonry's most respected authorities, *The Kentucky Monitor* declares plainly, "Freemasonry has come to us from the Ancient Mysteries of Osiris and Isis as celebrated in Egypt; that we owe much of our ritual to those old systems, and that from them and through them to even more remote sources we trace much of our doctrine."[48]

According to the consensus of Masonic authorities, the only pure form of religion that ever existed was that of the ancient pagan mysteries, and they were adulterated, contaminated, and forgotten by Hebrews and then Christians through the ages. Masonry, they teach, is a revival of those pagan mystery religions, an effort to rediscover their secrets and restore their perfection. J.D. Buck, in his classic book *Mystic Masonry*, expresses it this way:

"Drop the theological barnacles from the Religion of Jesus, as taught by Him, and by the Essenes and Gnostics of the first centuries, and it becomes Masonry. Masonry in its purity, derived as it is from the old Hebrew Kabalah as part of the Great Universal Wisdom Religion of remotest antiquity...."[49]

Their goal is that, through study and meditation, the mysteries will be restored to their ancient perfection and all men will gather to worship the nature gods and goddesses at only one altar, the altar of Masonry. Again, *The Kentucky Monitor* is clear:

"It [Freemasonry] makes no pretense of Christianity, and wars not against sectarian creeds or doctrines, but looks forward to the time when the labor of our ancient brethren shall be symbolized by the erection of a spiritual temple [worthy of] civilization. A temple in which there shall be one altar and but one worship, one common altar of Masonry ..." [50]

8. How and when did Masonry come to the United States?

All the early American lodges were chartered by the Grand Lodge of England. Here again, Masonic historians make different claims about which lodge was the first established in the colonies. The generally accepted version is that the first American lodge was established in 1730 in Boston, and the second in 1733 in Philadelphia. This first lodge in Philadelphia, of which Benjamin Franklin was an early member, met at Tun Tavern.

Historical Note. Tun Tavern in Philadelphia was also the site of the first recruitment of American Marines in 1775, and is considered to be the birthplace of the U.S. Marine Corps. Does this mean that there is a connection between Freemasonry and the Marine Corps? Absolutely not! It probably means that Tun Tavern was **the** place in Philadelphia where people gathered to eat, drink and be merry, and a recruiter goes where the crowd is. By the same logic, today there is **not** a Marine Corps Recruiting Station in Possum Trot, Kentucky. And, yes, there is such a village in southwestern Kentucky, populated by good people; but crowds do not gather there, except for church services and family reunions.

9. Why all the symbolic references to building?

The symbolic references to building have to do with the goal of self-improvement and character building in the members. They teach that the individual Mason, by his lessons in religion and morality and by his association with other Masons, is gradually perfected, both socially and spiritually. They proudly proclaim, "We make good men better" (which, significantly, makes no provision for making bad men good).

ENDNOTES

45 *The New Encyclopaedia Britannica*, 15th ed., s.v. "Freemasonry"; Malcolm C. Duncan, *Duncan 'S Masonic Ritual and Monitor,* 3rd ed. (New York: David McKay Co., Inc.), 29, 34, 35, 64-66, 94·96; see Chapter 13, "Masonry's Exclusiveness and Elitism."

46 Those who really believe this probably also believe in Santa Claus, the Tooth Fairy, and the essential goodness of man. "Even Blue Masonry cannot trace back its authentic history, with its present degrees, further than the year 1700, if so far," wrote Albert Pike in *Morals and Dogma,* rev. ed. (Washington, DC: House of the Temple, 1950), 208.

47 As is the case with much of Masonic doctrine, the authorities differ, with about as many "factual" accounts as there are writers, often in contradiction with one another. To pursue the subject seriously is to experience frustration and confusion.

48 Henry Pirtle, *The Kentucky Monitor,* 9th ed. (Louisville, KY: Standard Printing Co., 1921), xi, xii.

49 J.D. Buck, *Mystic Masonry,* 3rd ed. (Chicago: Chas T. Powner Co., 1925), 66, 67.

50 Pirtle, *The Kentucky Monitor*, 95.

The Scope of Freemasonry

A LITTLE LEAVEN LEAVENETH THE WHOLE LUMP.
GALATIANS 5:9

1. Is Masonry found only in England and the United States?

No. Freemasonry is worldwide, with lodges in every major nation except for Iran. The Ayatollah Khomeini closed the Iranian lodges after the shah was deposed. Until recent years, there were no lodges in China or Cuba, but lodges are now reopened in both. Because such political policies are constantly changing, what I have just written may have changed by the time you are reading it; but this will give you an understanding of the system. And there are always exceptions. In Roman Catholic Italy, Masonic lodges are against the law. And yet, there is a lodge called the P2 Lodge, operating in Rome. How could they get away with such a conspicuous violation of Italian law? It seems to be because some of the most powerful men in the World are members. One of them is Henry Kissinger.

Although the majority of Masons are in the United States, there are lodges around the world, with rituals largely the same.

2. In what other countries is Masonry strong?

Masonry is strongest in Great Britain, where it originated. In the Grand Lodge of England, the position of Grand Master is usually held by a member of the Royal Family. The current Grand Master of the Grand Lodge of England is His Royal Highness Prince Edward, Duke of Kent; he has been Grand Master since 1967. Masonry is also very strong in Western Europe and Scandinavia, where royalty also often rules in the Lodge. In France, Masonry has tended to be a political force and is considered by some to be a "rogue" branch of Masonry with very strong leanings toward the occult.

3. Is Masonry powerful in the United States?

Yes, it is, especially in some regions and in some social, political, and religious settings. For example, there are some places where one cannot be hired if not a Mason; elsewhere, promotions depend on the man's being a Mason. A man in Indiana related to the federal government that in eleven years of work with his employer, he had been denied promotion eight times because he refuses to join the Masonic Lodge. Masonry tends to be strong in police departments, and this creates problems in terms of fair and objective enforcement of the law. In Maryland, for example, automobile license plates have distinctive prefixes for Masons; since many, if not most, policemen are Masons, the problem is obvious. In recent years, this practice of special license plates for Masons, and for other groups, has spread to other states.

4. How many Masons are there?

No one but God really knows the answer to this question (with the exception, perhaps, of Satan) because there is no single, overall headquarters to keep track. Although the various grand lodges around the world cooperate and are networked, each tends to be autonomous with no one man or group in control of them all. However, an educated estimate is that there are between two and three million Masons in the United States and another one million in the rest of the world.

5. Are the Masons' numbers going up or down?

Masonic membership in the United States is in a steep decline; numbers are dropping, and with much fewer young men entering the Lodge, the average age is going up. According to the *Scottish Rite Journal*, Masonry's most prominent and authoritative periodical, the average age of American Masons is estimated at above seventy.[51] According to a report presented at the 1990 Conference of Grand Masters of Masons in North America, 40 percent of all Masons are over age sixty-five (compared with the general population of adult white males, where only 5 percent are over sixty-five). The same study estimates that overall membership will drop by 50 percent by the year 2000 and by an additional 50 percent by the year 2010.[52] At this rate, American Masonry would virtually cease to exist within the next thirty or forty years.

6. If numbers are declining, why is Masonry still a powerful force in the United States?

Despite the above figures, the lodge system is still a very powerful force in this country. The reason for this is that Masons still occupy positions of power and influence in the legal and judicial system, in local, state, and national government, law enforcement, business, certain parts of the armed forces, and in the churches.

In April 1993, a part of the U.S. Capitol Building was taken over for a day by the Supreme Council of the Thirty-third Degree. It was declared a Masonic Lodge and "tiled" (cleared of all non-Scottish Rite Masons), and George M. White, architect of the United States Capitol, was made a Thirty-second Degree Mason. Do you think your civic group, club, or church could do that? Don't bother to try.

The power of Masonry in the churches was brought out in the open in the conflict within the Southern Baptist Convention during 1992 and 1993, and in subsequent conventions. Although the convention admitted, on the record, that there are things about Masonry which are pagan, unscriptural, and in conflict with basic Christian beliefs, the delegates in June 1993 voted ten to one to compromise on the issue and take no stand against it.

7. If Masonry is in such a serious decline in numbers, why is it that so many powerful politicians and other prominent men are Masons?

The original members of English Masonry were aristocrats, and they quickly took in members of the royal family. Since "success begets success," politicians and other prominent people have been attracted to it ever since. An organization which can boast "important" men, past and present, readily attracts still more "important" men, and this success perpetuates itself. Even though fewer and fewer "ordinary" men are joining the Lodge, it still attracts the prominent and powerful (and those who seek to be). There are fewer and fewer "Indians" but a considerable number of "chiefs."

8. Is Masonry stronger in some parts of the country than in others?

Definitely. Although lodges are to be found in all states, territories, and the District of Columbia, Masonry tends to be much stronger in some parts of the country. Numbers of Masons are greater, and their influence stronger, in the South and Midwest, and much less so in the Northeast and Far West. In the South, especially, there is a great deal of blind and passionate loyalty to the Lodge. There are places in the South where a man can't be elected dogcatcher if he is not a Mason.

ENDNOTES

51 Thomas M. Boles, 33°, "Where Do You Do Your Shopping?," *Scottish Rite Journal* (July 1993): 53.
52 S. Brent Morris, 33°, "Unite in the Grand Design," *Scottish Rite Journal* (May 1990): 46-49.

American Freemasonry: The Blue Lodge and the Higher Degrees

FOR A GOOD TREE BRINGETH NOT FORTH CORRUPT FRUIT;
NEITHER DOTH A CORRUPT TREE BRING FORTH GOOD FRUIT.
LUKE 6:43

1. How is American Masonry organized?

American Masonry is a rather complex structure built on a broad foundation; that foundation is the local lodge, referred to by Masons as the Blue Lodge. This is the lodge in your home town. In the South and Midwest, there is likely to be one in even the smallest of towns. Further, in the South, if there are only three buildings in town besides the general store, they will probably be the Baptist church, the Methodist church, and the Masonic Lodge. This is perhaps an exaggeration, but if it is, it is only a slight one. In the local lodge (the Blue Lodge), the first three degrees ("Entered Apprentice", "Fellowcraft", and "Master Mason") are conferred and practiced. The third, or Master Mason Degree, is as far as most Masons go, meaning that their entire Masonic experience is limited to the local lodge and its three degrees. Traditionally, the vast majority of Masons has gone no farther.

Built upon the foundation of the local lodge are the higher degrees, the Shrine, all the special Masonic bodies, and the auxiliary groups for women, boys, and girls.[53]

2. What is the significance of the *Blue* in Blue Lodge?

This is a hazy area, even among Masonic writers, but it seems to derive from the significance of the sky overhead, and this in two ways. The tradition is that the ancient stonemasons' guilds met secretly on hilltops under the "starry canopy of the Heavens," so many Blue Lodges have blue ceilings (some blue ceilings have stars scattered about); some even have blue doors. Another reason for the "blue heaven" symbolism is that astrology is very important to Masonic philosophy. Additionally, the "ancient brethren" worshiped the heavens, especially the sun, from the highest hills—thus the blue sky and its starry host.[54]

Similarly, lodge halls are often above the ground floor, the custom descending from "high place" worship as well as for enhanced security. Daniel Sickles, venerable Masonic authority, explains: "Lodge meetings at the present day are usually held in upper chambers. Before the erection of Temples the celestial bodies [stars and planets] were worshipped on hills, and the terrestrial ones [Earth spirits] in the valleys."[55] *The Kentucky Monitor* adds, "It may be, however, that the custom had its origin in a practice illicitly observed by the ancient Jews (worshiping in the pagan "high places").. The ancient Jews were forbidden to worship in the high places of the pagans, but when they were backslidden (as was often the case) they adopted this practice from their pagan neighboring nations."[56]

3. What are the "higher degrees"?

As Freemasonry evolved, systems of additional degrees were conceived, and, to varying degrees, Masons accepted, embraced, and joined them. The basic concept was (and is) that there should be further steps toward perfection than were found in the original three degrees. An additional factor contributing to their development and acceptance is the elitist appeal of becoming one of the relative few who occupy higher positions than the rest.

In Freemasonry's early days, some systems of higher degrees failed to attract wide acceptance and died on the vine, while others grew. Since "success begets success," those degree systems which attracted more men tended then to attract still more. People love to join "the best," and some prospered while others withered and died.

To make the matter even more complex, some individual degrees in the "higher" systems attracted such a following that separate chapters were organized. The best example of this is the Royal Arch degree, the seventh degree of the York Rite, which has become a separate organization within the overall system, with its own books of ritual and doctrine, officers, regular meetings, dues, etc. It is interesting to me that the Royal Arch degree claims to be a "Christian" degree but is, in fact, probably the most wicked of earned degrees. (See chapter 4, "Freemasonry's 'Christian' Degrees.")

4. What are the systems for the "higher degrees" in America?

In American Masonry, two such systems of higher degrees prevail: the York Rite and the Scottish Rite. By far the larger and more influential of these is the Scottish Rite. The Scottish Rite is further divided into northern and southern jurisdictions. Although they cooperate, neither answers to the other.[57] The Southern Jurisdiction of the Scottish Rite is much larger and more powerful, including all states, territories, and trusts, except for the fourteen Midwest and Northeast states that comprise the Northern Jurisdiction.[58]

5. Who can join these systems and earn the higher degrees?

Until recent years, any Mason, after six months as a Master Mason (Third Degree), if he had the time and money, could enter either the York or Scottish Rite and begin the climb to "the top." In order to remain in either the York or Scottish Rite, the man must not only satisfy the requirements of that rite (attendance, dues, etc.) but must also continue to be a Master Mason in good standing in his local Blue Lodge. After being either a 32nd Degree Mason or a Knight Templar for six months, a man was eligible to join the Shrine.

There are no degrees in the Shrine; rather the Shriners are devoted to community service and fun. The Shriners are looked upon as the "party boys" of Masonry, and they have a well-deserved reputation for rowdy conventions and a lot of drinking. In harmony with this reputation, their local body is called a "Shrine Club" although they may call the building in which they meet a "temple." In recent times, because of dramatic membership losses, the Shrine lowered its membership requirements to allow men to enter the Shrine directly from the 3rd (Master Mason) Degree. This sent shock waves through the York and Scottish Rites because, until this change of Shrine policy, it had been necessary for a man to be a Master Mason for six months in order to be eligible to enter either the Scottish Rite or the York Rite. And the Mason then was required to become either a 32nd Degree Mason in the Scottish Rite, or a Knight Templar in the York Rite (its equivalent rank) in order to be eligible for the Shrine. Suddenly, Master Masons could go directly into the Shrine, bypassing the time and expense of going through the higher degrees of the York or Scottish Rites. Just as suddenly, there was a dramatic reduction in men petitioning to enter either of the traditional pathways to the Shrine. Apparently, many Masons were more interested in entering into the "fun" of the Shrine than the spiritual enlightenment of the higher degrees of the York or Scottish Right. For more on this, and other recent changes within Freemasonry, see the Epilogue to Part Two.

6. What is the difference between the York Rite and the Scottish Rite?

In the York Rite, the Mason climbs through a total of ten additional degrees, culminating in his becoming a "Knight Templar." He can then sign his name "Hiram A. Mason, KT." In the Scottish Rite, the Mason goes through twenty-nine additional degrees culminating in the Thirty-second Degree ("Sublime Prince of the Royal Secret"). The Thirty-second Degree Mason can then sign his name "John Q. Mason, 32°." The degree of Knight Templar is the equivalent of the Thirty-second Degree, so the two are viewed as being at the same level.

Some Masons, with extra time, money, and motivation, go through both the York and Scottish Rites. Such a man can then sign his name "Mason A. Cuttabuv, KT, 32°."

7. Is there a headquarters for Masonry in America?

No. Since each state and territory is a Grand Lodge, essentially sovereign and independent of the others, there is no single headquarters, nor a central authority recognized by all Masons. Despite this, the House of the Temple, headquarters of the Southern Jurisdiction of the Scottish Rite, seat of the Supreme Council of the Thirty-third Degree, tends to function as such de facto because of its size, influence, and power. In fact, this Supreme Council claims to be the "Mother Jurisdiction of the World," and former Sovereign Grand Commander of the Southern Jurisdiction, Albert Pike, took upon himself the title, "Supreme Pontiff of Universal Freemasonry."

ENDNOTES

53   "Busy, Brotherly World of Freemasonry," *LIFE Magazine* (8 October 1956): l04-122.

54   Albert Pike, *Morals and Dogma*, rev. ed. (Washington, DC: House of the Temple, 1950).

55 Daniel Sickles, *Ahiman Rhezon and Freemason's Guide* (New York: MaCoy Publishing Co., 1911), 75.

56 Henry Pirtle, *The Kentucky Monitor,* 9th ed. (Louisville, KY: Standard Printing Co., 1921), 36, 37. Mr. Pirtle is in error here; worshiping on high places was an ancient pagan practice adopted by backsliding Israelites. It did not originate with the Israelites.

57 "Busy, Brotherly World," 104-109.

58 The fourteen states of the Northern Jurisdiction are Illinois, Wisconsin, Indiana, Ohio, Michigan, Pennsylvania, New Jersey, New York, Connecticut, Rhode Island, Massachusetts, Vermont, New Hampshire, and Maine.

Freemasonry's "Christian" Degrees

I KNOW THY WORKS, THAT THOU HAST A NAME
THAT THOU LIVEST, AND ART DEAD.
REVELATION 3:1

1. Are there any Christian degrees in Masonry?

No, at least there is none that answers to the biblical definition of the word "Christian," because they are part of the overall Masonic system with its death oaths and deception. Masonry reduces the Bible to the level of equality with all other "holy books," no better than the Koran or the Hindu Vedas. It denies the uniqueness of Jesus Christ as the sole redeemer of lost mankind and reduces Him to the status of being merely one of many "exemplars" (great men of the past). There can be nothing truly Christian about any such system; nine gallons of ice cream and one gallon of dirt combine to make 10 gallons of dirty ice cream.

2. Do Masons claim to have Christian degrees?

Yes. York Rite (also called American Rite) Masons, when confronted with Masonry's obvious paganism, claim that theirs is different from all the rest of Masonry, that theirs is a Christian rite because Christ and Christian symbolism appear in some parts of their ritual. In fact, the degree of Knight Templar, the York Rite's highest degree, is open only to "professing Christians," and, in the ritual, the candidate promises that if he is called upon to "draw his sword in a religious cause," he will "give preference to the Christian religion" (which seems to me to be a strange and insipid commitment).

3. If York Rite Masons must profess to be Christians in order to receive their highest degree and must mention Christ in their ritual, doesn't that make it a Christian branch of Masonry?

While it is true that Jesus is mentioned in some of the York Rite degrees, the critical issues of man's essential sinfulness and the uniqueness of Jesus as the only means of redemption are never expressed. In only four of the ten degrees is Christ mentioned at all.

4. But, since Jesus is mentioned in at least some of their degrees, doesn't this still make the York Rite a Christian organization?

No, it does not, and, again, this is so for at least the following reasons:

a. To make references to Jesus in an organization's rituals and lessons, but as less than what He really is, as less than God the Son, unique Redeemer, the only means of reconciliation for lost and sinful mankind, is not only invalid but blasphemous. We cannot have Jesus Christ on our own terms. A watered-down concept of Jesus is no Jesus at all.

b. Prayers in the York Rite are the Christ-less "universal" prayers of the rest of Masonry, never prayed in the name of Jesus. Similarly, references to Jesus are excluded in the passages of Scripture used in the ritual. For example, in the charge to the chapter in the Royal Arch, 2 Thessalonians 3:6-16 is read, omitting the name of Jesus as if the passage had nothing to do with Him. In the fourth degree, 1 Peter 2:5 is used, but with the reference to Jesus omitted. The same passages are used, mutilated in the same way, in Blue Lodge Masonry. (See chapter 11, *Freemasonry and the Bible*.)

c. In the seventh (Royal Arch) degree, their blasphemous confession of the name of their god combines part of the sacred name of Yahweh (or Jehovah) with Baal or Bel, the pagan god ancient Israel was warned not to touch, and with On, representing Osiris, the Egyptian sun god (sex and fertility god), or Om, the generic Hindu name for their gods. In their most secret moment of ritual, they declare that the name of God is *YA·BEL·OM* or *JE·BUL·ON*. Spellings vary, but the supreme name of their god always combines the first sounds in Jehovah or Yahweh with Baal or Bel and On or Om *(Aum)*.[59] Some Royal Arch Masons will deny that their name for their deity is a combination of Jehovah with Baal and On or Om, but Albert Pike, the quintessential Masonic authority, knew that that is precisely what it is. It is interesting that even Pike, patron saint of the Scottish Rite and author of the thoroughly pagan Masonic classic *Morals and Dogma*, was offended by what he called this "mongrel" name for deity.[60]

d. Worse, I believe, is their use of the name of God as a password in the Royal Arch chapters, taking this sacred name upon themselves and identifying *themselves* as the God of Abraham, Isaac, and Jacob. The challenge is, "Are you a Royal Arch Mason?" The reply is, "I am that I am."[61] At this point your mouth should be dropping open as you gasp in unbelief! This is horrible blasphemy!

e. The York Rite initiate must drink wine from a human skull, calling down a curse, the death of Judas (suicide), upon himself should he ever betray any of the secret work. In this same way, he also calls down upon himself the sins of the one from whose skull he drinks, in addition to his own. The Bible makes no provision for calling down curses upon ourselves and makes it clear that we are responsible for our own sins and no one else's.

f. As in the rest of Masonry, there is a horrible death oath for each degree of York Rite Masonry, in which the candidate agrees that, should he violate any of the secrecy or other provisions of the oath, he will allow himself to be mutilated and killed. For example, in the oath of the "Christian" Royal Arch, he swears to "no less a penalty than that of having my skull smote off, and my brains exposed to the scorching rays of the noonday Sun."[62] In the oath of the "Christian" degree of Knight Templar, he accepts "no less a penalty than that of having my head struck off and placed upon the highest spire in Christendom."[63]

g. Even if the York Rite were truly Christian and did not contain such awful blasphemies and occult, pagan ritual, it would still be true that the York Rite cannot divorce itself from the rest of Masonry. To be a member of the York Rite a man must continue to be a Blue Lodge Mason in good standing. "Veneration for, and fidelity to" Blue Lodge Masonry are declared in his York Rite initiation, and he must drink "libations" (religious drink offerings) to the "illustrious Grand Masters of Ancient Craft Masonry."[64] In addition, a York Rite Mason may also belong to the Scottish Rite, and it is not uncommon for the most dedicated (or ambitious) Masons to belong to both.

5. Does the history of the Order of Knights Templar (York Rite) go back to the Crusaders of the Middle Ages?

No, some writers claim this, but Knight Templarism in Masonry, like the rest of speculative Masonry, dates only from the eighteenth century. The Knight Templar degree was first conferred in America in 1769.

6. What were the medieval Knights Templar?

The medieval order of Knights Templar went to Jerusalem as crusaders in the early twelfth century to protect pilgrims and defend the temple site, where they made their initial headquarters. They were a combination religious and military order. Their last leader (early fourteenth century) was Jacques DeMolay. Their latter history is a murky and controversial one.

The Masonic version is that DeMolay and his Templars were unselfish heroes, protecting and defending the Christian pilgrims journeying to Jerusalem, and that he was a martyr to the greed of the King of France and the Pope (who also was French), both of whom feared his power and wanted his wealth.[65]

History records that the Templars, who in the beginning took vows of poverty, diversified their activities and became immensely wealthy, becoming in fact the most wealthy group in the world, with properties scattered throughout Christendom. They became "the great international financiers and bankers of the age with their Paris temple the center of the world's money market," in which "popes and kings deposited their revenues."[66] Their military might protected their widespread banks and bullion transfers. Sworn to absolute secrecy concerning their internal affairs, their secret, mysterious ritual meetings were held at midnight. Accused of corruption, witchcraft, and victimizing the pilgrims they were supposed to protect, they were greatly feared.

In 1305, evidence of their Satanic corruption was obtained by means of a defector and spies sent by the king of France to infiltrate the order. On Friday, 13 October 1307, DeMolay and sixty templars were arrested in Paris.[67] DeMolay avoided torture and readily repented and tearfully confessed to "denying Christ and spitting on the cross." By joint order of the Pope and the King of France, he and the rest were burned at the stake before Notre Dame as criminals and enemies of the faith, effectively ending the Templars' power.[68] There is some evidence, however, that the enormous wealth of the Templars has survived and evolved into the power base of the most powerful international banks of today.[69]

7. Then, what do the Masonic Knights Templar have to do with the medieval crusaders?

York Rite Masons take much of their symbolism from the medieval crusaders (defending the faith with their swords, etc).

Although they also claim to trace their actual history from Jacques DeMolay and the Crusades, the most credible Masonic authorities deny this. Albert Mackey, author of the *Encyclopedia of Freemasonry,* called the idea "wholly unsupported by the authority of history."[70] Albert Pike agrees that "they have assumed a title to which they have not a shadow of a claim."[71]

ENDNOTES

59 Malcolm C. Duncan, *Duncan's Masonic Ritual and Monitor,* 3rd ed. (New York: David McKay Co., Inc., undated), 223-226.

60 Albert Pike, *The Holy Triad* (Washington, D.C., 1873).

61 Duncan, *Masonic Ritual,* 221.

62 Ibid., 230.

63 *In Hoc Signo Vincis,* 133, as quoted in Philip Lochaas, "American Rite Masonry" (Newtonville, NY: HRT Min, Inc., undated), 7-8.

64 Ibid., 139, 140.

65 This aspect of the story probably contains a certain amount of truth.

66 *Encyclopaedia Britannica,* vol. 21, 1957 ed., s.v. "Templars." There is an interesting theory to the effect that the templars found the hidden treasury of the temple, lost since Jerusalem was destroyed by Titus in A.D. 70, and that this was the beginning of their enormous wealth (for which there is no other known explanation).

67 This is believed by many to be the origin of the belief that Friday the thirteenth is an "unlucky" day.

68 The Order of DeMolay, the Masonic order for boys not yet old enough to join the Lodge, is named for this same Jacques DeMolay.

69 William T. Still, *New World Order* (Lafayette, LA: Huntington House, 1990), 112-114.

70 Albert Mackey, *Encyclopedia of Freemasonry,* rev. ed. s.v. "Templar" (Chicago, New York, London: Masonic History Co., 1927), 764.

71 Albert Pike, *Morals and Dogma,* rev. ed. (Washington, DC: House of the Temple, 1950), 821.

The Shrine:
Islam in Freemasonry

THEIR SORROWS SHALL BE MULTIPLIED THAT HASTEN AFTER
ANOTHER GOD: THEIR DRINK OFFERINGS OF BLOOD WILL I
NOT OFFER, NOR TAKE UP THEIR NAMES UNTO MY LIPS.
PSALMS 16:4

1. Are the Shriners part of Masonry?

Yes, the Shrine (the full name is Ancient Arabic Order,
Nobles of the Mystic Shrine) is a part of the Masonic system.
It is the Islamic expression of Freemasonry. (See question 8,
below.) It is one of the addendum groups within Masonry
which has attracted wide interest and acceptance and has
become a major fixture within Freemasonry. The Shrine was
first organized in New York in 1872.

2. Are these the men who wear the red hats with tassels and glittery decorations?

Yes, the Shrine is the most conspicuous part of Masonry;
in fact, it is the only conspicuous part of Masonry. While the
rest of Masonry is deliberately inconspicuous and maintains a
low public profile, the Shrine is deliberately conspicuous and
maintains a high public profile. They love to be in parades with

their little motor scooters, go-carts, donkeys, or elephants and take clown acts to hospitals and conduct circuses. People who know nothing of the rest of Masonry will usually have some awareness of the men in the red hats (fezzes), their circuses, all-star football games, and hospitals for children.

3. How is the Shrine related to the rest of Masonry?

Until July 2000, the Shrine's membership was restricted to those Masons who have advanced to the level of the Thirty-Second Degree or Knight Templar. After six months as either a Thirty-second Degree Mason or Knight Templar, a man might then apply to the Shrine. This may sound like the Shrine is the "top of the mountain" in Freemasonry, but it isn't; it is actually an organization off to the side. Because of dwindling numbers, major changes have taken place in the Shrine and its membership. These will be explained in the Epilogue to Part Two.

4. Is the Shrine a drawing card attracting men to Freemasonry?

Yes. Only God knows the hearts and motives of men, but there can be no doubt that some men have entered the Blue Lodge and gone on to become 32nd Degree Masons in the Scottish Rite, or Knights Templar in the York Rite, only because they wanted to become Shriners and enjoy the parades and the social life. There is one case of a man who petitioned to enter the Lodge, and the day after he was initiated into the first degree, Entered Apprentice, he went out and bought a midget car! He was probably two years away from being eligible to join the Shrine, but when that day came he would be ready for the fun. There can be no doubt about his motive for entering the Lodge.

5. Does the rest of Masonry acknowledge the validity of the Shrine?

Absolutely. Although some of the purist students of Masonry may look down upon it as a recent creation and a much-less-than-pure form of Masonry, the vast majority of Masons are proud of the Shrine. When anyone questions the rightness of Masonry, the first thing a Mason will cite to prove its goodness will be either George Washington (see Chapter 19, *Masonry, Presidents, and the Founding Fathers*) or the good works of the Shriners.

6. What are the most common criticisms of the Shrine by other Masons?

There are no degrees in the Shrine, no lessons in religion and morality. In fact, the position of being a Shriner is not even a degree; he becomes a "Noble," but this is not a degree. Also, the Shriners take a very lighthearted approach to what they do, seeking "fun" in all gatherings, and they have a well-deserved reputation for drinking a lot and conducting rowdy conventions. In fact, for this reason some cities are reluctant to host their conventions.[72] They are commonly referred to by other Masons as "the party animals of Masonry." It is significant that the proper name for their local organization is "club," in spite of the fact that their building is called a "temple." Their initiation ceremonies are particularly childish, rowdy, and often vulgar, featuring degrading, "bathroom" humor. (See question 8, below.) These initiations can be physically dangerous to the extent that a Shrine candidate must go through health screening prior to initiation. In 1991, a Shriner sued his local Shrine club and six of its members for physical and emotional injury resulting from electric shock during his initiation.[73]

The Grand Lodge of England, where they take their Masonry very seriously, forbids its members to join such "fun" Masonic orders on penalty of dismissal. They definitely **do not** recognize the Shrine as a legitimate branch of Freemasonry.

7. What are the good works that offset all these criticisms?

The Shriners build and operate orthopedic hospitals and burn centers for children in the United States, Canada, and Mexico; the care is free for those who cannot pay. The cornerstone for the first Shrine hospital was laid in 1922 in Shreveport, Louisiana. In the year 2010 the total number of Shrine hospitals was twenty-two.

8. So, how could there be anything wrong with a group that builds hospitals for children and provides free care?

The fact that a group does one thing that is good doesn't mean that everything else the group does is right.

9. Then, what about the Shrine is wrong?

What is wrong with the Shrine begins with the fact that it is part of the overall Masonic system. A man can't be a Shriner without being first, and continuously, a member in good standing of his Blue Lodge.

Additionally (and uniquely), the Shrine is the Islamic expression of Freemasonry, making it clearly anti-Christian. Everything about the Shrine is based on the Muslim faith and Arabic symbolism. One soon notices that their costumes, symbols, and even the architecture and names of their temples are usually Arabic or Muslim.

The candidate for initiation is greeted by the high priest, who says, "By the existence of Allah and the Creed of Mohammed, by the legendary sanctity of the Tabernacle at Mecca we greet you...." The candidate must kneel before a Muslim altar, put his hand on the Koran (in some cases, also a Bible), and take his horrible death oath, calling upon the pagan god, Allah, for help: "May Allah, the god of the Arab, Moslim [sic] and Mohammedan, the god of our fathers, support me to the entire fulfillment of the same, Amen, Amen, Amen."[74]

In the recognition test ritual for a Shriner seeking to enter a Shrine meeting in a temple not his own, he is asked, among other things, at what Shrine he worships. He must answer, "At the Shrine of Islam."[75]

The Shrine ritual declares that Islam is truth: "Whoso seeketh Islam earnestly seeks true direction."[76] Since Islam and its holy book, the Koran, teach that Jesus was only a minor prophet, subordinate to Mohammed, that God has no sons, and that all "infidels" (and that definitely includes us Christians) who will not renounce their faiths and convert to Islam are to be put to death, this creates a serious contradiction for the Christian Shriner.[77]

A minor and repulsive fact about the Shrine is its preoccupation with urination. In the roughhouse setting of the initiation, it appears to be merely bathroom humor, a matter of childish bad taste. The blindfolded candidate is sprayed with warm water and made to believe that he is being urinated upon by a dog or another man. Yet, in the serious matter of their "secret work," the recognition test by which a Shriner may be admitted to a lodge where he is not known refers to his having to "contribute a few drops of urine" in order to gain access to the meeting, reducing the Shriner to the cultural level of a sniffing dog.[78]

10. If the initiate must kneel before a Muslim altar and call upon Allah, the god of Mohammed, are there actually Christians who do this?

It seems impossible for a Christian to do such an obviously wrong and sinful thing, but they do. Pastors do. With not only the obvious theological contradiction, but also the historic determination of the Muslims to eradicate the Jews and possess the land of Israel, it seems unthinkable that a Jew should also do this, but they do. Rabbis do.

In the case of most Shrine candidates, I believe that they don't take the Muslim matter or the oath seriously; they are just going through it all, getting it over with, so they can get on with the good works and the parties. But a pastor, priest, or rabbi who does such a thing must be one who is already terribly confused theologically, perhaps a universalist who thinks everyone will go to heaven, if there is such a place, that all gods are one, and that "all roads lead to the same mountaintop." They are wrong; and forever is a long time to be wrong.

11. But, what about the Shrine as a charity?

Here again, reality falls way short of the image they seek to project. Here also is an example of the kind of deception I have found throughout the Masonic system. In the first place, the impression that they seek to make is that every dime contributed to their hospital charities goes to help little children. That is certainly the belief of the person who gets stuck at the street intersection "roadblock" where he drops his money into the bucket marked "HELP CRIPPLED CHILDREN." Worse still, in a way, is that the Shriner standing there in the heat, cold, or rain, wearing his red fez and shaking the bucket at you with hope, also believes that every dime dropped in his bucket does go to help children. The reality is something quite different.

In 1986, the *Orlando Sentinel* published a landmark investigative series on the Florida Shrine and found that **as little as two percent of the money** collected in all of their fundraising efforts actually went for building and operating their hospitals. The rest went to promotion, entertainment, publicity, operation of private bars, restaurants, and golf courses, travel, and conventions. An estimated 15.5 million dollars was spent on parties and conventions in 1986 alone, according to the Internal Revenue Service. This brings us to another interesting point.

The Shrine is an extremely wealthy "charity." (To me, this seems to be a very great contradiction in terms.) In 1985, the IRS reported it as the wealthiest in the United States, with an estimated war chest of 2 billion dollars, approximately twice as wealthy as the one in second place, the American Red Cross, and four times as wealthy as the one in third place, the American Cancer Society. The Red Cross, however, spent four times as much in 1985 as the Shrine. In that year, according to the IRS, the Shrine spent only 29.8 percent of its income on program services, while the Red Cross spent 84 percent and the American Cancer Society spent 67.2 percent. In fact, no other charity in the top fourteen gave as little to designated assistance programs as the Shrine, the wealthiest of them all!

In 1985, according to IRS reports filed by the Shrine, they spent more money (15 million dollars) on parties and gala conventions than they did on their hospitals (12 million dollars). The same investigation (none of which was denied by the Shrine) disclosed that "Shrine hospitals get little support from Shrine Circuses, but most Shrine Temples could not pay their bills without an annual circus." An even more startling revelation of Shrine values was that "a Shriner may spend as much as $180,000 to get elected to the Imperial Divan, the organization's national board of directors. Once elected, however, years of perks help make up for the cost."[79]

12. Does the Shrine require a death oath for membership?

Yes. Like the true degrees in Masonry, the Shrine also requires the candidate to take a death oath of obligation. In fact, this one is particularly gruesome, even when compared with the rest of Masonry's bloody oaths. In this oath, the candidate accepts the penalty of: "… having my eyeballs pierced to the center with a three edged blade, with my feet flayed [sliced across in thin strips], and I be forced to walk the hot sands upon the sterile shores of the Red Sea until the flaming Sun shall strike me with livid plague."[80]

13. What is the significance of the red cap (the fez)?

The red cap is called a *fez*. It will usually have the name of the local Shrine club on the front in gold embroidery or sequins and is the essential item of dress for a Shriner. Some are extremely ornate (and expensive) and a matter of great personal pride. The red fez is the national headwear in Turkey, Egypt, and other Muslim countries. (It is interesting that in these countries, as in the Shrine, the fez may only be worn by men.)

The fez gets its name (and color) from the city of Fez in Morocco. Until the Muslim invaders overran it in the eighth century, Fez was a Christian city. When the city fell, the Muslim conquerors slaughtered thirty-five thousand Christians—men, women, and children—and their blood literally ran in the streets. The exultant Muslims celebrated their victory by dipping their wool caps in the Christians' blood and then wearing them in triumph. This is why it is called a fez, and this is why it is always red.

By wearing the red fez, Shriners are, in a sense, celebrating the slaughter of those Moroccan Christians. Most Shriners, of course, don't know this; if they did, most would laugh it off, saying, "We don't mean any such thing; we're just having fun," the classic Shriner justification for most of what they do.

14. But, don't some Masons excuse all this by saying that the Shrine isn't "official" Masonry?

Yes. When confronted with all this ugly truth, some knowledgeable Masons will try to explain it away by saying that the Shrine isn't really an "official" part of Masonry. For that matter, there is probably nothing in all the vast, complex system of Masonic orders and degrees that is "pure" Masonry except for the Blue Lodge, the first three degrees. But, if you go to the huge Masonic National Memorial, Masonry's national showpiece, towering just inside the beltway in Alexandria, Virginia, you will see a large portion of their space proudly devoted to the Ancient Arabic Order, Nobles of the Mystic Shrine. You will also find a Shrine room at the House of the Temple in Washington, D.C.

No, the Shrine, where Allah is their god, Mohammed is their prophet, and fun is their principal occupation, is not only an inseparable part of American Freemasonry, it is probably the part of which Masons are most proud.

ENDNOTES

72 In 1993, the question of whether or not to allow them to return was a hotly contested issue in New Orleans (certainly not an intolerant city), with many testimonies to irresponsible, destructive behavior by convening Shriners in the past.

73 Associated Press, *The Columbus Dispatch* (lO December 1991): 4-A.

74 *The Mystic Shrine, an Illustrated Ritual of the Ancient Arabic Order, Nobles of the Mystic Shrine*, rev. ed. (Chicago, IL: Ezra Cook Publishers, 1975), 18, 22.

75 *Shriners Recognition Test* (Chicago, IL: Ezra Cook Publishers, undated), 2.

76 Cook, *The Mystic Shrine*, 19.

77 The Koran, Surah 9:4, 5.

78 Cook, *Shriners Recognition Test*, 1.

79 John Wark and Gary Marx, "Shrine," *The Orlando Sentinel* (29 June 1986, AI; 30 June 1986, AI; 1 July 1986, AI).

80 Cook, *The Mystic Shrine*, 22.

For several years, a Masonic lodge and this church were housed in the same building north of Birmingham, Alabama. The shared sign suggests they are one and the same. Notice the Masonic symbols above the sign.

Adoptive Freemasonry: Masonic Groups for Women and Children

BEHOLD, THERE SAT WOMEN WEEPING FOR TAMMUZ [OSIRIS}.
THEN HE SAID TO ME ... THOU SHALT SEE GREATER
ABOMINATIONS THAN THESE. AND HE BROUGHT ME INTO THE
INNER COURT OF THE LORD'S HOUSE, AND BEHOLD ...
FIVE AND TWENTY MEN WITH THEIR BACKS TOWARD THE
TEMPLE OF THE LORD, AND THEIR FACES TOWARD THE EAST;
AND THEY WORSHIPPED THE SUN TOWARD THE EAST.
EZEKIEL 9:14-16

THE LORD GOD ... WILL BY NO MEANS CLEAR THE GUILTY;
VISITING THE INIQUITY OF THE FATHERS UPON THE CHILDREN.
EXODUS 34:6-7

1. Can women and children be Masons?

No. Membership in the Masonic Lodge is only for men. However, there are other groups related to the Masonic Lodge that are for women and children. These groups are the subject of this chapter.

Bizarre Exceptions. As a matter of interest, however, it is recorded that several women, due to unusual circumstances, have been initiated into one or more of the Blue Lodge degrees. One woman was initiated into the First Degree (Entered Apprentice). This amazing event took place in Ireland, in Masonry's early days. Even more bizarre is the case of a woman in Kentucky who took all three of the Blue Lodge degrees and was "raised" as a Master Mason. For more on this issue see Chapter Thirteen, "Freemasonry's Exclusiveness and Elitism," and Appendix A, "Female "Brothers" in the Lodge."

2. What is the group for women?

Actually, there are several groups for women, including the Order of the Eastern Star, the Daughters of Isis, and the Daughters of the Nile. The Eastern Star is open to all women who are directly related to Master Masons in good standing (or to those who died in good standing). Some groups are more exclusive: the Daughters of Isis and the Daughters of the Nile are open only to the wives of Shriners, and the latter is by invitation only.

3. Are all these women's groups about the same?

No. although they are all basically the same in that they are Masonry-related and this Masonic influence is apparent in their exclusiveness, secrecy, lofty titles, and pompous ceremony. The Eastern Star is relatively benign in its rituals, its oath is not bloody, much use is made of Scripture, and most of its members think it is Christian. The Daughters of Isis, on the other hand, is obviously pagan. The ritual is entirely based on the legend and worship of Isis and Osiris, its initiation is more like Blue Lodge Masonry, there is a horrible death oath, they must kiss the Koran and "the Red Stone of Horus," and not even the most deceived member would consider it "Christian."[81]

4. What is the Order of the Eastern Star?

The Order of the Eastern Star, open to all Mason-related women of age eighteen and above, is by far the largest women's group. "The Star," as it is familiarly called, was the creation of Rob Morris, a prominent Kentucky Mason, poet, philosopher, and teacher, who wrote its degrees in 1850. Mississippi lays claim to being its birthplace, as the degrees were written and the first meeting was conducted by Morris in a rural Mississippi school building (which also served as the Masonic Lodge) while he was principal there. "The Little Red Schoolhouse" still stands and is preserved as an Eastern Star shrine in Holmes County, about ten miles south of Lexington, Mississippi, on State Route 17.[82] Today, the Eastern Star has grand chapters at state level, in U.S. territories, and several foreign countries, and a general grand chapter, with general authority, headquartered at the International Eastern Star Temple in Washington, D.C.

Women in the Eastern Star and the other groups "go through the chairs" (advance through the offices) just like their male sponsors in the Masonic Lodge.

5. Is the Eastern Star a Christian organization?

No, although most women who belong believe that it is. It can't be Christian, for it is based upon and is a part of the overall Masonic Lodge system. Like the parent Blue Lodge of Masonry, their prayers are the Christ-less "universal" prayers of the rest of Masonry. Although there are references to Christ in the ritual, they are always indirect or implied; the name of Jesus does not appear, even in their Eastern Star burial service.[83]

6. Why then do most of the members think "the Star" is a Christian organization?

Like most Blue Lodge Masons, members of the Eastern Star believe that it is a Christian organization because they were told this upon entering the order by sincere people who believed it to be true. Those who told them believed it because an earlier generation of sincere people told it to them, and so the deception is perpetuated from one generation to the next. With a strong belief in the Star as Christian and a right thing to do, they thenceforth blind themselves to a lot of facts that contradict their assumption.

It is important to understand that they accept it because they are like most people who don't stop and think through what it means to be "Christian." If a Bible is involved, or Bible stories and characters included prominently in the rituals, and prayers (even if they are Christ-less prayers), most will call it "Christian." The exclusion of Jesus by name, secrecy, exclusiveness, references to the Cabala, and other non-Christian characteristics go unnoticed by most.

Finally, their ritual statement, "We have seen his star in the East and are come to worship him," is assumed by practically all to refer to the Star of Bethlehem and the child, Jesus. It doesn't. As in the Masonic Lodge, the position of honor and worship is the east, not the west; the throne chairs of the Worthy Matron and Worthy Patron are against the east wall, under the symbol of deity. The Magi (wise men) of the Nativity of Jesus, however, came *from* the East. The star they saw and followed *was west of them;* they traveled from cast to west and found the child Jesus in the west, not in the east.

Although few Eastern Star ladies realize it, east is their direction of honor and worship because the sun rises in the east. Since ancient times, pagan worshipers of nature and fertility have faced eastward and worshiped the reproductive, life-giving power of the sun. Unwittingly, those nice ladies in their fine attire, with their candles and music, many of them well-meaning Christians, are reenacting this ancient pagan sex worship.[84] According to the most revered Masonic authorities, they are unwittingly participating in the worship of Isis and Osiris, which is phallic worship.[85] (See Chapter Seventeen, Freemasonry and Its Symbols, and Chapter Twenty One, Freemasonry and the Occult.)

7. Can men belong to the Eastern Star?

Yes. Most people don't realize this, but men can also belong to the Eastern Star if they are Master Masons in good standing. Although the Star is thought of as strictly a women's group, it was founded by men, the degrees and rituals were written by men, and a meeting can't even be conducted without the supervising presence of men. Each Eastern Star chapter has a male officer called "Worthy Patron" who oversees the functioning of the Worthy Matron (senior female leader). It is a violation of Eastern Star law to conduct any initiation without the Worthy Patron's presence, and such a thing may only be done under extraordinary circumstances, and with special permission.

8. What is the meaning of the pin, the five-pointed star emblem of the Eastern Star?

The five-pointed star is the basic emblem of the Order of the Eastern Star; it must be worn with the single point down. Each point is a different color and represents the virtues of the heroine of each of the five degrees of the order. The five-pointed star with the single point down is called a pentagram.

Although most members of the Eastern Star are unaware of it, there is a major theological and spiritual problem with their basic symbol. The five-pointed star with the single point down is the ancient and evil symbol of the Goat of Mendes, pagan god of lust, and, ultimately, Lucifer.[86]

Although Masonic historians are aware of this, it seems to be virtually unknown among the ladies of the Eastern Star. In fact, the pentagram is the most significant symbol in Satanism; this symbol, stamped in gold on the cover of the white Eastern Star Bible, is likewise to be found on the cover of the Satanic Bible!

9. Is there a Masonic group for girls?

Yes. In fact, like the women, there are several Masonic orders for girls, including Job's Daughters and the Order of the Rainbow. The largest of these is the Order of the Rainbow, usually referred to as "Rainbow Girls." Rainbow Girls, affiliated with the Eastern Star, is for girls from age twelve to seventeen and is in a real way the "prep school" for the Eastern Star. The girls' orders have state and national structure, and the girls "go through the chairs" just like the women in the Eastern Star and their male sponsors in the Masonic Lodge. They even have their own (Christ-less) burial service!

10. And, what is there for boys?

For boys between the ages of fourteen and twenty there is the Order of DeMolay. As in the case of the Rainbow Girls, it can be thought of as the "prep school" for the Masonic Lodge. The boys in the Order of DeMolay wear black, scarlet-lined, "Dracula" type capes in their meetings, "go through the chairs," and have a national structure. The order is named for the famous (or infamous) Crusader, Jacques DeMolay, and its degrees are based on the Masonic version of his death. (See chapter Four, "Freemasonry's 'Christian' Degrees.")

11. Are these Masonic orders for women and children secret societies, or are their meetings open?

Like their parent organization, the Masonic Lodge system, they are secret societies. Their meetings are closed to the public, and they are sworn to secrecy concerning the ritual, key words, grips, signs, etc.

12. Can anyone of the right age join these groups?

Definitely not. Again, like their parent organization, the Masonic Lodge system, memberships in these "adoptive" orders are denied to certain groups and individuals.

13. What is the purpose of these groups?

In Masonic language, these Masonic orders for women and children are collectively called "adoptive Masonry." The name means just what it sounds like; these groups are "add-on" groups, not really part of Freemasonry as such, but adopted—externally attached, sponsored, and controlled by Masons. The idea of adoptive Masonry had its beginnings in France, where Masons wanted some way to include women in the Lodge. Rob Morris brought the idea to America and refined it. His stated purpose was to enable "worthy wives, widows, daughters and sisters of Freemasons" to be exposed to what he believed to be the beneficial influences of the Lodge and its teachings, without actually being initiated into its secrets.

14. What are their meetings like?

Like Masonic Lodge meetings, the meetings of the "adoptive" orders are extremely formal, wordy, pompous, and boring. Their titles are exalted, and the rituals complex. The lessons, lectures, and prayers are all "canned" and are recited from memory or read from script. They take themselves very seriously. Their ceremonies in costume or uniform can be lavish and colorful, and, in the women's and girls' groups, they can be beautiful, featuring pretty dresses, flowers, ribbons, candles, and pretty music.

Also, their meetings, initiations, and other rituals include the basic framework and much of the language of the parent Masonic Lodge. So much of the Masonic ritual and language has carried over into the groups for women and children that it has been a source of controversy among Masons, some fearing that their "secrecy" is thus partially compromised. If the women or children could go into a meeting of a Masonic Lodge, they would probably be amazed at the similarity, recognizing much of the ritual and language as their own and feeling right at home. Of course, in many ways they really would be, for their meetings are not only similar to those of the Masons but are often held in the very same room.

15. Is there a Masonic organization on college campuses?

Yes, "Acacia" is a social fraternity on many college and university campuses. It was organized at the University of

Michigan in 1904 and was originally restricted to Masons on college campuses. Since 1933, however, its membership has been opened to include non-Mason males by invitation only. Its name is significant. Acacia is an important part of Masonic symbolism and ritual, representing redemption and everlasting life. The Acacia is an evergreen tree, common in Africa and the Middle East, similar in appearance to the American locust tree. It figures significantly in the legend of Osiris in the Egyptian mystery religions.[87] (See also Chapter Twelve, *Freemasonry and Religion*.)

ENDNOTES

81 National Imperial Court of the Daughters of Isis, "Ritual," (Chicago: Ezra Cook, undated): 1-16.

82 The name is misleading: "The Little Red Schoolhouse" is actually a fine, two-story brick building on a stone foundation, a veritable palace in light of its rural mid-nineteenth century surroundings.

83 General Grand Chapter, Order of the Eastern Star, *Ritual of the Order of the Eastern Star,* 22d ed. (Chicago, 1911), 119-133.

84 Albert Mackey, *Symbolism of Freemasonry* (Chicago: Chas. T. Powner Co., 1975), 333.

85 Ibid., 351,352; Albert Pike, *Morals and Dogma,* rev. ed. (Washington, DC: House of the Temple, 1950), 5, 757, 758, 771, 772.

86 Albert Mackey, *Encyclopedia of Freemasonry* (Masonic History Co.: Chicago, New York, London), rev. ed. s.v. "Pentagram," 1927, p. 553; L.C. Hascall, *History of the Ancient and Honorable Fraternity of Free* and *Accepted Masons, and Concordant Orders* (Boston and London: The Fraternity Publishing Co., 1891), 49, 101.

87 Mackey, *Symbolism of Freemasonry,* 313, 314.

Freemasonry and Other Fraternal Orders

FOR EVERY TREE IS KNOWN BY HIS OWN FRUIT.
LUKE 6:44

1. Is Masonry connected with other fraternal orders like the Elks, Moose, Eagles, and Knights of Columbus?

No, at least they are not in any practical way. In terms of their origins, they can all be traced to the same pagan roots; but in terms of what they actually are today, with the exception of the Knights of Columbus, the others are very different from Masonry. The others have evolved to the place where they are primarily social, with very little emphasis on spiritual or moral matters. Initiation rites are similar but not taken nearly so seriously; likewise, matters of loyalty are not nearly as compelling.[88]

But, these things can't be said of the Knights of Columbus. The Order of the Knights of Columbus is so different from all the others as to need separate treatment. (See questions five through eight, below.)

2. Are these other groups as influential as the Masons?

No, not nearly. This is partly due to their "less serious" approach to themselves, but, in a practical way, it is primarily because of fewer numbers. In the same way that "success begets success," the opposite is true. As their numbers have dwindled, so has their attraction for new members. For the same reasons, the influential, prominent, and powerful are not attracted to these groups as they are to Masonry, a trend which perpetuates and magnifies itself.

3. Are they trying to reverse this trend?

They seem to be trying to capture some notice and gain credibility by taking on major public concerns. Of course, Masonry has stolen a gigantic march on them all with the Shriners' hospitals, but the others seem to be trying to find similar issues with which to identify. For example, the Elks clubs have taken up the battle against drugs.

4. Why do men join these other fraternal orders?

One reason men join the Elks, Moose, Eagles, Woodmen of the World, Odd Fellows, the Grange, and similar groups is for insurance purposes. Most of these fraternal orders, if not all, offer group insurance programs. A few initiates do seem interested in the spiritual aspect, however, and pursue that to some extent. Another major reason for joining these groups is social fulfillment. Such organizations usually maintain a clubhouse and carry on a busy program of social functions. In a dry county or district, where alcoholic beverages are otherwise prohibited, such a private club may be the only place where liquor may be bought and consumed; for some, this is sufficient motivation to cause a man to join.

5. Are the Knights of Columbus part of the Masonic Lodge system?

Definitely not. Although there are some similarities, the Knights of Columbus is a separate system, in no way connected with Freemasonry.

6. In what way are the Knights of Columbus and Freemasonry similar?

The Order of Knights of Columbus is a closed fraternal order similar to Blue Lodge Masonry in that they have secret initiation rites, recognition signs, passwords, and grips. There is a commitment, as in all fraternal orders, to support and protect one another. The Order also has national organization, with local and regional authorities, published rituals, etc.

7. How then are the Knights of Columbus different from Masonry?

They are as different, almost, as night and day. Masonry is non-Christian (and as such, actually anti-Christian), nonsectarian, and universalist; Knights of Columbus is decidedly Christian in the sense that it is within the ecclesiastical system of the Roman Catholic church. It is under the authority of the Roman Catholic church, and one of its basic purposes is to promote the Catholic faith. Jesus, rejected and blasphemed in Freemasonry, is welcome in the Order of the Knights of Columbus where He is acknowledged as the divine Redeemer and second person of the Trinity.

Also, Knights of Columbus does offer an insurance program for its members, and Masonry never has.

Because of the long-standing papal prohibition of Catholics from joining the Masonic Lodge, the Knights of Columbus and the Masonic Lodge are about as far apart in terms of doctrine as possible, in spite of superficial similarities.

It seems that there are always exceptions to rules. I have known of one man who was a conservative Roman Catholic who attended only the Latin Mass. Not surprisingly, he was an active member of the Knights of Columbus. Somewhat astonishing, however, is that he was also a Freemason in good standing in the local Blue Lodge. The man was a judge, active in politics, and I believe that he attended the Latin mass because he was truly devout and theologically conservative. He probably joined the Knights of Columbus and the Masonic Lodge for political reasons.

He and his wife were murdered, almost certainly by the Dixie Mafia. After the murders, when I was researching the book, *Please Tell Me,* I interviewed the judge's bishop, who was also the judge's close friend. He assured me that what I have written here is true.

8. Do the Knights of Columbus have to take bloody death oaths like the Masons do?

No, they do not, at least not for basic membership (three degrees). There is only one oath for all three degrees, and it is only one paragraph long. In the oath, the initiate promises to keep the secrets, to be loyal to the order and to the Church, to be courteous to all, and to be true to God, the Church, and his country. I find it interesting, however, that the oath is not taken in the name of Jesus, nor in the name of the Triune God (Father, Son, and Holy Spirit).

The greatest threat to the initiate in the ritual is that he is reminded that the order is approved by and under the authority of the church so that to betray the order would be to betray the church, bringing a curse upon him (but not one for which he could not be forgiven). Otherwise the "secret work" (password, recognition signs, grips, etc.) is relatively simple and brief.[89]

ENDNOTES

88   *Secret Societies Illustrated* (Chicago, IL: Ezra Cook Publications, undated), 59-99.
89   Thomas C. Knight, *Knights of Columbus, Illustrated* (Chicago, IL: Ezra Cook Publications, 1974), 89-93.

Freemasonry's Membership: Why Men Join

THERE IS A WAY THAT SEEMETH RIGHT UNTO A MAN, BUT THE
END THEREOF ARE THE WAYS OF DEATH.
PROVERBS 16:25

1. Why do men join the Masonic Lodge?

Men join the Masonic Lodge for a variety of reasons. Some join because of the mystique; it appeals to them to belong to something exclusive and "secretive." Very few will join for spiritual reasons, seeking occult knowledge, or simply looking for God and don't know where to find Him. Many join because of peer pressure. Perhaps the most common reason for joining is to gain social, political, or business advantage.

2. Do Masons actually join for personal gain?

Definitely. Most candidates have been told, or have simply observed, that "things go better" for those who are Masons. Although, theoretically, men are not supposed to join for such self-serving reasons, any honest Mason will admit that this is probably the most common motivation. Prior to being initiated into the first degree, the candidate is asked if he is joining for any self-serving reason. Most have been told about this question in advance by their friends in the Lodge and are told to answer, "No." It is interesting to me that this is the only part of the initiation about which the candidate is told in advance, and this single exception is made so that he can be prompted to lie if necessary.

3. Is there real advantage in being a Mason?

Absolutely. It is true that Masons give preferential treatment to other Masons. If two men are competing for the same contract, appointment, scholarship, promotion, etc., and one is a Mason, the other isn't, and the one who makes the decision is also a Mason, the Masonic candidate will probably be selected. If the setting is a civil or criminal court, the consequences can be much more serious. (See Chapter 20, Freemasonry and Divided Loyalties.)

4. Does Masonry run in some families?

Yes. A very common and powerful motivation for joining the Lodge, especially in the South, is family tradition. When a man's father, uncles, and grandfathers have been Masons, there is great pressure to conform to the family tradition and enter the Lodge. Joining is often something assumed, and most such young men wouldn't even consider not joining, for to fail to join would be an affront, or at least a disappointment, to his Masonic ancestors. I really believe that this is why my father became a York Rite Mason. He entered the Lodge as a very young man, apparently to please the older men in the family, and then he left it behind. In my memory, He never went to meetings or spoke of it.

5. Do some join for the social life?

Yes, and the social life, the fellowship, is real. There is very close fellowship in the Lodge, a kind of social bonding that comes from shared experience and commitment. Also, there is an ongoing round of carry-in dinners, parties, and other social functions associated with the Lodge, not just for the Mason, but also for his family. A man becomes part of it all when he joins (and, incidentally, he usually loses it all if he should leave the Lodge).

6. Do some men join because they have to?

No one is literally forced to become a Mason. However, in some cases the pressure to join can amount to the same thing. In some settings and industries, a man will not be hired if he is not a Mason. One man, now a pastor, told me that as a young man he was forced to join the Lodge in order to be hired by a railroad, and he said that to his knowledge this requirement was virtually universal at the time throughout the railroad industry. But are men ever literally forced to join? The answer is no.

7. Is there ever pressure on ministers to join the Lodge?

Oh, yes. This occurs especially in some denominational groups. Although some denominations forbid their ministers and priests to join the Masonic Lodge, in others there is a considerable pressure to join. Young Baptist ministers are often told by the older ones that if they want to "succeed," they should join the Lodge. The same is true, if not more so, among United Methodist ministers, where Masonry is well entrenched.

8. What about the armed forces?

There is pressure to join the Lodge in the armed forces; in fact, "Sojourners" is a Masonic group just for members of the armed forces, in effect a traveling lodge. In my experience, this pressure manifests itself most often in the Air Force and the Army, and is more common in the upper enlisted ranks, where it can have an impact on promotion, especially in the very highest grades. Interestingly, in all my years as a Marine, both enlisted and commissioned, I never saw any sign of Masonry's presence or influence in the Marine Corps. I never heard it mentioned—not once.

Freemasonry's Membership: How Men Join

AN INHERITANCE MAY BE GOTTEN HASTILY AT THE BEGINNING; BUT THE END THEREOF SHALL NOT BE BLESSED. PROVERBS 20:21

1. How does a man enter the Masonic Lodge?

In theory, the candidate must inquire. He must somehow notice the existence of Masonry—perhaps the ring, guarded conversations from which he is excluded, the exchange of coded expressions and knowing looks, etc. He must then ask about Masonry and how he may join.

This is the theory. Theory and reality are sometimes very different, and this is especially true of this tradition, as we shall see.

2. Do the Masons ever recruit new members?

In theory, Masonry doesn't recruit; one must ask to be a Mason, for he will not be invited to join. You may see bumper stickers that say, somewhat cryptically, "2 B 1 ASK 1." If you see such a bumper sticker, it will be on a Mason's car, and this bumper sticker is a typical Masonic contradiction. The expanded translation of the coded message is "To be one of us, you must ask one of us." Since this invites the curious to ask what it means and then ask about joining, it is a recruiting device, *doing exactly what it says must not be done.*

3. But, do they really recruit—actually go after new members?

Yes, at times, they do just that. The recruiting approach can be very subtle, very aggressive, or something in between. Masons can subtly engage in suggestive conversation around a prospect, conversation designed to inspire curiosity so that he will ask about the Lodge. A very common occurrence, and a step beyond this approach, is for a Mason simply to say to a prospect that Masonry is a fine institution and ask if he isn't interested in finding out about it. It is not uncommon for a Mason to say to a friend something like, "The Lodge is a fine organization, it has been good for me, and you would be wise to look into it."

Sometimes, as we have already seen in Chapter Eight, recruiting becomes outright coercion. A man is given to understand, one way or another, that if he wants to "get ahead" (or even be hired), he must join the Masonic Lodge.

In recent years, with more and more unflattering truth being made public about Masonry, they have taken to billboard advertisements. Some have a photo of a prominent person and his testimony as to the benefits Masonry has brought into his life; others simply state the claims of the institution ("Masonry builds character in men") or trumpet the good works (e.g., Shrine hospitals, Masonic retirement homes, orphanages, etc.).

As the Masonry-wide problem of declining membership gets worse, recruiting becomes more open and aggressive. It is unusual, but there are times when a temporary Masonic lodge room is set up in an over-the-road truck trailer, in a busy shopping center parking lot and men are recruited and initiated right there on the spot. For more on this subject, see Epilogue to Part Two.

4. Once a man expresses interest or willingness to join the Lodge, what happens next?

After the inquirer expresses interest in Masonry, or a willingness to join, he is told a little about the group, enough to get him started. He must find two Masons willing to sponsor him and recommend him in writing to the local lodge.[90] Within a few days, he will be visited by an investigating committee; the purpose of the visit is to ascertain whether or not the candidate is "good enough" to become a Mason.[91] If the man is acceptable, he is subsequently contacted and told when to report to the lodge hall for initiation.

5. If the visiting committee finds the candidate acceptable, is he automatically taken into the Lodge?

No. A ballot of the Lodge membership is taken. Balloting is strictly secret and is done by means of dropping a small ball into a ballot box. A white ball is a "yes" vote, and a black ball is a "no" vote. To be taken into the Lodge, the "yes" vote must be unanimous. If all the balls are white, the ballot is said to be "clear," and the man is accepted. If there is even one black ball, the candidate is rejected. In Masonic language, that man has been "blackballed."

6. What does it cost to become a Mason?

Costs vary from state to state (grand lodge to grand lodge) and even from local lodge to local lodge within a state (grand lodge); but, regardless of the variation, there will always be an initiation fee for each degree. It is common to pay for all three degrees of the Blue Lodge at once, before being initiated into the first degree. If a man goes on into the higher degrees of the York Rite or the Scottish Rite, there are additional initiation fees for those degrees (usually paid for in degree "groups" in the higher degrees). If he then goes into the Shrine, there is still another fee for that. The same is true of the Order of the Eastern Star, Tall Cedars of Lebanon, Jesters, or other appendant groups, should a Mason join them. In addition to the initiation fees, there are annual dues for each affiliation (separate dues for the Blue Lodge, the York Rite, the Scottish Rite, the Eastern Star, etc.).

The total cost for one who goes on into the higher degrees can be a thousand dollars or more, depending on how high he goes and how many related groups he joins. The initiation fees must be paid for each order, degree, or group of degrees before initiation begins. In addition to the initiation fees, there are the annual dues, which the man is to go on paying for life.

7. Are there any tests or examinations to pass in order to join?

Yes, in the Blue Lodge there are. There is considerable memory work to be done in the Blue degrees, and a member of the Lodge is appointed to be the instructor for each incoming group of initiates. (Ordinarily, two or more men will be initiated together.) This instructor meets with the candidates on appointed nights in the lodge hall and helps them memorize the "secret work" of the degree into which they have just been initiated. This is very much like the way candidates for confirmation in a liturgical church are taught the catechism in preparation for examination and confirmation by the bishop, except that in a church the instruction precedes the confirmation. When the candidates are ready, they must recite acceptably before the assembled members of the lodge in order to be initiated into the next degree. Again, due to dwindling membership, in some jurisdictions there is less-demanding memory work, so as to make entrance easier. And, at times, it may be abandoned altogether. For more on this and other changes, see the Epilogue to Part Two.

8. What is it that they must learn?

They must learn the Masonic catechism. For example, they are asked, "What makes you a Mason?" The correct answer is "My obligation." In addition to this, they must memorize the "secret work" of the degree, such as the grip, penalty sign, dueguard, password, etc. The most difficult learning challenge is the oath of obligation, which is to be memorize word for word. This memorizing is done, it must be pointed out, after the oath has been taken. The candidate is never told of the oath before he takes it at his initiation, repeating a few words at a time, after the Worshipful Master.

9. Must they do all this memorizing for the higher degrees?

No. Although there is a death oath of obligation, grip, and password for each higher degree, they are demonstrated only and there is no memorization to do once the oath is taken. Blue Lodge Masons who don't know this imagine the awesome work involved in becoming a Thirty-second Degree Mason because they know how much they had to work to memorize all that stuff for the three degrees. Receiving the higher degrees is mostly a matter of sitting in a theater, watching as the degree is presented in a drama ("exemplified") or merely listening to it as a lecture ("communicated"), and then taking the oath. Higher degree Masons seldom remember the oaths they have taken because they take so many in a short time and they do not have to memorize them.

10. How long does it take to go through all this and get the degrees?

In the Blue Lodge, the time required varies, depending on how long it takes the incoming initiates to learn the material. A man could go through all three of the Blue degrees in as little as a few weeks or as long as a few months. Perhaps five or six weeks would be the average time for the entire process in the Blue Lodge.

In the higher degrees, a group initiation is done in one weekend. In the Scottish Rite, this is normally done in two successive weekends, with the fourth through the fourteenth degrees taken the first weekend and the fifteenth through the

Thirty-second degrees taken in the second weekend. This occurs twice a year, normally fall and spring, and they call these convocations "reunions." In the York Rite, the process is essentially the same, with the degrees organized into three groups: Capitular Rite, Cryptic Rite, and Chivalric Rite.

11. Is a man given his Masonic ring when he is taken into the Lodge?

No. With the exception of the Scottish Rite, rings are not presented, they are selected and purchased privately. All those Masonic rings one sees, with a colored stone embossed in gold with the Masonic emblem, are purchased by the individual Mason. That's why there are so many variations in color and style; manufacturers simply make them and distributors market them, and anyone can buy one, as is the case with lapel pins and other Masonic jewelry. It is not even necessary to be a Mason in order to buy such things since Masonic rings and other jewelry can be bought through catalogs. The same is true of the jewelry for the Eastern Star and other "adoptive" Masonic groups. There is no such thing, outside the Scottish Rite, as an "official" Masonic ring.

In the Scottish Rite, the Thirty-second Degree ring is normally presented with the Fourteenth Degree at the end of the first reunion weekend. (You probably think this is a typographical error, but it isn't; they really do present the Thirty-second Degree ring with the Fourteenth Degree, strange as it seems, and some Masons call it the Fourteenth Degree ring.) This ring is a plain, flat, gold band exactly like a plain gold wedding ring except that it has a small triangle with the Hebrew letter *yod* stamped in it. There is a second such ring, given with the Thirty-third Degree, and it looks just the same except that it has "33" inside the triangle.

It is interesting to me that the only real Masonic ring would never be recognized as such without some insider knowledge of Masonry (which, of course, you now possess).

12. Is it true that a married man must remove his wedding ring in order to be initiated into the Masonic Lodge?

Yes, and most wives would be offended if they knew this. The initiate must remove all his rings and other jewelry, along with his clothes, in order to be initiated into the Blue Lodge.

13. Do you mean that Masons must take off their clothes to be initiated?

Yes. This is to make the point that the initiate brings nothing to the process of initiation; rather, he is poor, naked, helpless, has nothing "going for him," and is totally dependent on the Worshipful Master and the Lodge to redeem him and bring him out of his present wretched condition.

14. Does he go through the initiation naked?

No, it is more like he is half-naked. In the preparation room, after he takes his own clothes off, he is given a simple cotton shirt and trousers, much like pajamas, and he is told to put them on. In each of the first two degrees, he has one or the other leg rolled up high and the shirt half off his torso; in the third degree, he has both legs rolled up high and the shirt completely off. In all three degrees, he is completely blindfolded and is led (i.e., jerked, dragged) around the room by a rope called a "cabletow." In the first degree (the most frightening), the rope is tied around his neck. In the second degree, it is around his shoulder. In the third degree, it is tied around his waist.[92]

15. Why is he blindfolded?

This is probably the most important aspect of the initiation, especially for a Christian. The blindfold makes the point that the candidate is in complete spiritual darkness and needs the Worshipful Master and the Lodge to bring him out of spiritual darkness and into the light of redemption. For a Christian to do this is a blasphemous denial of his true Redeemer and an outright denial of Scripture such as John 8: 12, "I am the light of the world; he that followeth me shall not walk in darkness, but shall have the light of life."

Incidentally, the proper Masonic term for the blindfold is "hoodwink," and an initiate so blindfolded is said in Masonic terminology to be "hoodwinked."

16. Is there really a rope tied around his neck?

Absolutely, but only in the first degree. In the second and third degrees, it is tied around the shoulder and the waist, respectively, as we have already noted. In many lodges, this rope, called a "cabletow," is blue.

17. But, what is its purpose?

With this rope, the hoodwinked candidate is led around the room during the ritual of initiation like a blind dog on a leash.

18. But, what is the purpose of all this? Why is the man treated this way?

The effect, and its apparent purpose, is humiliation. The candidate is "reduced to nothing" in this way; he is poor, blind, naked, helpless, confused, and afraid. In addition, he has no idea of where he is, who is watching him, or how many there are. It is a powerful means of subjugation and mind control and may have a permanent detrimental effect on the man, binding him mentally and spiritually to the Lodge and its authority.

19. Does the candidate know in advance what his initiation will be like?

Definitely not. This seems to be part of its impact, at least in the first degree. There is, naturally, less surprise in the second and third degrees, having already experienced the first degree.

20. Does the candidate know about the death oath in advance?

No, he does not. He doesn't even know that there will be an oath, let alone the horrible, bloody nature of it. He may suspect such oaths in the second and third degrees, after experiencing the first; but he is definitely never told in advance the wording, or even the nature of the oaths of obligation.

Disoriented, blindfolded, half naked, and with a rope around his neck, the candidate is told to kneel and place his left hand under the Bible (or other "holy book"), and his right hand on the square and compass on top of the Bible. Then, an authoritative voice in front of him (it is the Worshipful Master, but he doesn't know that) says, "Repeat after me…," and the candidate repeats the oath, a few words at a time.[93]

In this way, the Ku Klux Klan is more honorable and straightforward than the Masonic Lodge. In the Klan, a candidate not only knows in advance that there will be an oath, he is required to read it in advance so that he will know, exactly, that to which he is going to swear. And, the oath of the Klan is not a bloody death oath as is the one in the Lodge.

21. Does the candidate, once he learns what the initiation is really like, ever just get up and leave?

Almost never. Once the process is begun, the emotional and spiritual pressures to continue are very great. Even a Christian, under immediate conviction that what he is doing is wrong, will almost always go through with it. He knows that all the Masons whom he knows, perhaps including his father, grandfather, deacons, elders, or pastor of his church, went through with it, so he thinks that it must be alright, although his mind and the Holy Spirit are telling him that it is wrong.

22. Can a man become a Mason without going through initiations?

Yes. Becoming a Mason without being initiated is called being made a Mason "at sight." This is ordinarily done only for very important people, such as high-ranking political figures, heads of state, celebrities, etc. The process can vary from jurisdiction to jurisdiction but usually consists of a Grand

Master (or another man of lofty position) going to the office of the honoree (or some other suitable location), reading the ritual, and declaring the individual to be a Mason.[94] William Howard Taft was made a Mason "at sight" in 1901, but was never an active member.

ENDNOTES

90   It is interesting that this recommendation is called "a recommend" (using a verb as if it were a noun), the same odd name given in Mormonism to the document needed to enter the temple. There is an intimate relationship between Masonry and Mormonism. (See Chapter 22, "Freemasonry and Mormonism.")

91   The candidate is almost always found to be acceptable; there must be something very wrong with a man in order for him to be rejected.

92   Malcolm C. Duncan, *Duncan's Masonic Ritual and Monitor*, 3rd ed. (New York: David McKay Co., undated), 7-96.

93   Ibid.

94   George W. Chase, *Digest of Masonic Law*, 8th ed. (Boston: Pollard and Leighton, 1869), 60-65. Pollard and Leighton, 1869).

Freemasonry's Membership: How Men Leave the Lodge

BE YE NOT UNEQUALLY YOKED TOGETHER WITH UNBELIEVERS;
FOR WHAT FELLOWSHIP HATH RIGHTEOUSNESS WITH
UNRIGHTEOUSNESS? AND WHAT COMMUNION HATH LIGHT
WITH DARKNESS? AND WHAT CONCORD HATH CHRIST WITH
BELIAL, OR WHAT PART HATH HE THAT BELIEVETH WITH AN
INFIDEL? ... WHEREFORE COME OUT FROM AMONG THEM,
AND BE YE SEPARATE, SAITH THE LORD, AND
TOUCH NOT THE UNCLEAN THING....
2 CORINTHIANS 6:14-17

1. Do men ever leave the Lodge?

Yes. There have probably been men leaving the Lodge from the time of Freemasonry's beginnings. The great mass exodus from Freemasonry, however, was in the period immediately following the kidnapping and Masonic execution of Captain William Morgan in 1826. We shall see his story in Chapter Eighteen ("Death Oaths and Masonic Executions"). From time to time men have continued to leave Freemasonry, ending their relationship with the Craft.

2. Why do Masons leave the Lodge?

Most men who leave the Lodge do so because they discover Masonry's roots in paganism and realize its rejection and denial of Jesus Christ. Some leave even before they finish taking the Blue Lodge degrees; in the case of others, some may wrestle with their convictions and consciences for years before finally leaving the Lodge. There will always be a few whose departure is the result of some personal problem; but the vast majority of those men (and women in the "adoptive" organizations of Freemasonry) who leave the Lodge do so for matters of conscience.

3. How do Masons Leave the Lodge?

a. By Demit. Most Masons who leave the Lodge do so by submitting, to the local lodge, a formal statement to that effect called a "demit." This term is derived from the Latin word, "dimittere," meaning to release, or to send away. From this Latin word we derive our English word, "dismiss." Those of you who are familiar with Anglican, Catholic or other liturgical worship services will recognize the connection to the "Nunc Dimittis," the liturgical song taken from Luke 2:29-32, in which the aged Simeon takes the infant Jesus into his arms and says to the Lord, "Now lettest thou thy servant **depart** [emphasis mine] in peace...for mine eyes have seen thy salvation..."

The demit, however, does not sever a Mason's connection with the Lodge; in fact, it does just the opposite. What a demit does is to make the Mason inactive; but it also keeps him in good standing in case he wishes to become active again in the future. Most Masons don't realize this; they think that the demit is a permanent break with Freemasonry. It isn't.

In most jurisdictions there is flexibility concerning the exact form of the demit; even an informal letter will usually suffice. For a more formal request, the following is an example of the form.

AN EXAMPLE OF A FORMAL REQUEST FOR DEMIT STATUS

Request for Demit

Date:_____, 20_____

To the Master, Wardens, and Secretary of _____

_____Lodge Number_____, Located at:

Mailing Address: _____

_____

Greetings,

The undersigned respectfully announces his intention to withdraw from membership in this, his Lodge, and requests a Demit to this effect.

Name: _____

Street Address: _____

City: _____ State: _____ ZIP:_____

Respectfully yours,

Signature: _____ Date: _____

b. By Resignation. The best way to sever the relationship with the Lodge is by submitting a letter (or letters) of resignation. This leaves no room for doubt or misunderstanding. Such a letter should be sent to the Secretary of the local lodge. In addition, such a letter should be sent to each Lodge activity of which the Mason has been a part (Scottish Rite, York Rite, Eastern Star, Royal Arch, etc.).

c. By Expulsion. A Mason can have his membership terminated by expulsion from the Lodge for reasons of misconduct. This, however, is an exceedingly rare event. Although I am sure that it happens, in all of my years of studying the Masonic system, and discussing it with the public on talk programs, I have never heard of an example of expulsion's actually being carried out.

Freemasonry and the Bible

EVERY WORD OF GOD IS PURE ... ADD THOU NOT
UNTO HIS WORDS.
PROVERBS 30:5

1. Is Masonry based upon the Bible?

No. One of the most common misconceptions about
Freemasonry, especially among Masons, is that it is based on
the Bible. Nothing could be farther from the truth.

2. Do Masons believe that Masonry is based on the Bible?

With few exceptions, those of the Blue Lodge definitely
do. One of the first things most Masons will say to defend the
"rightness" of belonging to the Masonic Lodge is that it can't
be wrong, for it is based on the Bible. Among the rank and file,
where one is most likely to hear this assertion, they truly believe
this. Those who have taken the higher degrees and become
32nd Degree Masons or Knights Templar should know that
Freemasonry is not based on the Bible, but even among them
very few do.

3. If Masonry isn't based on the Bible, why do most Masons believe that it is?

Most Masons, especially in the "Bible Belt," are told at the outset that Masonry is based on the Bible. Virtually all of them believe this, and go on believing this, in spite of the fact that so much of what they see and hear for the rest of their Masonic lives indicates that it isn't. Except for a few serious students of Masonry, they go on believing this because the Bible is always on the altar, because some verses of Scripture are used in the ritual, and because Bible characters and events are used in some of the degrees. There is even a Masonic Bible, usually presented to the newly made Master Mason, and this strengthens the deception.

4. If there is a Bible open on the altar, why do you say that Masonry is not based on the Bible?

The fact that the Bible is on the altar in the Masonic Lodge no more proves that the Lodge is based on it than a Bible on a coffee table means that the family is Christian and living according to the Bible. Even if it did, then how do we explain all those lodges where they have the Koran, the Hindu Vedas, or some other "holy book" on the altar in place of the Bible?[95] Even in those lodges where there is an open Bible on the altar, there are also the Masonic square and compass, lying on top of it, in the superior position.

5. What then is the official status of the Bible in the Masonic Lodge?

Masonic literature refers to the Bible as a part of the "furniture" of the lodge. In lodges where the Bible is used, candidates put their hands on the Bible to take their oaths of obligation and then are required to kiss it.

In the Blue Lodge (the first three degrees), candidates are taught that the Bible is "the rule and guide for faith and practice" (some say, "*a* rule and guide—not "*the* rule and guide ...") and that it is one of the three "Great Lights of Masonry."[96]

6. If they say that the Bible is their rule and guide for faith and practice and one of their great lights, doesn't that mean that Masonry is based on the Bible?

No, in fact this is one of the many contradictions in Masonic doctrine. They say that the Bible is "the rule and guide for faith and practice" yet reject or ignore much of its clear teachings, especially those concerning Jesus, redemption, and its claims about itself (i.e. its uniqueness, divine inspiration, etc).[97]

The Bible is very clear in saying that there is only one true and living God, only one Mediator between God and men (the man, Christ Jesus), that every part of the Bible is inspired ("God-breathed"), and that no one is to take away from or add to it. Yet, Masonry honors pagan gods, reduces the God of Abraham, Isaac and Jacob to the level of Buddha or Krishna, and worships a generic god called the Great Architect of the Universe. Masonry denies the divinity and uniqueness of Jesus as Savior, reducing Him to the status of just one of the great men of the past. And, Masonry's policy makers feel free to alter Scripture by removing references to Jesus from New Testament verses used in the ritual, even though the Bible clearly forbids this.[98]

Herein is a most significant and revealing thing about Masonry, expressing clearly the true attitude of the Masonic philosophers toward both Jesus and the Bible. The removal of references to Jesus from verses of the New Testament used in the ritual is an eloquent expression of Masonry's contempt for both Jesus and the Bible. An example is the verse used in the charge to a regular meeting of the Blue Lodge, II Thessalonians 3:6: "Now we command you brethren, in the name of our Lord Jesus Christ, that ye withdraw yourselves from every brother that walketh disorderly, and not after the tradition that ye received from us." In the Lodge ritual, the words "in the name of our Lord Jesus Christ" are arbitrarily removed from the verse, as if it had nothing to do with Him. This butchering of such references to Jesus out of the Bible (and this is not the only one) is a blasphemous insult both to Him and to the Word of God, a direct violation of the Bible's teachings about itself. Albert Mackey, revered Masonic authority, called such mutilations of Scripture "slight, but necessary, modifications."[99]

Yet, this same Albert Mackey, in his authoritative work, *Jurisprudence of Freemasonry,* says that the Masonic writings are perfect and must not be changed in any way! Let's hear him in his own words: "The Landmarks (fundamental doctrines) of Masonry are so perfect that they neither need nor will permit of the slightest amendment."[100]

A related and revealing fact is that while the Bible is the unique, unchanging, inspired Word of God to the Christian, in Masonry the Bible is only one of their "three great lights." The square and compass are the other two, and remember where they are: on top of the Bible, in the superior position, on the Masonic altar. And, that's not all. In lodges where the Koran, Hindu Vedas or some other "holy book" is on the altar in place of the Bible, the square and compass must **always** be there. The square and compass are clearly more important in Masonry than the Bible.

Do you still need convincing? Let's hear again from Albert Mackey: "An attempt has been made by some Grand Lodges to add to these simple, moral and religious qualifications, another, which requires a belief in the divine authenticity of the Scriptures. It is much to be regretted...." [101]

So, for Masonry to say that the Bible is the (or even *a*) rule and guide for faith and practice and then to ignore and violate its most important teachings, is an obvious and outrageous contradiction. No—in no way is Masonry "based on the Bible."

7. Do any of the leading Masonic authorities say that Masonry is based on the Bible?

No, in fact, they say just the opposite. I will quote only four, but there are many more.

"The place of the Bible in Freemasonry is as difficult to fix as are some of the [religious] beliefs adverted to above" (Henry Wilson Coil).[102]

"The Bible is an indispensable part of the furniture of a Christian lodge only because it is the sacred book of the Christian religion. The Hebrew Pentateuch in a Hebrew lodge, and the Koran in the Mohammedan one, belong on the altar; and [any] one of these, and the Square and Compass, properly understood, are the Great Lights by which a Mason must walk" (Albert Pike).[103]

"Thus the Trestleboard [blueprint for life] of the Jews is the Old Testament; of the Mohammedan, the Koran; the Vedas Scriptures of Hinduism and the writings of Baha-ullah are just as good as the Word of the Christians' God, for the fact is that all religions are never as good as the pure teachings of Freemasonry" (Albert Mackey).[104]

"The Jews, the Chinese, the Turks, each reject either the New Testament, the Old, or both, and yet we see no good reason why they should not be made Masons. In fact, Blue Lodge Masonry has nothing whatever to do with the Bible. It is not founded on the Bible; if it was it would not be Masonry, it would be something else" (George W. Chase).[105]

8. What is the Masonic Bible?

The Masonic Bible is merely the King James Version of the Bible with the basic Masonic symbol on the cover and a section of Masonic teachings in the front. One of the most interesting things about the Masonic Bible is that the Masonic teachings in the front of their Bible are in direct contradiction with the Bible itself. Two examples of this are the "Masonic Creed" and the section on "The Great Light in Masonry." Let me explain.

The Masonic Creed. This is their statement of basic beliefs and, right there at the beginning of their Bible, it presents another glaring contradiction in Masonry. Of these six statements of fundamental Masonic belief, three are in conflict with the Bible itself, and another is simply untrue:

(1) "There is one God, the Father of all men." But, the Bible says that God is the creator of all men, but is no one's father until redeemed by faith in Christ Jesus.

279

(2) "Character determines destiny." In simple words, this means that "good" people go to heaven, "bad" people go to hell, and we must save ourselves by being "good." Jesus is unnecessary in this plan of salvation. (See chapter 14, "Freemasonry and Jesus Christ.")

(3) "Prayer, communion of man with God, is helpful." Helpful? This anemic statement is in fact a subtle lie; the Bible doesn't say that prayer is "helpful," the Bible says that prayer is essential, and commands it!

(4) The statement that is simply untrue is that the Bible is the great light in Masonry and the rule and guide for faith and practice. (See question 6, above.)

The Great Light in Masonry. This belief statement on the Bible is written by the revered Masonic authority, the Rev. Dr. Joseph Fort Newton. The pertinent passages are too extensive to quote here, but he states that the Bible is merely "a symbol" of the will of God, a part of man's ever-changing understanding of God, that it teaches us to revere the "book of faith" of the Muslim and Hindu, and that the Christian and all the pagan religions worship the same "Nameless one of a hundred names," praying to the same "God and Father of us all." He says that "Masonry knows, what so many forget, that religions are many, but Religion is one." (In other words, all religions are actually the same and of equal value.) He then goes on to agree with the poet Lowell, that the true Bible is not a book written on paper, but is the ongoing accumulation of human experience and wisdom.

As is the case with Jesus, here is a very serious problem: A watered-down Bible is no Bible at all.

9. If Masonry is not based on the Bible, then on what is it based?

Masonry is based on the Kaballa (variously spelled as Caballa, Quaballah, etc.). I could fill this book with authentication on just this one subject. That, of course, would be impractical; so let's allow two of Masonry's most honored philosophers to speak briefly on this subject.

Albert Pike, the preeminent Masonic philosopher, made clear the position of the Kaballa: "Masonry is a search after light. That search leads us back, as you see, to the Kaballah."[106]

"All truly dogmatic religions have issued from the Kaballah, and return to it; everything scientific and grand in the religious dreams of the Illuminati, Jacob Boeheme, Swedenborg, St. Martin and others, is borrowed from the Kaballah; all Masonic associations owe to it their secrets and their symbols."[107]

J.D. Buck, highly esteemed Masonic philosopher, concurs: "The Kabalah alone consecrates the alliance of the Universal Reason and Divine Word; it establishes ... the eternal balance of being; it alone reconciles Reason with Faith, Power with Liberty, Science with Mystery; it has the keys to the Present, the Past and the Future. The Bible, with all the allegories it contains, expresses, in an incomplete and veiled manner only, the religious science of the Hebrews."[108]

Again, Buck explains: "Drop the theological barnacles from the Religion of Jesus, as taught by Him, and by the Essenes and Gnostics of the first centuries, and it becomes Masonry. Masonry in its purity, derived as it is from the old Hebrew Kabalah...."[109]

Even in the doctrine of the relatively benign Order of the Eastern Star, their code word is called their "Cabbalistic [based on the Cabala] Word."[110] [111]

10. If Masonry is based on something called "the Kabala," what is the Kabala?

The Kabala is a medieval Jewish book of occult philosophy and magic based on mystical interpretations of the Old Testament.[112] It is sometimes published in more than one volume and sometimes in applicable portions. "Kabalistic" (also variously spelled) is the adjective form denoting anything derived from the Kabala. The Kabala is popular with, and important to, magicians, sorcerers, witches, and Satanists, as well as Masonic philosophers. It is, interestingly, also very important to Hasidic Jews. The Hasidim (the legalistic ones with the black hats and one pigtail on the side of the head) are thought of as the most strictly fundamentalist Jews; yet, in their use of "scriptures," they are very far from the Word of God delivered to Moses and the Prophets.

11. Then, what does Masonry really teach about the Bible?
There are three themes that are consistent in what the most respected Masonic philosophers write; in very brief form, they are as follows:

(1) The Bible is merely one of the "holy books" of the world's religions, no better or worse than the Koran, the Hindu scriptures, the Book of Mormon, or the Tibetan Book of the Dead. (See questions 7 and 8, above.)

(2) The Bible is not the final, complete revelation of the will and Word of God. Rather, they teach that the Bible is incomplete, distorted, and merely "a symbol" of both. The real Bible, they teach, is the ongoing accumulation of human knowledge of the nature and will of God. (See question 8, above, *The Great Light in Masonry*.)

(3) The obvious meaning of the Bible, that is, what it actually says, is not true. As in all doctrinal matters, Masonic writers recognize two meanings of all teachings: The outer, obvious meaning, and the inner, hidden meaning. Because of their love for impressive language, they call the outer, obvious meaning the *exoteric* meaning. The inner, hidden meaning they call the *esoteric* meaning.

The hidden meaning (the esoteric meaning) is always the true one, and the obvious meaning (the exoteric meaning) is untrue and only for the ignorant, unthinking masses. Albert Pike, that preeminent Masonic authority, wrote much on this, including the following about the Bible: "What is truth to the philosopher would not be truth, nor have the effect of truth, to the peasant. The religion of many [the ordinary people] must necessarily be more incorrect than that of the refined and reflective few.... The doctrines of the Bible are often not clothed in the language of strict truth, but in that which was fittest to convey to a rude and ignorant people ... the doctrine.[113] ... The literal meaning [of the Bible] is for the vulgar only."[114]

ENDNOTES

95 In Muslim lodges, Hindu lodges, and the lodges of other non-Judeo·Christian faiths, there will be on the altar their "holy book" in place of the Bible; in a Jewish lodge, there will be the Old Testament only.

96 According to Masonic doctrine, the "Three Great Lights of Masonry" are the Square, the Compass, and the Bible. The "Three Lesser Lights of Masonry" are the Sun, the Moon, and the Worshipful Master of the Lodge.

97 Deuteronomy 4:35, 32:39; 1 Timothy 2:5; John 14:6; Acts 4:12; Psalms 12:6,7; 2 Timothy 3:16; Revelations 22:18,19; et a1.

98 Ibid.

99 Albert Mackey, *The Masonic Ritualist* (New York: MaCoy Publishing Co., 1903), 272.

100 Albert Mackey *Jurisprudence of Freemasonry,* rev. and enlarged ed. Book II (Chicago: Chas T. Powner Co., 1975), 57.

101 Ibid.

102 Henry W. Coil, *Masonic Encyclopedia,* s.v. "Religion" (New York: MaCoy Publishing Co., 1961), 518.

103 Albert Pike, *Morals and Dogma,* rev. ed. (Washington, DC: House of the Temple, 1950), 11.

104 Mackey, *The Masonic Ritualist,* 59.

105 George W. Chase, *Digest of Masonic Law,* 8th ed. (Boston: Pollard and Leighton, 1869), 207, 208.

106 Pike, *Morals and Dogma,* 741.

107 Ibid., 744.

108 J.D. Buck, *Mystic Masonry,* 3rd ed. (Chicago: Chas T. Powner Co., 1925), 42.

109 Ibid., 66.

110 Their secret "Cabbalistic word" is *Fatal,* meaning "Fairest among thousands, altogether lovely."

111 Robert MaCoy, *Adoptive Rite Ritual* (New York: MaCoy Publishing and Masonic Supply Co., 1942), 87; *Order of the Eastern Star Recognition Test* (Chicago, IL: Ezra Cook Publications, 1975), 2, 3.

112 Cabala or Cabbala: "An occult theosophy of rabbinical origin, widely transmitted in medieval Europe, based on an esoteric interpretation of the Hebrew Scriptures. A secret doctrine..." *American Heritage Dictionary*, 2d college ed., "cabala; cabbala"; "a medieval and modern system of theosophy, mysticism, and thaumaturgy (magic)," *Merriam Webster's Collegiate Dictionary* 10th ed., s.v. "cabala."

113 Pike, *Morals and Dogma*, 224.

114 Ibid., 166.

Freemasonry and Religion

And the children of Israel did evil in the sight of the
LORD and served Baalim: and they forsook the LORD
God of their fathers ... and followed other gods, of
the people that were round about them, and bowed
themselves unto them ... And they forsook the LORD
and served Baal and Ashtoreth.
Judges 2:11-13

1. Is Masonry a religion?

Yes. Although most Masons will deny this, Masonry is
indeed a religion. What else could it be, when:
- they meet in temples (and call the largest ones *cathedrals);*
- they open and close each meeting with prayer;
- they have an altar with a Bible or other "holy book" opened on it;
- they have deacons;
- they call their leaders such things as "Worshipful Master" and "High Priest";
- they claim to bring the initiate from spiritual darkness to spiritual light;

- they conduct formal burial services in which the Worshipful Master acts as High Priest;
- they present a plan of salvation and cleansing from sin; and, in some degrees, they serve communion and baptize one another?

How, if one examines the evidence at all, could Masonry *not* be a religion?

2. How then do Masons deny that Masonry is a religion?

They manage it with typical Masonic double talk. The most common argument is that, "We are an order of religious men, but not a religion." (In the same way, they deny being a secret society, saying, "We are a society with secrets, but not a secret society.")

3. Do they really believe this?

Yes, they do; at least most of the rank-and-file, Blue Lodge Masons do. Even though their position holds no water when the evidence is examined, most are sincere when they say that Masonry is not a religion.

4. How can they be so wrong and still be sincere?

There are two principal reasons. First, most of them belong to a religious denomination of some kind, and even though they may seldom or never go to church, to consciously embrace "another religion" would to them seem a betrayal. Second, they believe it because they were told upon entering the Lodge that, whatever their religion, Masonry would not conflict with or contradict it. They believed this because sincere men told them so. Those sincere men who told them so believed it because an earlier generation of sincere men had told them the very same thing. And so this deception, which originated as a lie in Masonry's dark beginnings, is perpetuated generation after generation.

5. What is your basis for saying that Masonry is a religion?

The answer to question 1, above, should suffice, but there is more.

It is common knowledge (at least among those who bother to take notice) that many Masons lose interest in church (if they ever had any such interest) and cease to attend. When asked about it, or urged to return to their church, they will usually reply, "I don't need to go to church; the Lodge is a good enough religion for me."

This, I believe, is powerful evidence that Masons are taught, one way or another, that Masonry is not only a religion, but the best, and that the Lodge will meet all their spiritual needs, including salvation. If such teachings, explicit and implicit, didn't run through Masonic ritual and instruction, such a widespread belief by sincere men would not be possible. The result, well known within the Lodge and without, is valid and powerful evidence of the process.

But, in addition to this interesting feature of Masonic culture, Masonry's most respected teachers and writers of doctrine themselves identify Masonry as a religion.

"Every Masonic Lodge is a temple of religion; and its teachings are instruction in religion" (Albert Pike).[115]

"These two essentials, belief in a Supreme being and reverence for his Word, establish beyond question the character of the fraternity as a religious institution" (Joseph Fort Newton).[116]

"A meeting of a Masonic lodge is a religious ceremony" (Webb's Monitor).[117]

"The candidate ... is shown through the Kabalah or Secret Doctrine that at the heart of every great religion lie the same eternal truths.... Masonry is not only a universal science, but a world-wide religion.... Masonry is the Universal Religion...." (J.D. Buck).[118]

"But the religion of Masonry is not sectarian. It admits men of every creed within its hospitable bosom, rejecting none and approving none for his peculiar faith" (Albert Mackey).[119]

And Henry Wilson Coil, revered author of *Coil's Masonic Encyclopedia*, apparently with tongue in cheek, observed, "If Freemasonry is not a religion, nothing would have to be added to make it such;" and he offered the Masonic funeral service, of which he disapproved, as sufficient evidence that Freemasonry is a religion.

Coil went on to say, "… A man may be born without religious ceremony; he may be married without religious ceremony; he may live a long life without religious ceremony; but one moment comes to every man when he feels the need of that missing thing—when he comes to crossing into the great beyond. Freemasonry has a religious service to commit the body of a deceased brother to the dust whence it came and to speed the liberated spirit back to the Great Source of Light. Many Masons make this flight with no other guarantee of a safe landing than their belief in the religion of Freemasonry. If that is a false hope, the Fraternity should abandon funeral services…."[120]

6. Does Masonry have any form of a priesthood?

Absolutely. Although there is no single priesthood to which some Masons are ordained, there are several forms of priesthood within the order, both functional and symbolic. For example, the title of the leader in the local lodge (Blue Lodge) is "Worshipful Master," and, according to Masonic teachings, "The Master of the Lodge is its priest, and the director of its religious ceremonies."[121]

In addition, the Worshipful Master in the Blue Lodge, when officiating at a Masonic funeral, assumes the role of "High Priest." In the Royal Arch chapter, the presiding officer's (leader's) title is "High Priest." According to the doctrine, he is "the representative of Joshua, the High Priest who, with

Zerubbabel, Prince of Judah, and Haggai, the Scribe, laid the foundations of the second temple...."[122] In the Nineteenth Degree (Grand Pontiff) of the Scottish Rite, the candidate is anointed with oil, and it is declared, "Be thou a priest forever, after the order of Melchizedek." In the Thirty-second Degree of Scottish Rite Masonry (Sublime Prince of the Royal Secret), the initiate is again anointed with oil, and it is declared, "Thou art a priest and a prophet."[123]

7. Does Masonry present to the initiate a plan of salvation?

Yes, and it does this over and over. Although there may be no single document entitled "Masonic Plan of Salvation" bearing the imprimatur of a World Headquarters of Freemasonry, there might as well be. Over and over, in Masonic degrees, lessons, ritual, and revered source books, there is clearly expressed a plan of salvation. As is the case with most of Masonry, there are some internal contradictions, but the basic concept is well established, and only the most indifferent or spiritually blinded could miss it.

8. If there is a Masonic plan of salvation, what is it?

The Masonic plan of salvation is a three-part plan of self-redemption. The Mason is redeemed (made spiritually perfect and sinless) by (a) being enlightened (having both secret knowledge and the proper understanding of it), (b) faithfulness to his oaths of obligation (death oaths), and (c) his virtuous life (by "being good"). Each man's salvation is his own responsibility; he is his own savior (and isn't *that* a wretched, frightening prospect!?!?).

Although Masonry promises, from the very first degree, to bring the candidate to "the light," ultimately, he will learn, he must find the light himself. This to me is extremely interesting. In the climactic moment of the Thirty-second Degree, when the candidate has finally reached the top of the Masonic mountain, he is told that the mountain top is covered with mist and clouds, that the light is out there somewhere, and that he must find it for himself. After all that memorizing and stress in the Blue Lodge, after all the time and money spent there and in the Scottish Rite initiations, being promised at every step that he would be brought to the light, he is finally told that he still isn't there, and that he will have to find it on his own. This seems like an outrageous deception and an outrageous rip-off!

Added to and underlying the basic plan of Masonic salvation, there is reincarnation. Although not prominently displayed, reincarnation is a part of Masonic teaching, appearing especially in the Scottish Rite. By means of this doctrine, the individual goes through an indefinite cycle of lives (incarnations), dying and being reborn for another life, becoming a little more "perfect" in each incarnation (life), or at least having the opportunity to do so, until he finally becomes "perfect."

9. What is your basis for saying these things?

The basis, once again, consists of the ritual, teachings, and the writings of the Masonic authorities; among others, there are:

"May we be received into Thine everlasting kingdom, to enjoy, in union with the souls of our departed friends, the just reward of a pious and virtuous life. Amen. So mote it be" (M. Taylor, *Texas Monitor*). [124]

"*Acacian*: a term signifying a Mason who by living in strict obedience to obligations and precepts of the fraternity is free from sin" (Albert Mackey). [125]

"Initiation and regeneration are synonymous terms" (J.D. Buck).[126]

"I [Masonry] am a way of common men to God" (Carl Claudy, *Kentucky Monitor*).[127]

"This principle of Brotherhood and the perfectibility of man's nature through evolution necessitates Reincarnation ... all conditions in each life being determined by previous living" (J.D. Buck).[128]

And, in the Rituals, representative selections:

1. Worshipful Master: "In your present, blind condition, what do you most desire?" Initiate to the First Degree: "Light."

2. Priest (in the Shrine initiation): "Our Oriental will now conduct the Sons of the Desert to our purifying cavern in the South. It is the fountain of Mecca. Let them there wash their hands in innocency, cleansing themselves of the snares of sin and vice that may have surrounded them, and let them be returned to us free from the stains of iniquity."

10. Does Masonry view all candidates for initiation as unregenerate sinners when they come to the Lodge?

Yes; all non-Masons are considered "profane" (unclean). In Albert Mackey's *Manual of the Lodge,* he says: "There he stands without our portals, on the threshold of the new Masonic life, in darkness, helplessness, and ignorance. Having been wandering amid the errors and covered with the pollutions of the outer and profane world, he comes inquiringly to our doors seeking the new birth."[129]

Even professing Christians, ministers, priests, and rabbis are declared unclean and must get on their knees, confess their lost and polluted condition, and call on the Worshipful Master and the lodge to bring them out of deepest spiritual darkness and into the "new birth" of enlightenment!

11. How does Masonry view other religions?

Masonry sees all religions as being only very imperfect remnants of the ancient pagan mystery religions, distorted and changed for the worse through the ages, until they have lost most of their validity and value. It even sees itself as by far the best of them all and the only hope for regaining the grandeur and perfection of the "real thing," the ancient, pagan mysteries. For two examples:

(1) "Drop the theological barnacles from the religion of Jesus, as taught by Him, and by the Essenes and Gnostics of

the first centuries, and it becomes Masonry. Masonry in its purity, derived as it is from the old Hebrew Kabalah as part of the Great Universal Wisdom-Religion of remotest antiquity."[130]

(2) "Though Masonry is identical with the ancient Mysteries, it is so only in this qualified sense: That it presents but an imperfect image of their brilliancy, the ruins only of their grandeur ... (its) alterations the fruits of ... the ambitious imbecility of its improvers."[131]

12. Does Masonry have a vision for a world religion?

Yes. If you consider all the Masonic teachings and expressions of doctrine and put them all together, the clear conclusion is that Masonry's goal is to recover the ancient pagan mystery religion, restore it to its original "purity," and unite all mankind around its altar. *The Kentucky Monitor* expresses it thusly: "It [Masonry] makes no profession of Christianity, and wars not against sectarian creeds or doctrines, but looks forward to the time when ... there shall be but one altar, one worship, one common altar of Masonry...."[132]

Of course, there is a problem here, a very great problem. That problem is that only "good" men can be admitted to this ultimate, perfect religion once it is rediscovered, leaving no hope of redemption for women, children, and "bad" men. But, perhaps reincarnation can take care of this, with the "bad" men eventually becoming "good," and the women and children eventually becoming men.

ENDNOTES

115 Albert Pike, *Morals and Dogma*, rev. ed. (Washington, DC: House of the Temple, 1950), 113.

116 Joseph Fort Newton, "The Great Light of Masonry," *Masonic Bible* (A. J. Holmes Co., 1968), unnumbered page.

117 "Chaplain," *Webb's Freemason's Monitor* (LaGrange, KY: Rob Morris Publishers, 1862), 231.

118 J.D. Buck, *Mystic Masonry*, 3rd ed. (Chicago: Chas T. Powner Publishing Co., 1925), 46, 47.
119 Albert Mackey, *Encyclopedia of Freemasonry*, rev. ed. s.v. "religion" (Chicago, New York, London: Masonic History Co., 1927), 619.
120 Coil, Henry W., *Masonic Encyclopedia* (New York: MaCoy Publishing Co., 1961), 512.
121 Webb, *Freemason's Monitor,* 280.
122 Albert Mackey, *Lexicon of Freemasonry*, 2nd Ed., s.v. "high priest" (Charleston, SC: Walker and James, 1852), 195.
123 J. Blanchard, *Scottish Rite Masonry, Illustrated,* vol. II (Chicago: Chas T. Powner Publishing Co., 1972), 26.
124 M. Taylor, "Masonic Burial Service," *Texas Monitor* (Houston, TX: Grand Lodge of Texas, 1883), 147.
125 Albert Mackey, *Lexicon of Freemasonry*, 2nd ed., s.v. "acacian."
126 Buck, *Mystic Masonry*, 44.
127 Carl Claudy, "Spirit of Masonry" *The Kentucky Monitor* (Louisville, KY: Standard Printing Co., 1921), xx, xxi.
128 Buck, *Mystic Masonry,* 63.
129 Albert Mackey, *Manual of the Lodge* (New York: MaCoy Publishing Co., 1903), 22-23.
130 Buck, *Mystic Masonry,* 66-67.
131 Pike, *Morals and Dogma*, 23.
132 Henry Pirtle,*The Kentucky Monitor* (Louisville, KY: Standard Printing Co., 1921), 95.

PART TWO — CHAPTER THIRTEEN

Freemasonry's Exclusiveness and Elitism

AND THE SPIRIT AND THE BRIDE SAY COME … AND LET HIM
THAT IS ATHIRST COME. AND WHOSOEVER WILL,
LET HIM TAKE THE WATER OF LIFE FREELY.
REVELATION 22: 17

AND YE MASTERS [REMEMBER] THAT YOUR MASTER
ALSO IS IN HEAVEN; NEITHER IS THERE ANY RESPECT OF
PERSONS WITH HIM.
EPHESIANS 6:9

1. Is Masonry open to anyone who wants to join?

Absolutely not! Exclusiveness has been a hallmark of
Freemasonry since its earliest beginnings. Socially, it was
founded by English aristocrats and was open only to the socially
elite; the first Grand Master (1717) is identified in the records as
"Anthony Sayer, Gentleman," not "Anthony Sayer, Bricklayer."

Spiritually, the mystery religions, the roots of Masonry, have
always been for only an elite, favored few. These elite insiders
were the only ones with the knowledge of the secrets, the secrets
were the keys to power, and they only admitted those to their
elite group who had been chosen and initiated.

The social snobbery may be offensive, but it is harmless. The spiritual snobbery is a much more serious matter.

2. Then, does a man have to be an aristocrat in order to join the Masonic Lodge today?

No, definitely not, or their numbers would be very much smaller than they are; but, the principle of elitism and exclusiveness prevails throughout the system.

In England, the high offices are still occupied by the aristocracy. The office of Grand Master of the United Grand Lodge of England is often occupied by a member of the royal family, as it now is. The current Grand Master is His Royal Highness, Prince Edward, Duke of Kent; he has been Grand Master since 1967.

Yet, even in England, men of ordinary means and humble birth may today be admitted to the Lodge (although they will seldom, if ever, achieve high office).

In the United States, men of very humble birth and little education are readily taken into the Lodge. Theoretically, any man can rise to the top levels of leadership within the Lodge system; but those of wealth and prominence definitely have the edge, and an honest Mason will tell you this. There are some offices, and even some organizations, in American Masonry which the "ordinary" Masons will never achieve because by their very nature the positions require wealth and social level. As George Orwell wrote in *Animal Farm,* "All animals are equal; but some are more equal than others."

This is especially true of the Shrine. In the Shrine, even the local leader (Illustrious Potentate) is expected to have the wealth and position to be socially active and sufficiently impressive to visiting dignitaries. No matter how hard a man may work, no matter how totally committed he may be, if he doesn't have money, a nice home, social position, etc., he will probably never occupy high office in the Shrine.

In fact, there are even some Masonic organizations with such a high "snob factor" that the ordinary working man will not be allowed to join; some of the most prestigious auxiliary groups in the Shrine are "by invitation only." It seems unbelievable, but a Shriner may have to spend more than one hundred thousand dollars to be elected to the national leadership's "Imperial Divan." (See Chapter Five.) This excludes thousands of Masons from even hoping to rise to top level leadership.

3. Who then may join the Lodge?

To summarize, Freemasonry is open only to men (no women may be initiated) who are "good" ("of good report"), who are "freeborn" (neither born in slavery nor bond-service, nor the son of such a person not born free), white, without physical disability, without mental impairment or emotional sickness, who have the money required, who are "of full age" (twenty-one or older) but not "old," and not an atheist.[133]

4. Are these restrictions on membership literally true?

Yes. One of the things a Master Mason swears to, on penalty of mutilation and death, is that he will not take part in the initiation of a "clandestine" Mason (a black or a woman), "a young man in his nonage" (underage), or "an old man in his dotage" (feeble, senile, or simply old), or one emotionally disturbed or mentally ill ("a madman or a fool").[134]

When the candidate for the first degree is presented for initiation, the Junior Deacon is asked of the candidate's qualifications "to gain admission" to the Lodge. He answers, "By being a man, freeborn, white and of full age."[135]

5. How do Masons justify this exclusiveness?

They can't, and they don't like being asked about it. When they are asked about their exclusion of certain types of people, they will usually react as they do to other negative aspects of

Masonry: they will either deny it or say that they are not allowed to discuss it. It's either, "It isn't so," or "I can't talk about that."

6. Why does Masonry exclude these kinds of people?

In terms of their basic policy of exclusiveness ("We make good men better"), it seems to be traceable to Masonry's beginnings as an order for just the well born, well educated, and reputable. This, I believe, is the origin of their exclusiveness in social terms. But, in a way much more sinister, their exclusiveness is readily traceable to the pagan mystery religions with secret initiations and elite priesthoods, the spiritual and ceremonial roots of Masonry. Elitism was, and is, the central characteristic of the pagan mystery religions

7. Is there any practical reason for their excluding these people?

Yes and no. They exclude women and blacks simply because they consider them unsuitable or undesirable. They exclude the deaf because they can't hear the passwords, recognition, and distress signs. They exclude the physically disabled (amputees, paralytics, etc) because they can't assume the proper body positions for dueguards, penalty signs, etc. They exclude the blind because they can't see the dueguards, penalty signs, etc. They exclude the poor because they can't pay, or occupy too low a level in society. They exclude the emotionally troubled because they can't be trusted with their secrets. And, they exclude (at least theoretically) the sinner because their system is only for "good" men who want to be made better. There are, of course, variations in these matters, from jurisdiction to jurisdiction, and from case to case; but this is the way it generally is.

8. What is so wrong about this?

Early in my study of Masonry, it occurred to me that these groups which Masonry automatically rejects are the groups that Jesus went after. He sought out sinners in general, and his time and energy were primarily expended on the unwanted, the blind, the deaf, the crippled, the poor, and the emotionally disturbed. These people, who in most cases need not even apply to the Masonic Lodge, were the ones in which Jesus specialized, those to whom He most readily opened his arms and said, "Come unto me."

I find this contrast extremely interesting and enormously significant.

9. But, still, if some men want to have an organization for social reasons and limit its membership only to certain people or types of people, isn't that their right?

Absolutely. I believe strongly in the right of association (or non-association). I believe that if it is merely a social organization or club and its policy is to accept into their membership only left-handed white men with red hair and blue eyes who are graduates of MIT in odd-numbered years (make up any set of restrictions you like here, the principle is the same), the organization should have every right to do so. Even if they want to consider themselves superior to the rest of us, that's perfectly alright with me. They would also have a right to do so, and I couldn't care less.

Not only is the right to free association a hallmark of free societies, it is also a scriptural principle that two cannot "walk together except they be agreed" (Amos 3:3).

10. Then, what's so wrong with Masonry for accepting only certain types of people?

What makes this question different with Masonry is that it presents itself as a means of spiritual redemption. Philosophically and logically, it is indefensible to declare on the one hand, "We are the only ones with the true spiritual light, the only ones with the truth," and then to say on the other hand, "What we have is not for everyone." It is like saying, "I am the man on the ship with the life preservers; but when the ship sinks, I'm only going to give them to a few of my friends."

11. Why does Masonry reject blacks?

This exclusion undoubtedly has its beginnings in the prevailing social and political attitudes and customs at the time of Masonry's origin in eighteenth century England, continuing into its spread into the American colonies. Blacks were looked upon as being inferior and socially unacceptable.

12. But, how do Masons justify this form of racial discrimination today?

They usually don't try to. When confronted with Masonry's historic rejection of blacks, most Masons will deny it and say that there are blacks in Masonry. But, what they are referring to (although they probably won't want to tell you) is the *entirely separate* black Masonic system called "Prince Hall" Masonry.

13. What is Prince Hall Masonry?

Prince Hall Masonry is the Masonic system for blacks. It is exactly like "white" Masonry, with the same rituals, same "secrets," all the same systems for higher degrees; it has its own Shrine and the same "adoptive" orders (e.g., Eastern Star, Rainbow Girls, etc.). It also has its own problems, including the same pagan roots.

14. Doesn't this mean that Masonry is open to blacks?

Definitely not; Freemasonry (the "legitimate" system) looks upon Prince Hall Masonry as counterfeit, an illegitimate imitation of the real thing. Prince Hall Masonry is classified as "clandestine" Masonry, one of the things in which a Master Mason swears to take no part, under penalty of death.

15. How did Prince Hall Masonry come to exist?

It all seems to have begun with a black man named Prince Hall. The exact history is hazy, but it is probably true that the British army, for reasons of its own, authorized Prince Hall and thirteen other black men to organize a lodge called "African

Lodge," in Boston, Massachusetts. This lodge, not recognized by the Grand Lodge of Massachusetts, refused to acknowledge any allegiance to that Grand Lodge and continued to operate in some form until the death of Prince Hall and his colleagues. In 1827, the system was revived. Receiving no recognition from the Grand Lodge of England, the men decided to acknowledge no Masonic authority but their own. They decided that "with what knowledge they possessed of Masonry, and as people of color by themselves, they were, and ought by rights to be, free and independent of other Lodges." From this beginning, a complete Masonic system developed and spread to Canada, Liberia, and other foreign countries. Today, because of an American military presence, there are Prince Hall lodges in Europe, and elsewhere overseas.

This elaborate Masonic system, a perfect parallel with white, "legitimate" Masonry, is still classified as illegitimate, clandestine, and off-limits to all white Masons. Albert Mackey, one of the most important Masonic writers of doctrine, summed it up thusly: "It cannot be denied that the unrecognized self revival of 1827, and the subsequent assumption of Grand Lodge powers, were illegal and rendered both the Prince Hall Grand Lodge and all the Lodges which emanated from it clandestine. And this has been the unanimous opinion of all [white] Masonic jurists in America." [136]

It is interesting, but not surprising, that the same attitude of superiority and spirit of snobbery exists among Prince Hall Masons toward those blacks outside the Lodge system, as that which has prevailed among white Masons towards blacks and others outside its confines. People are, after all, people.

16. Do white men join Prince Hall Lodges?

Until recent times this would have been unthinkable; had you asked me this, I would have said, "Impossible!" After 300 years of rejection by traditional, white Masonry, and because of the justifiable pride Prince Hall masons take in their fraternity, I would have said that it could never happen. But it has happened. I now know of one Prince Hall lodge that has "initiated, passed and raised" white men. A man whom I knew in my church, now deceased, was initiated into a Prince Hall lodge at Camp Darby, an American Army base in Italy, while he was a senior non-commissioned officer stationed there. After his arrival at Camp Darby he had been approached by the local white lodge about joining; and he was interested, until he discovered that the lodge would not accept blacks. This offended him and, to make a statement against racial segregation, he petitioned the local Prince Hall lodge and was accepted. He served that lodge as Lodge Secretary for the three years that he was stationed there. During that time he entered the Prince Hall Scottish Rite and rose to the 32nd Degree. Upon his transfer from that base he returned to the U.S. and retired. In retirement he became an inactive Mason and never attended another meeting. His widow states that there was one other white man in that Prince Hall lodge while they were stationed at Camp Darby.

In addition to the lodge at Camp Darby, there have been white and Hispanic men taken into other Prince Hall military lodges in Europe and elsewhere overseas, under at least three jurisdictions. The walls of Masonic segregation appear to be crumbling.

17. Are there ever exceptions in local lodges to these rules of exclusion in membership?

Yes, there are, but they are definitely exceptions and not the rule. I was told by one Mason in New York, at least 15 years ago, that his lodge had taken in a black man, and it has happened elsewhere. Because of changes in social mores and political pressures, change seems inevitable, and the resulting social adjustments will be increasingly painful, emotional, and divisive. Looming before Masonry, as a whole, is a growing problem of enormous proportions.

For example, the Grand Lodge of West Virginia recently issued an edict "forbidding members of the Most Worshipful Grand Lodge of West Virginia, Ancient Free and Accepted Masons to visit lodges under the Grand Lodges" of seven northern and western states because of their openness to recognizing Prince Hall Masonry as legitimate.[137] Today, the Grand Lodge of New York recognizes Prince Hall Masonry as legitimate. For more on this, see the Epilogue to Part Two, "Recent Developments."

18. Are there ever exceptions to the other exclusions for membership in the local lodge?

Yes, or at least so I am told, and I am inclined to believe it. A man called me on one talk show and told me that he was a Mason, although he was blind, and had been blind when taken into the lodge. Another man called on another such broadcast and told me that his lodge had taken in a man in a wheelchair. But, I emphasize, these are exceptions and not the rule. Once a local lodge has taken in such a man, initiated him, and given him the "secrets" of a Master Mason, the Grand Lodge is presented with a *fait accompli* and has no choice but to allow him to stay (or kill him—and the probability of this solution is very near zero).

Concerning the poor, there are definitely cases in which a man who cannot afford the initiation fees will have them paid for him by a member of the lodge, in order to be able to take him in. But, such a man will be expected to stand on his own financial feet from that time on. Again, such cases are the exception and not the rule. There is definitely a cost to entering and remaining in the Lodge.

19. Do you know of any men who have been denied membership because of disability?

Yes, several. One man I remember was blinded as a Marine in the battle for Iwo Jima in World War II. When he returned to civilian life, he applied for membership in his local lodge. He was rejected because of his blindness.

The most poignant and powerful example of this that I know is that of a man in Tampa, Florida. He had grown up in a Masonic family, had been an ardent member of the Order of DeMolay, had gone through the chairs and held all its offices, and loved it. He was living for the day when he would reach his twenty-first birthday so he could enter the Lodge. When he was nineteen, he was drafted into the army and sent to Korea, where he was terribly wounded, bayoneted, and left by the enemy for dead. He survived but was blinded, lost one leg, and one arm was paralyzed. By the time he recovered from his wounds and returned home, he was twenty-one. He immediately petitioned his local lodge for membership, the fulfillment of his lifelong dream, and was summarily rejected because of his disabilities. He told me that, at the time, this rejection by the Masonic system he so loved hurt him more than all his physical wounds. Now, however, he is a Christian and says that their rejection of him was his gain and their loss.

20. But, what about women; are they ever taken into the Lodge?

Never! To my knowledge, this is the exception never made, which is interesting. With the exception of Mrs. Aldworth (Elizabeth St. Leger) and a few other bizarre and questionable cases, including Annie Besant, famed English mystic, occultist, and socialist, Masonic history is consistent and emphatic: women have never been admitted to Freemasonry. Concerning this, see Appendix A, "Female 'Brothers' in the Lodge." "Androgynous" Masonry, including both women and men, has been largely a French idea, as has been the case of purely female Masonry; neither has ever found acceptance by Freemasonry in general.

English Freemasonry (along with its American, European, and Asian off-springs) has from its earliest beginnings excluded women.[138] This "ancient landmark" has never been shaken. Most Masons won't know why this has always been done. Those who are familiar with the argument will tell you that it is because the work of operative stonemasons (the real ones, from which they draw much of their symbolism) required the physical strength of men, and speculative Masons (the guys in the Lodge) have carried on the ancient tradition of excluding women. The truth may be much darker, as explained in Appendix A.

21. What is meant by the Masonic expression "profane world"?

This is an extremely important question; one that goes to the heart of Masonic exclusiveness and elitism. The word *profane* derives from the Latin word *profanus* meaning "outside, or excluded from, the Temple." The expanded meaning refers to one who is unclean, polluted, unholy, and entirely unacceptable. In Masonic teachings, anyone not an initiated Mason is *profane*, and there is frequent reference in their ritual and conversations to "the profane" (people) or "the profane world," which means all of the non-Masonic world around them.

Here is still another thing most Masons seem never to think of, but this doctrine of basic snobbery means that their wives, mothers, daughters, and grandmothers are all "unclean and unfit for fellowship." So also are their sons, fathers, brothers, and grandfathers if not Masons. This is a point worth pondering.

ENDNOTES

133 Albert Mackey, *Jurisprudence of Freemasonry*, rev. and enlarged ed. Book II (Chicago: Chas T. Powner Co., 1975), 14; Henry W. Coil, *Masonic Encyclopedia* (New York: MaCoy Publishing Co., 1961),494-496.
134 Malcolm C. Duncan, *Duncan's Masonic Ritual and Monitor*, 3rd ed. (New York: David McKay Co., undated), 94·96.

135 Ibid., 28-29; this response is modified today in some parts of
the country to: "By being a man, freeborn, of a full age, and of
a good reputation." In the South, the original wording is still
common.

136 Albert Mackey, *Encyclopedia of Freemasonry,* rev. ed. s.v.
(Chicago, New York, London: Masonic History Co., 1927),
508,509.

137 Connecticut, Wisconsin, Nebraska, Washington, Colorado,
Minnesota, and North Dakota.

138 The charges compiled by Anderson and Desaguliers (founders
of speculative Masonry) were explicit in this regard: "the
persons admitted members of a Lodge must be good and true
men." Mackey, *Encyclopedia of Freemasonry,* s.v. "woman,"
855.

Freemasonry and Jesus Christ

WHOSOEVER DENIETH THE SON,
THE SAME HATH NOT THE FATHER.
1 JOHN 3:23

1. Does Masonry acknowledge Jesus as Lord and Savior?

The answer to this question is what propelled me into the study of Freemasonry twenty years ago. As I reluctantly began to read the introduction to *The Kentucky Monitor,* a "secret" Masonic book, in order to please a friend, it immediately got my attention, aroused my interest, and then it nearly knocked me off my chair!

My first "Masonic shock" was learning that Masonry is not just a fraternal order given to good works but is, in fact, a revival of the pagan mystery religions of Egypt and the East.[139]

My second "Masonic shock" was learning that Masonry denies the divinity and uniqueness of Jesus, equating Him to "other saviors" of history.[140]

My third and greatest "Masonic shock" was learning that Masonry has its own messiah, someone called "Hiram."[141]

2. Then, where does Jesus fit into the Masonic system and doctrine?

He is presented as just one of what they call the "exemplars," the great men of the past, on the same level with Buddha, Confucious, Mohammed, and Aristotle. Listen to the words of Albert Pike: "It (Masonry) reverences all the great reformers. It sees Moses, the lawgiver to the Jews, in Confucious and Zoroaster, in Jesus of Nazareth, and in the Arabian Iconoclast (Mohammed), great teachers of morality, and eminent reformers, if no more."[142]

As a matter of fact, when we consider the Shrine, Masonry views Jesus to be even lower than the other "exemplars" because, in Islam, Jesus is recognized as only a minor prophet, decidedly inferior to Mohammed.

3. Is this true, even in Lodges where all or most of the members are Christian?

Definitely; of course, many who would classify themselves as Christians may not be truly born-again into the family of God. (I was such a nominal Christian for most of my life.) But, even if all of the members of a local Lodge were born-again Christians, it wouldn't change in any way the status of Jesus in their Lodge. He could not be honored as the unique Savior of lost mankind, nor could prayers be offered in His name. Masonic doctrine is Masonic doctrine, regardless of the religious persuasion of a Lodge's membership.

4. Do you mean that Masons are not allowed to honor Jesus as Lord in the Lodge?

Absolutely! At least, not out loud. Some of them may truly honor Him in their hearts, but they are not allowed in any way to acknowledge Him outwardly as Lord in the Lodge.

5. Why is this so?

Because, very simply, Freemasonry is **not** Christian. In addition, as the usual justification goes, it would be offensive to the non-Christians in the Lodge. Some Lodges have a mix of Christians, Deists, Mormons, Muslims, etc., and the principle is that they must not be offended by having Jesus honored as Lord.

In a classic example of this Masonic syncretism, my late friend Mick Oxley, while on active duty as an officer in the Royal Air Force, belonged to a lodge in Singapore under the English Constitutions (chartered by the United Grand Lodge of England). In that lodge the Worshipful Master was a Muslim, the Senior Warden was a Muslim, the Junior Warden was a Hindu, the Senior Deacon was a Hindu, the Junior Deacon was a Taoist, and the Tiler was a Sikh.

6. But, doesn't this make sense? Shouldn't the Christian Masons be tolerant of their non-Christian brothers?

In human terms, this seems reasonable and right; but, from a scriptural point of view, it is very wrong. To fail to acknowledge and confess Jesus is to deny Him, and to deny Him is a spiritually fatal error.

As a matter of fact, Christians shouldn't even have "non-Christian brothers" because of the scriptural admonition not to be unequally yoked with unbelievers; nor are we to have fellowship with the unfruitful works of darkness.[143] And, in the Lodge, Christians are not just associating with unbelievers in social functions and community service, they are literally bound together with them by "unbreakable" death oaths, sworn to give them unfair preference in all dealings and to conceal their crimes. (See Chapter Eighteen, "Death Oaths and Masonic Execution.")

For those who would seek refuge behind the defense that they only belong to a local lodge whose members are all Christians, I point out that every Mason who has ever taken even the first oath of obligation is spiritually bound in brotherhood to every other Mason who ever lived.[144]

7. Is it true that prayers in the Masonic Lodge are not offered in Jesus' name?

This is definitely true! The prayers of Masonry must be kept "universal" so as not to offend any of the non-Christians in the system. This happens even in the so-called "Christian" degrees of the York Rite. The Reverend Harmon Taylor, Past Grand Chaplain of the Grand Lodge of New York, testifies that, in that office, he was given only one instruction, and that he was given that one many times. This oft-repeated direction was that he was never, under any circumstance, to offer prayers in Masonic gatherings in Jesus' name.[145]

This prohibition also prevails in the Eastern Star, which most of its members believe to be Christian. Even in the Rainbow Girls, the prayers are "universal" and Christ-less. Their burial service (yes, those little girls really do have one) makes reference to "the master teacher," who could be Aristotle, Zoroaster, or the teacher of the year in Possum Trot, Kentucky—and this is as close as they get to honoring Jesus.

8. Are prayers ever offered in Jesus' name in a Masonic Lodge?

Yes. There are sometimes exceptions to this rule, but they are definitely exceptions and not the rule. Let me explain. There are some small town lodges, especially in the South, where this rule is sometimes broken. In such a small town, where all the churches are at least nominally Christian and there is no one offended by such prayer, the chaplain may, in some cases, offer prayer in Jesus' name. However, if a visitor reports it, or if in any other way word of this reaches the Grand Lodge headquarters in that state, the local lodge will be forced to stop praying in Jesus' name or have its charter revoked.

9. Do you mean that a Masonic Lodge could actually have its charter revoked if its leaders insisted on honoring Jesus in the Lodge or offering prayers in His name?

Yes. This, I think, is an eloquent expression of Masonry's position on Jesus. Masonry is not only non-Christian, but, because it denies His rightful place in the Universe, Masonry is actually anti-Christian. Jesus Himself said that those who are not for Him are against Him.

10. Do Masons have their own system for reckoning time?

Yes, and it is yet another way in which Jesus is denied in the Lodge. Virtually all the rest of the civilized world counts years from the birth of Jesus, before and since. "B.C." is an abbreviation of the words "before Christ." "A.D." is an abbreviation of the words "Anno Domini," Latin for "the year of our Lord." Julius Caesar was born 100 B.C.; Jerusalem fell to the Roman General Titus in A.D. 70, and Abraham Lincoln was murdered in A.D. 1865. That's the way most of us reckon time, and I love it because, in so doing, the entire civilized world acknowledges and honors Jesus, even calling Him "our Lord."

But, Freemasonry does not do this—not even in the "Christian" degrees of the York Rite. Masons use a different system, and their system leaves Jesus completely out. In Masonry, current time is reckoned, not from the birth of Jesus, but from the supposed time of creation, 4,000 years B.C. So, Masonic time is reckoned by adding four thousand to the current year and calling it "Anno Lucis" (in the year of light), abbreviated "A.L." By their system, A.D. 1993 becomes A.L. 5993. You may confirm this by looking at the engraved date on any cornerstone laid by Masons.[146]

11. Does Masonry teach the need for any personal savior?

No. Concisely and simply stated, Masonry teaches that we must save ourselves by initiation into Freemasonry, by growing in knowledge ("light") through its degrees, by obedience to the oaths of obligation, and by leading a virtuous life ("being good"). To help with all this, there is the doctrine of reincarnation.

Faith is not only not required, but the concept of salvation by faith is considered to be an "ignorant perversion" of the truth, and the Apostles who first taught it "dunces." Nowhere in all Masonic teachings is there declared (or even implied) a need for basically sinful man to have a personal savior, and if there is even an oblique reference to a personal savior, it is Hiram Abiff—not Jesus.[147] And, if one is "redeemed" by Hiram, it is not by faith in him, but by gaining knowledge of him, a very different matter indeed.

12. Can you document that amazing statement?

I realize that all this sounds bizarre, especially to the Christian, but let's allow the Masonic philosophers to speak for themselves. Once again, I could fill this book with documentation to this effect, but that obviously would not be workable; a few examples must suffice:

"By the Lambskin [apron] the Mason is reminded of that purity of life and rectitude of conduct which are so essentially necessary to his gaining admission into the Celestial Lodge above [Heaven], where the Supreme Architect of the Universe presides" (Albert Mackey).[148]

"And in Thy favor may we be received into Thine everlasting kingdom to enjoy, in union with the souls of our departed friends, the just reward of a pious and virtuous life. Amen. So mote it be" (M. Taylor, *Texas Monitor*).[149]

"Acacian: a term signifying a Mason who, by living in strict obedience to the obligations [oaths] and precepts [teachings] of the fraternity, is free from sin" (Albert Mackey).[150]

"The rite of induction signifies the end of a profane and vicious life, the palingenisis [new birth] of corrupt human nature, the death of vice and all bad passions, and the introduction to the new life of purity and virtue" (Daniel Sickles).[151]

"These three degrees [First, Second, and Third] thus form a perfect and harmonious whole, nor can it be conceived that anything can be suggested more, which the soul of man requires" (Daniel Sickles).[152]

"Step by step men must advance towards Perfection, and each Masonic Degree is meant to be one of those steps" (Albert Pike).[153]

"Salvation by faith and the vicarious atonement were not taught as now interpreted by Jesus, nor are these doctrines taught in the esoteric [hidden] scriptures. They are later and ignorant perversions of the original doctrines" (J.D. Buck).[154]

"The dunces who led primitive Christianity astray [the Church's Apostolic Fathers], by substituting faith for science, reverie for experience, the fantastic for the reality; and the inquisitors who for so many ages waged against Magism [magic, sorcery] a war of extermination, have succeeded in shrouding in darkness the ancient discoveries of the human mind" (Albert Pike).[155]

"All antiquity believed … in a Mediator or Redeemer, by means of whom the Evil Principle was to be overcome and the Supreme Deity reconciled to His creatures. The belief was general that he was to be born of a virgin and suffer a painful death. The Hindus called him Krishna; the Chinese, Kiountse; the Persians, Sosiosch; the Scandinavians, Balder; the Christians, Jesus; the Masons, Hiram" (Pirtle, *Kentucky Monitor*).[156]

"It is Christos or Hiram, the Mediator between the soul, or physical man, and the Great Spirit—the Father in Heaven" (J.D. Buck).[157]

"It is far more important that men should strive to become Christs than that they should believe that Jesus was Christ" (J.D. Buck).[158]

"Theologians … tore the Christos from the hearts of all humanity in order to deify Jesus, that they might have a God-man peculiarly their own!" (J.D. Buck).[159]

"In the early church, as in the secret doctrine, there was not a personal Christ for the whole world but a potential Christ in every living being. Hence Masons believe in the Architect of the Universe, but positively not in Jesus the man as the only Son of God" (J.D. Buck).[160]

"This principle of Brotherhood and the perfectibility of man's nature through evolution necessitate Reincarnation... Hence the doctrine of pre-existence taught in all the Mysteries applies to "every child of woman born; all conditions in each life being determined by previous living" (J.D. Buck).[161]

To achieve it [Heaven], the Mason must first attain a solid conviction, founded on reason, that he hath within him a spiritual nature, a soul that is not to die when the body is dissolved, but is to continue to exist and to advance toward perfection through all the ages of eternity .... This [reincarnation], the Philosophy of the Ancient and Accepted Rite teaches him" (Albert Pike).[162]

"In deifying Jesus the whole of humanity is bereft of Christos as an eternal potency within every human soul, a latent Christ in every man. In thus deifying one man, they [the Christians] have orphaned the whole of humanity! On the other hand Masonry, in making every man personify Hiram, has preserved the original teaching.... Few candidates may be aware that Hiram whom they have represented and personified, is ideally and precisely the same as Christ. Yet such is undoubtedly the case" (J.D. Buck).[163]

13. Does Masonry really teach that Jesus is not unique, but is just one of many "redeemers"?

Absolutely. For openers, see question 12, cite eighteen, above; there, in the introduction to *The Kentucky Monitor*, it is plainly (if a bit obliquely) said that there is really nothing special about Jesus, that all civilizations have had a myth of such a messiah, born of a virgin, suffered, and died, and so on. For more, let's again allow the leading Masonic writers to speak for themselves:

"Krishna, the Hindoo[sic] Redeemer, was cradled and educated among shepherds. A tyrant, at the time of his birth, ordered all the male children to be slain. He performed miracles, say his legends, even raising the dead. He washed the feet of the Brahmins. It was on a cruciform tree [a cross] that Krishna was said to have expired, pierced with arrows. He descended into Hell, rose again, ascended to Heaven, charged his disciples to teach his doctrines, and gave them the gift of miracles" (Pirtle, *Kentucky Monitor*).[164] Does this sound familiar to you Christians? It should.

"Every act in the drama of the life of Jesus, and every quality assigned to Christ, is to be found in the life of Krishna and in the legend of all the Sun Gods from the remotest antiquity" (J.D. Buck).[165]

"The true Mason is not creed-bound. He realizes with the divine illumination [light] of his lodge that as a Mason his religion must be universal; Christ, Buddha, or Mohammed, the name means little, for he recognizes only the light and not the bearer. He worships at every shrine, bows before every altar, whether in temple, mosque, or cathedral...." (Manley P. Hall).[166]

"In his private devotions, a man may petition God or Jehovah, Allah or Buddha, Mohammed or Jesus; he may call upon the God of Israel or the First Great Cause.... A hundred paths may wind upward around a mountain; at the top they meet" (Carl H. Claudy).[167]

"Is Jesus any the less Christos because Christna [sic] was called "The Good Shepherd?" or because the Mexican Christ was crucified between two thieves? or because Hiram was three days in a grave before he was resurrected? (J.D. Buck).[168]

14. Who is this Hiram who seems to be so important in Masonry?

Hiram Abiff is the central character in the legend of the third degree of the Blue Lodge; as such, he is the most important person in Blue Lodge Masonry. According to Masonic tradition, Hiram was the chief architect in the building of the temple in Jerusalem by King Solomon. He is called "Hiram, the Widow's son" and is a mythological character consisting of a mixture of fact and fiction.

There are two Hirams in the scriptural account of the building of Solomon's Temple. One was Hiram, King of Tyre, friend of King David and of his son, King Solomon. This King Hiram provided much of the material for the temple's construction; he also sent to Solomon a man named Hiram, a widow's son, of the tribe of Naphtali. This Hiram was a skilled worker in metals, who was brought to the construction project to make objects of brass. This second Hiram, a remarkable craftsman and artist, made all the wonderful brass objects and implements for the temple, "made an end of all his work" for the temple, and apparently went back home to Tyre and lived happily ever after.[169]

The Hiram of Masonic legend is supposed to have been the chief architect of the temple project. He was also, in some way, a master mason, and the "grand master" of all the stonemasons working on the temple. The story is (typically) confused because Hiram is called "our first Grand Master," yet both King Solomon and King Hiram are also referred to as grand masters. Nevertheless, as the story goes, Hiram knew the "Master's Word," a secret the working masons wouldn't be qualified to receive until the temple was finished. Several of the masons ("ruffians") decided that they wanted to know the word before they finished, and trying to scare or beat the secret out of Hiram, they ultimately killed him. After three days the truth was revealed, the "ruffians" were caught, and the grave was opened. King Solomon, with Masonic technique, raises Hiram from the dead. This, in greatly abbreviated form, is the legend of Hiram Abiff.

15. But, what does this have to do with Jesus?

Everything—or nothing at all—depending on how one views it. In the climactic part of the third degree initiation, the legend of Hiram is enacted as a play in the lodge hall, with the bewildered, hoodwinked candidate playing the role of Hiram (about whom he knows nothing at all). As is the case with all the rest of his initiations, the candidate knows nothing of this in advance. In fact, he has already been led to believe that his initiation is finished. Then he must again take off his clothes and be re-hoodwinked. He is led through the bewildering skit, about which he knows nothing, being jerked around by three consecutive "ruffians" (who really do get rough), is "buried" under "rubble of the Temple," and then resurrected by the Worshipful Master, playing the role of Solomon.

Almost none of this is scriptural, almost none of it is true, and some of it is downright blasphemous. God Himself was the architect of the temple, laying down plans and specifications to the last minute detail. And, there was no "rubble" in the building of the temple; every stone was cut to fit at a distant site and merely put in place in the temple. And, what is even more outrageous, in the legend Hiram takes his lunch break in the Holy of Holies! All serious Masonic historians acknowledge that it is pure myth and legend; yet, most Masons believe that it is all true. The shock effect, confusion, and fear leave the hoodwinked candidate vulnerable to deep spiritual bondage.

And here is how it relates to Jesus. Hiram Abiff actually represents Osiris, the Egyptian sun and sex god. In order to receive the Masonic "new birth" and ascend from spiritual darkness to light, the candidate must enter into the death, burial, and resurrection of Hiram Abiff (Osiris), Masonry's bogus redeemer. To quote just one of the Masonic philosophers, "In the third degree the candidate impersonates Hiram, who has been shown to be identical with Christos of the Greeks, and with the Sun-Gods of all other nations."[170]

This is a blasphemous parody of genuine redemption by faith in Christ Jesus.

If you would like to know more about the legend of Hiram Abiff, how it relates to Isis and Osiris, its real spiritual implications concerning our Redeemer, Jesus Christ, and what

Masonic scholars say about it, see Appendix D to Part One of this book.

ENDNOTES

139 Henry Pirtle, "The Spirit of Masonry," *The Kentucky Monitor* (Louisville, KY: Standard Printing Co., 1921), xi, xii.

140 Ibid., xiv, xv.

141 Ibid., xv.

142 Albert Pike, *Morals and Dogma,* rev. ed. (Washington, DC: House of the Temple, 1950), 525.

143 2 Corinthians 6:14-18; Ephesians 5:6-11.

144 Albert Pike, *Morals and Dogma*, 726.

145 Harmon R. Taylor, *Oil and Water* (Newtonville, NY: HRT Ministries, undated pamphlet; Personal Interview, Knoxville, TN: 5 June 1993).

146 Here again there is contradiction and confusion in Masonry. Blue Lodge Masonry uses this basic system (Anno Lucis); the York Rite uses another (Anno Ordinis, "the Year of the Order," dating from the year 1118, which is subtracted from the A.D. year); the Scottish Rite uses still another (Anno Mundi, "the Year of the World," adding 3,760 to the A.D. year, approximately the same as the Jewish system); and there are even more!

147 Pirtle, *The Kentucky Monitor*, xv; J.D. Buck, *Mystic Masonry*, 3rd ed. (Chicago: Chas T. Powner Co., 1925), 133.

148 Albert Mackey, *Encyclopedia of Freemasonry,* rev ed. s.v. "apron," (Chicago, New York, London: Masonic History Co., 1927), 72- 74.

149 M. Taylor, "Masonic Burial Service," *Texas Monitor* (Houston, TX: Grand Lodge of Texas, 1883), 147.

150 Albert Mackey, *Lexicon of Freemasonry,* 2nd ed., s.v. "Acacian," 6.

151 Daniel Sickles, *Ahiman Rhezon and Freemason's Guide* (New York: MaCoy Publishing Co., 1911), 54.

152 Ibid., 196.

153 Pike, *Morals and Dogma*, 136.

154 Buck, *Mystic Masonry*, 57.

155 Pike, *Morals and Dogma*, 732.

156 Pirtle, *Kentucky Monitor*, 14, 15.
157 Buck, *Mystic Masonry*, 45.
158 Ibid., P 62.
159 Ibid., P 57.
160 Ibid.
161 Ibid., 63; S.R. Parchment, *Ancient Operative Masonry* (San Francisco: San Francisco Center-Rosicrucian Fellowship, 1930), 35.
162 Pike, *Morals and Dogma*, 855.
163 Buck, *Mystic Masonry*, 63.
164 Pirtle, *Kentucky Monitor*, xv.
165 Buck, *Mystic Masonry*, 63.
166 Manley P. Hall, *The Lost Keys of Freemasonry* (Richmond, VA: MaCoy Publishing Co., 1976), 65.
167 Carl H. Claudy, *Introduction to Freemasonry* (Washington, DC: Temple Publishers, 1939), 38.
168 Buck, *Mystic Masonry*, 47.
169 1 Kings 7:13-40.
170 Buck, *Mystic Masonry*, 133.

This Methodist church in Dundee, Kentucky, was converted into a Masonic lodge hall and meetingi place for the Order of the Eastern Star. Notice the goat on the steeple in place of a cross.

Freemasonry and Secrecy

I [JESUS] SPAKE OPENLY TO THE WORLD;
I EVER TAUGHT IN THE SYNAGOGUE AND IN THE TEMPLE ...
AND IN SECRET HAVE I SAID NOTHING.
JOHN 18:20

1. Why do Masons seem so mysterious and secretive about what they do?

They are so mysterious and secretive because secrecy has been a basic characteristic of Freemasonry since its founding. As a matter of fact, this is part of its foundational law, one of its "landmarks." (See question 7, below.) This is the feature that makes Masonry appealing to many Masons; they enjoy being part of an exclusive group with secrets that others "aren't in on."

2. Why has Masonry been secretive since its beginnings?

The secrecy has remained entrenched for two reasons. First, the medieval stonemasons' guilds, from which Masonry takes so much of its symbolism, met in secret in order to protect their trade secrets.

Second, and more important, Masonry is based on, and is a revival of, the ancient pagan mystery religions of the East, especially those of Egypt. The ancient mysteries were for only an elite few; secrecy and exclusiveness were characteristic. According to the *Encyclopedia of Freemasonry* (s.v., "ancient mysteries"), they were: "... the secret worship rites of the Pagan gods. Each of the Pagan gods had, besides the public and open, a secret worship paid to him, to which none were admitted but those who had been selected by preparatory ceremonies called Initiation."

Concerning those mystery religions, the *Encyclopedia* goes on to say: "Secret ceremonies were practiced in honor of certain gods, and whose secret was known to the initiates alone, who were admitted only after long and painful trials, which it was more than their life was worth to reveal.... The most important of these mysteries were the Osiric [those of Osiris and Isis] in Egypt."[171]

3. Is Masonry a secret society?

Absolutely; according to the *Encyclopaedia Britannica,* Freemasonry is not only a secret society but the world's largest.[172]

4. Do Masons ever deny that theirs is a secret society?

Yes, they will almost always deny being a secret society, if they answer the question at all.

5. Is the statement in the *Encyclopaedia Britannica* true?

Definitely. The article in the *Britannica* is definitely not a piece of anti-Mason propaganda; as a matter of fact, it is just the opposite, written to cast the most favorable light on Masonry. Not surprisingly, the article was written by a dedicated, high-ranking English Mason. So, yes, the statement is trustworthy.

6. Then, on what basis do Masons deny being a secret society?

They do so by classic, typically Masonic, double talk. They will usually defend their position by saying, "We are a society with secrets, but not a secret society." This is comparable to saying, "I am a farmer with thousands of cattle, but I am not a cattle farmer."

While they deny being a secret society, they meet behind painted or draped windows and a closed, guarded door, and everything they do there is secret and protected by death oaths. They will admit this, but point out that the fact of their existence is not a secret. Therefore, they say, they are not a secret society. It doesn't require a logician or a linguist to determine that this is merely word juggling.

7. What do the Masonic authorities say about secrecy?

They are unanimous about the necessity for secrecy and the gravity of any violation of the secrecy. Secrecy has been a hallmark of Masonry since its beginning; it is one of its "landmarks," and they take it very seriously.[173]

Albert Mackey, one of Masonry's most authoritative writers, said in his *Textbook of Masonic Jurisprudence,*

"The secrecy of this institution is another and most important landmark.... If divested of its secret character, it would lose its identity, and would cease to be Freemasonry.... Death of the Order would follow its legalized exposure. Freemasonry, as a secret association, has lived unchanged for centuries; as an open society it would not last for as many years."[174]

8. Then, why would Masons want to deny being a secret society?

They seem to be increasingly defensive about Masonry as a whole and are anxious to reassure those outside the Lodge that they are a fine, virtuous, and benevolent organization. Because of this, they are quick to deny the existence of anything negative in the public's perception of the institution. A secret society must have dark and sinister things to hide (which of course is true); for this reason, they don't like being known as a secret society.

9. Are the doors really guarded during their meetings?

Definitely; as a matter of fact, this guarding of the door is another of the "ancient landmarks." The guardian of the door is an officer of the lodge, and his title is "Tiler." The spelling of this word varies, like so much in Freemasonry, but this is the most common spelling. The origin of the word is uncertain, but most Masons, if they have knowledge of it at all, will tell you that the name comes from the fact that an otherwise finished roof must be "tiled" on its ridge, or rain and snow can come through. Thus, a "tiled" lodge is one in which the Worshipful Master can be assured that there is no one in the lodge hall except Masons of the appropriate degree and that no one else can enter or hear what is being said and done. With this in mind, the Tiler is usually armed, symbolically, with a sword.

10. Do Masons have to take an oath of secrecy?

Absolutely. A portion of the bloody and horrible death oaths for each degree is the promise to keep not only the secrets of the order's rituals and lessons but also the secrets of one another's crimes. Over and over, the Mason must swear, on penalty of mutilation and death, to "ever conceal and never reveal" any such secrets.

11. If the Masons want to have secrets, what's so wrong with that?

There is nothing at all wrong with secrecy *per se;* there are times when secrecy is the wise and right course. But, here again is that Masonic spirit of exclusiveness and elitism. What makes secrecy so wrong and such a contradiction, in this case, is that Masonry is supposed to have the answers to life, death, and eternity. In this sense, it is hideously wrong to take the position that "We have the secrets to life, death, and eternity, we are the only ones who know these things, and rather than hasten to share these wonderful secrets with all of mankind, we are going to keep most of the world from knowing our wonderful, life-giving secrets, let them wander in darkness, and be damned. We will share these wonderful, all-important secrets with only a few of our friends." As I said before, logically and ethically, this is indefensible.

The Christian imperative, since we really do possess the answers to life, death, and eternity, is to shout the Good News from the house tops and invite the entire human race into our redeeming truth and fellowship. The true gospel is for "whosoever;" the invitation of Jesus is for everyone who is thirsty and wants His unspeakable gift to come and take the water of life freely. And, He has commanded us to spread this good news all over the world. Now, *this* makes sense!

There are mysteries in God's Kingdom; *but there are no secrets!*

12. Do they really have secrets?

No. Most Masons believe that all their "secret work" is unknown outside Masonic circles, and they will fight—literally—to protect their "secrets," but, as in so many other ways, they are deceived.

13. How can Masons think that their matters are secret if they aren't?

They believe so for the same combination of reasons that they believe that Masonry is Christian, is based on the Bible, and is not a religion. They have been told that no one but a Mason could possibly know anything about Masonry's secrets because none of the "secret work" is in writing. To reinforce this, the Mason must swear that he will never write down any of the "secret work." This, like so much else that Masons are told, is simply untrue; it can all be found, one way or another, in writing. But, they believe that it doesn't exist in writing, and very, very few of them will take the time or trouble to investigate, read, and think for himself on the matter.

The truth of the matter is that there is only one well-kept Masonic secret, and that is that **there are no Masonic secrets!** If this were not so, how then could I have written this book?

14. How can these secret things of Masonry be seen and read?

I was amazed to learn how easily most of this material can be obtained. Some of it can simply be found in libraries. Such Masonic books may often be found in used book stores. (Many such stores will have a Masonic section.) I have bought some key Masonic reference books off the shelf in new book stores. (Here, also, they will frequently be found in the "Occult" section.) Some classics may be picked up at yard sales, and many are left behind by relatives when they die. But, the most amazing thing of all for me was the discovery that Masonic publishers will sell these books **to anyone!** I have ordered many over the years and have never had to tell them whether or not I am a Mason (nor have I ever been asked!). I have found that at least one Masonic publisher will even sell the books of "secret work" and ritual written by anti-Masonic writers.

For example, there is a published version of the secret recognition test for Shriners (the test a Shriner from a different club, a stranger, must pass in order to be admitted to a meeting as a visitor). I bought a copy for twenty cents! The most difficult book to obtain is Albert Pike's classic, *Morals and Dogma.* This book is given only to Scottish Rite Masons with the Thirty-second Degree and comes with the requirement that it must be protected from unauthorized eyes, and provision must be made for it to be returned to the Scottish Rite upon death of the owner. (In some places, this requirement is "on penalty of death.") Even this one can be bought when a used copy is available.

Yes, anyone who really wants to, can obtain all these "secret" books; yet the average Blue Lodge Mason not only believes that someone like you and I could not possibly have one of these books, *he doesn't even believe that they exist!*

15. How have their secrets come to be known outside the Lodge?

Since about 1830, there have been no Masonic secrets. After the kidnapping and murder of Captain Morgan in 1826 and the posthumous publication of his book (the first expose' of Freemasonry), there was a tidal wave of angry reaction to Masonry.[175] In addition to the revealing of all the Blue Lodge "secret work" in Morgan's book, influential Masons all over the country deliberately went to court and made public all the higher degrees as well. From that time on, a succession of books has been published, plainly revealing all that once was truly secret.

So, since about 1830, it is true that they have no secrets. But, you will have a tough time convincing most Blue Lodge Masons of this fact. (See Chapter 18, "Death Oaths and Masonic Execution.")

ENDNOTES

171 Albert Mackey, *Encyclopedia of Freemasonry*, rev. ed. s.v. "Mysteries, Ancient" (Chicago, New York, London: Masonic History Co., 1927), 497-500.

172 *The New Encyclopaedia Britannica,* 15th ed., s.v. "freemasonry," 302.

173 Landmarks are foundational, indispensable matters of Ma· sonic law, dating, in one form or another, since the first codification of Masonic doctrine in the early eighteenth century. The landmarks (i.e., secrecy, men only, belief in a "Supreme Being," obedience to the Worshipful Master, etc.) are sometimes called "The Unwritten Law of Masonry," as opposed to the Constitutions, which are called "The Written Law of Masonry." There is much reference in Masonic writings to "The Ancient landmarks"; however, as in all of Masonry, there is much confusion and contradiction concerning the landmarks, with varying numbers, from seven (according to Massachusetts) to fifty-four (according to Kentucky). Henry W. Coil *Encyclopedia of Freemasonry*

includes not only various lists of landmarks, but includes twenty-five definitions of the word!

174   Albert Mackey, "23rd Landmark: Secrecy," *Jurisprudence of Freemasonry,* rev. and enlarged ed., Book II (Chicago: Chas T. Powner Co., 1975), 17.

175   William Morgan, *Illustrations of Masonry,* printed for the Proprietor, republished (Batavia, NY: 1827).

Freemasonry and Deception

DELIVER MY SOUL, O LORD, FROM LYING LIPS
AND FROM A DECEITFUL TONGUE.
PSALMS 120:2

1. Is there deception in Masonry?

Yes there is, from top to bottom. In fact, the more I learn of Freemasonry, the more deception I see, both in small matters and in large ones.

2. What do you mean by that?

The public is completely deceived (at least, that is Masonry's intention and the attempt) as to the basic nature of Masonry, its teachings, and the "secret" things they do. In addition, there is vast and widespread deception of the public in terms of Masonic charities and how the public's money is spent. The worst example of this known to me is the Shrine. (See Chapter Five, *The Shrine: Islam in Freemasonry*.)

But, worse than this, by far, is the deception by Masonry of its own members.

3. In what way are the members of the Lodge deceived?

Freemasonry is, for the vast majority of its members, a lifelong succession of deceptions. Here are a few examples:

The first deception usually occurs when the prospective member, still only a prospect, is assured that Masonry is not a religion, is based on the Bible, will make him a better man, and, if he is a Christian, that the Lodge will make him a better Christian.

The initiations are deceptions in that the candidate is not told in advance of the death oaths, let alone their terrible content. The Ku Klux Klan is, in this way, much more honorable than the Lodge; for their oath is not a death oath, and the candidate is not only told of the oath in advance, he is required to read it, so there can be no misunderstanding concerning the obligation he is about to undertake.

The candidate is deceived in that he is told, just before taking his first oath of obligation, that there will be nothing in the oath that would conflict in any way with his personal religious faith. Here he is being lied to when the very taking of the oath is such a violation for a Christian or a religious Jew, forbidden both in the New Testament and the Old. And, this is to say nothing of its unscriptural content, promising to conceal other men's crimes and containing hideous penalties one writer has described as those "of which a common cannibal would be ashamed."[176] (See also Chapter Eighteen, "Death Oaths and Masonic Execution.")

Here, in the administration of the oath, is not only a deception but an enormous flaw in logic which leaps at me, yet it always seems to go unnoticed by those involved. When the Worshipful Master assures the initiate, just before administering the oath, that there will be nothing in the oath that will be in conflict with his personal religious faith, he hasn't asked the initiate what his personal religious faith is!

The initiate is deceived when led through his oath of obligation as a Master Mason and swears to uphold certain aspects of personal morality. The wording of the oath is extremely deceptive because of its very subtle immoral meaning.

He must swear never to "cheat, wrong or defraud" another Master Mason or a lodge of Master Masons, "I knowing them to be such." Sound good? It isn't. Note that this leaves the Master Mason free to "cheat, wrong or defraud" anyone else in the world, as long as it isn't another Master Mason, and even that will be alright as long as he doesn't know that he is dealing with a Mason.

Likewise, he must swear not to "violate the chastity of a Master Mason's wife, his mother, sister or daughter, I knowing them to be such." Sound honorable? It isn't. This leaves the initiate free to commit fornication or adultery with anyone else's wife, mother, daughter, or sister, or even those of another Master Mason as long as he is not aware of their Masonic connection. And, even a woman with a known Masonic connection is fair game if she has no chastity to violate.

These things are deceptive! These things are wrong!

The initiate is doubly deceived in the third degree (Master Mason):

(1) First, he is deceived in an emotionally cruel way by being led to believe that the initiation is finished when it is hardly begun. He takes his oath, gets his instruction, goes back to the preparation room, puts his clothes on, is given a "Jewel" (badge of office) to wear, and thinks he is a Master Mason. Then, he is taken back into the lodge hall, is rebuked by the Worshipful Master for wearing an "unauthorized jewel," is threatened, and is sent back to the preparation room. There he has to again remove his clothes, is again blindfolded, and is led by the cabletow back into the lodge hall for the traumatic remainder of the ritual.

(2) Second, he is deceived by being led to believe that the legend of Hiram Abiff involved in the second part of his initiation is historical and has no spiritual significance. Actually, the story he must reenact, portraying Hiram, is pure myth; worse than that, it is terribly significant paganism. The unwitting candidate is required to portray Hiram, not having

331

the slightest idea what it is all about, entering into the death, burial, and resurrection of the Masonic messiah, Hiram Abiff, who is actually Osiris, the Egyptian sex god.

Sound impossible? Unbelievable? Let's allow a few of Masonry's respected historians to speak for themselves:

"That part of the rite [third degree initiation] which is connected with the legend of the Tyrian Artist [Hiram Abiff] should be studied as a myth and not as a fact.... Outside of Masonic tradition there is no proof that an event such as is related in connection with the "Temple Builder" ever transpired and, besides, the ceremony is older by more than a thousand years than the age of Solomon.... It is thoroughly Egyptian" (Daniel Sickles).[177]

"It [the legend of Hiram Abiff] is thoroughly Egyptian, and is closely allied to the Supreme Rite [Third Degree] of the Isianic Mysteries [the pagan mystery religion of Isis and Osiris]" (Albert Mackey).[178]

"We readily recognize in Hiram Abiff the Osiris of the Egyptians" (A.T.C. Pierson).[179]

"Osiris and the Tyrian Architect [Hiram Abiff] are one and the same" (Daniel Sickles).[180]

It couldn't be much plainer than this, could it?

The initiate is deceived when he is promised that his initiation will bring him from darkness into the light; yet, he never quite gets to the light. From degree to degree he is promised light, he searches for it, and, finally, at the culminating moment in the Scottish Rite, the lecture of the Thirty-second Degree, he is told that the light is "out there somewhere" and that he must go find it on his own.

The Mason is deceived when his money is taken in dues and initiation fees and accumulated in vast sums by high-level leadership, where it is used for things of which the individual Mason is unaware, and of which most would not approve. Not only is the money used to provide luxurious offices, chauffeur-driven limousines, and memberships in expensive clubs for high-level leaders, but, much worse, it seems true that the power the money represents is ultimately applied to ungodly global political and spiritual matters. (See also Chapter Twenty Two, "Freemasonry, the New Age, and the New World Order.")

The individual Shriner is deceived when he solicits money at intersections for the Shrine's famous charities. He, with rare exception, believes sincerely that every penny of the money he collects in his bucket will go to build and operate those hospitals, when the truth is that as much as 98 cents of every dollar collected may go to pay for promotion, luxurious travel and parties for the top-level leaders.

The individual Mason is deceived as to the true nature of Masonry, believing that his degrees and lessons in the Blue Lodge are wholesome, moral, and based on the Bible; he doesn't know that he is participating in the rankest paganism. He doesn't realize, when he is required to kiss the Bible to seal his oath that he is, as former Mason Jim Shaw so eloquently expressed it, "kissing Jesus goodbye at the altar of Baal."

When you see the familiar film footage of Vice President Truman's swearing-in as president upon the death of Franklin Roosevelt, watch very carefully. You will see him complete the oath; and then he takes the Bible in both hands and kisses it, just as the Chief Justice of the Supreme Court reaches forward with his right hand outstretched, to shake hands with Truman. Truman ignores the hand of the Chief Justice, so intent is he upon kissing that Bible. He never did shake the Chief Justice's hand. This kissing of the Bible is *not* part of the swearing-in ceremony; but it is definitely part of Masonic ritual when taking an oath, and Harry Truman was a dedicated Mason. He was Past Grand Master of the Grand Lodge of Missouri, and was a master and teacher of Masonic ritual.

The individual Mason is deceived when he is taught, subtly and repeatedly, that he can earn his way to heaven by his moral living, good works, and obedience to his oaths.

4. Do the local Lodge leaders realize that they are deceiving their members in these ways?

They usually don't. If they would stop to think about what they say and do, as you and I are doing now, they would realize that they were being deceptive. But, for the most part, they are simply reciting the same things they have heard and said, over and over, assuming that they are right and good, and they, themselves, are in this way victims of this self-perpetuating deception.

5. Do the leaders at the very top realize that they are deceiving the rank and file members of Blue Lodge Masonry?

They definitely do realize that they are deceiving Masonry's rank and file, but I must qualify this statement. There are many of Masonry's high-level leaders, including Grand Masters and other officers at Grand Lodge level, who are themselves so deceived that they, like most officers in the Blue Lodges, believe that what they are doing is right. There is definitely a spiritual blindness that, in time, puts a veil over the minds of Masons so that things which are obvious to those of us on the outside, are hidden from them.

6. Can you give an example of this?

Yes. Again, I could cite many, but that would be unworkable, and one must suffice. The late Rev. Dr. Forrest D. Haggard was for many years pastor of the Overland Park Christian Church (Disciples of Christ) in Overland Park, Kansas. One year after his ordination in the Church of Christ in 1949, he was made a Master Mason. He was an ardent Mason from that day on, was Past Grand Master of the Grand Lodge of Kansas, and rose to the Thirty-third Degree. He received the Grand Cross, Scottish Rite Masonry's highest honor. He was the author of *The Clergy and the Craft,* a book of the Masonic view of the "harmony" between Masonry and the Church. He was, by anyone's standards, a prominent Masonic leader.

In the spring of 1993, in the midst of the intense conflict within the Southern Baptist Convention over Freemasonry, the *Scottish Rite Journal* published a series of articles by clergymen and others identified with "organized religion," all defending Masonry and declaring its compatibility with being a Christian. In the May issue, the inside front cover is a full color portrait of the Rev. Dr. Haggard, resplendent in his colorful clerical robe, and his is the lead article. His title is "Freemasonry and Religion Are Compatible," and the illustration of the article consists of a Christian cross, the crescent and star of Islam, the Star of David of Judaism, and, in the center, the Masonic square and compass. With my first glance at the story, I saw an obvious contradiction! I didn't have to think it over, I didn't have to meditate, ponder, or consult the major reference works. On its face, it was a total refutation of the entire premise of his article! It doesn't require a doctorate in systematic theology to realize that orthodox Christianity, Islam, and Judaism are hopelessly incompatible with one another, absolutely mutually exclusive! And, yet, Haggard, with all his learning and experience, is telling the world that the opposite is true. Any member of a Bible-believing Christian church (or, for that matter, a synagogue or mosque) should know that you can't have Jesus and Mohammed, or Jesus and rabbinical denials of Him, and you certainly can't have Islam and Judaism in the same camp! And, yet, the Reverend Dr. Haggard, with all his education and a lifetime in the pulpit, was saying that you can.

How can this be explained? How can we understand this? There are only two possibilities: either Haggard is a wicked, sinister, devious man, deliberately publishing propaganda intended to deceive and lead good men to everlasting damnation; or he is a sincere, nice guy who thinks that he is doing right—a good man, but terribly deceived. I choose to believe the latter and find no reason to doubt it. I see Rev. Dr. Haggard as a classic example of the self-perpetuating, deadly deception, even among prominent Masonic leaders.

7. But, are there also leaders at the top who do know that they are deceiving the rank and file?

Yes, and in this is found the most evil, most despicable, and most outrageous deception in all of Freemasonry's dark repository of lies. Blue Lodge Masons, the multitudes of the rank and file, make possible the entire Masonic system, with its hierarchy of degrees, orders, and offices. They give the money (an enormous amount when totaled) that makes it all possible, they give their loyalty (which is priceless), they believe in it, defend it, and go to their graves believing that they have been doing something honorable. Nothing could be farther from the truth, and, in this, they are deliberately and cynically deceived by those at the pinnacles of Masonic power. And those men, like the men at the pinnacles of power in Mormonism, definitely know the truth of what they are doing, and they must conceal and deny it in order to perpetuate the system.

8. How are the ordinary Masons deceived in this way?

Blue Lodge Masons are deliberately taught false meanings of the symbols in their degrees and lessons.

9. But, what is so important about the meanings of the symbols?

In Masonry, as in all occult sciences, symbols are not just important, they are the very essence of the teachings. Masonry describes its teachings as being a system "expressed in symbols and veiled in allegory." At the root, there is a basic love for big words in Masonry (their philosophers, it seems, can always be counted on to say "expectorate" or "masticate" when "spit" or "chew" would suffice); but, in this case, their words are instructive.

Their teachings in Blue Lodge consist primarily of lessons in morality and religion, including the explanation of the meanings of symbols. (See Chapter Seventeen, "Freemasonry and Its Symbols.") The meanings presented to the Blue Lodge Mason are, without exception, wholesome and healthy, stressing such things as responsibility, self-control, and fairness in dealing with others. Ah, but what about the part that their teachings are "veiled in allegory"? This means that the elements and words are symbolic, go to another level for more meaning, and are only suggested or hinted at by the teachings. The true meanings, in other words, are something else, something hidden, something other than what they are being taught.

10. But, what is so wrong with that; maybe the leaders just want the members to learn to think?

No, that's not all there is to it. The truth is much more sinister, much more evil, much more outrageously wrong. To fully grasp the significance of this, it is necessary to know that the temple of Solomon is the central symbol of Blue Lodge Masonry, ultimately representing Freemasonry's wisdom and knowledge. The portico (porch) of the temple was the outermost part, a place where the common people could go; the really important things took place on the inside. And, remember that the Masonic plan of salvation requires one to be enlightened, which means to gain the knowledge of the true meanings of the symbols.

In his classic Masonic reference work, *Morals and Dogma,* Albert Pike, Supreme Pontiff of Universal Freemasonry, Sovereign Grand Commander of the Supreme Council of the Thirty-third Degree, Mother Council of the World, etc., that preeminent Masonic authority, makes the following, amazing statement: "Masonry, like all the religions, all the mysteries, Hermeticism and Alchemy, *conceals* [emphasis his] its secrets from all except the Adepts and Sages, or the Elect, and uses false explanations and misinterpretations of its symbols to mislead those who only deserve to be misled; to conceal the Truth, which it calls Light, from them, and to draw them away from it."[181]

Does this sound outrageous? Unbelievable? It is. But, wait, it gets still worse. Pike goes on: "The Blue Degrees are but the outer court or portico of the Temple. Part of the symbols are displayed there to the initiate, but he is intentionally misled by false interpretations. It is not intended that he shall understand them; but it is intended that he shall imagine he understands them. Their true explication [explanation/meaning] is reserved for the Adepts, the Princes of Masonry. It is well enough for the mass of those called Masons, to imagine that all is contained in the Blue Degrees; and whoso attempts to undeceive them will labor in vain, and without any true reward violate his obligations as an Adept."[182]

If words have any meaning (and they do), this is the most outrageously wrong statement in all my knowledge of Masonry. Here this quintessential Masonic elitist is saying that the peasant masses of the Blue Lodge Masons are inside Masonry (the temple), but just barely (restricted to the common people's porch). This far, it is classic elitist snobbery, but not wickedness. But, then, he goes on to say that only a portion of the symbols the Mason must understand are shown to him, not all, though he thinks he has them all (this is worse). Then, he says, very plainly, that the Blue Lodge masses are deliberately taught false meanings. This is outrageous! This means that the occult adepts, the aristocracy of Masonry who believe that a true understanding of Masonry's symbols is required for enlightenment and acceptance in the "Celestial Lodge on High where the Great Architect of the Universe presides," deliberately withhold some of the symbols from the rank-and-file Masons and, much worse, condemn them to darkness by deliberately teaching them false meanings of the ones they do have!

I can't imagine anything more immoral! It is like teaching a gullible, trusting man that he can swim by merely wiggling his ears, adding that he must not move his arms or legs, and, then, dropping him in the ocean, miles from shore, with his hands and feet tied. The Masonic form of deception is worse, however, for it is an eternal dip in the sea. And, forever is a long time to be wrong.

Incidentally, Pike was prophetic in saying that those who might try to "undeceive" the peasantry of Masonry "will labor in vain." It has been my experience that most Masons, when presented with the truth about Freemasonry, even this statement by Pike, refuse to hear it. They just take offense, close their minds, and go on trying to learn to swim with their ears.

Endnotes

176 Martin L. Wagner, *Freemasonry, an Interpretation*, republished, (Grosse Pointe, MI: Seminar Tapes and Books, 1912), 556.

177 Daniel Sickles, *Ahiman Rhezon and Freemason's Guide* (New York: MaCoy Publishing Co., 1911), 195.

178 Albert Mackey, *Lexicon of Freemasonry* (Charleston, SC: Walker and James, 1852), 195.

179 A.T.C. Pierson, *Traditions of Freemasonry* (New York: Anderson and Co., 1865), 240.

180 Sickles, *Ahiman Rhezon*, 236.

181 Albert Pike, *Morals and Dogma*, rev. ed. (Washington, DC: House of the Temple, 1950), 104, 105.

182 Ibid., 819.

Freemasonry's influence in Mt. Liberty Baptist Church of Murphy, North Carolina, is apparent from the stained glass windows. This one is the Masonic symbol for the "All-seeing Eye" (the eye of Osiris).

Freemasonry and Its Symbols

A WISE MAN WILL HEAR, AND WILL INCREASE LEARNING ...
TO UNDERSTAND A PROVERB, AND THE INTERPRETATION;
THE WORDS OF THE WISE, AND THEIR DARK SAYINGS.
PROVERBS 1:5-6

1. What is the meaning of the Masonic symbol commonly seen on men's lapels, rings, autos, etc.?

Before I can answer that question, one thing must be made very clear: All Masonic symbols have two meanings. There is the outer, obvious meaning, which Masonry calls the *exoteric* meaning, and there is the inner, hidden meaning, which Masonry calls the *esoteric* meaning. As in all of Masonic symbolism, the true meaning is the hidden, esoteric one. Once again, we witness that spirit of elitism that runs through all of Masonry, seeing the Masonic rank and file as unenlightened, gullible, "vulgar" (common) masses compared to the elite, knowledgeable, wise "adepts."

Hear the words of Albert Pike: "The symbols of the wise are the idols of the vulgar, or else as meaningless as the hieroglyphics of Egypt to the nomadic Arabs. There must always be a common-place interpretation for the mass of initiates, of the symbols that are [by comparison] eloquent to the Adepts."[183]

When you ask about the Masonic symbol, you probably mean the familiar square and compass, with the G in the center. This is undoubtedly the most familiar of all Masonic symbols. Like all the other Masonic symbols, this one has both an esoteric and an exoteric meaning; to make things a little simpler, let's call them the apparent meaning and the true meaning.

2. What is the apparent meaning of the symbol?

It is the combination of the square, which teaches Masons to "be square" in all their dealings, especially with other Masons, and the compass, which teaches Masons to "circumscribe their passions," meaning to exercise self-control.

3. And, what is the meaning of the letter G?

Here is an excellent example of Masonic contradiction, yet one which seems to go unchallenged by Masons. In the first degree, the initiate is told that the G represents deity, that is God. But, in the second degree, he is assured that it represents geometry, "the first and noblest of science," by means of which the secrets of the universe may be discovered.

This was the only thing concerning Masonry which my father ever said to me, and he didn't bring it up. I once asked him what the G meant, and he answered simply, "God." This single word was the only word he ever spoke to me, or to anyone in my presence, about Masonry. And, for my father to lie was unthinkable; he was the most honest, honorable man I ever knew.

4. If these are the outer meanings, then what are the true, inner meanings?

At this point, in order to answer your question, we must plunge directly into the murky heart of the matter of Masonic symbolism, and, I promise you that, unless you already have some knowledge of it, this will be heavy going.

Since the true meaning of Freemasonry lies in its being descended from, and a revival of, the mystery religions of ancient Egypt, especially the worship of Isis and Osiris, the true meanings of its symbols are sexual. Shocking as this may be, I suppose that we shouldn't be surprised since the cult of Isis and Osiris was a fertility (i.e., sex) cult. In plain language, those pagans worshipped sex and reproductive power ("fecundity").

The sun, worshipped by nearly all pagan groups, represented life-giving sexual reproductive power, the active, male, generative force, with its rays penetrating the passive, female earth, causing new life to come forth. The personified image of the sun, usually worshipped in such fertility cults, was (and is) the phallus, the male reproductive organ, and their "worship" services were often orgies. It was to just such a scene that Moses returned when he came down off Mount Sinai after forty days with God. That golden calf wasn't just a sweet little baby cow, it was a bull calf with fearsome horns and conspicuous genital equipment. It was the personification of dominant male strength and reproductive power commonly worshipped in the fertility cults of the East.

Realizing these foundational facts, sickening though they be, the rest of the answers about Masonic symbols will make more sense to you, once your head ceases to spin.

5. Then, what about that basic Masonic symbol, the square, compass, and "G"?

According to Masonry's top authorities, the symbol represents sexual reproduction. The Compass represents the dominant, active, male "reproductive principle." The square, inverted, represents the passive, receptive, female "reproductive principle," and the relative positions, the one above and the other beneath, is no accident. The combination, thus arranged, represents the sun penetrating and impregnating the earth to bring forth new life. The Compass also represents loftier, spiritual functions, while the Square represents the more earthly, carnal, and base functions.

In the Entered Apprentice symbol, the points of the Compass are usually beneath the Square; in the Fellowcraft symbol, one point is usually above and one below; in the Master Mason symbol, both points of the Compass are usually above the Square, symbolizing complete dominance.[184] These changes seem to represent the progression of revelation, with the relative positions of the square and compass becoming increasingly correct as the three degrees are received.

It doesn't take much thought to see that not only are the Square and Compass symbols of the ancient worship of nature and sex, but that the female is in the decidedly inferior position.

6. Then, what about the letter "G" in the center; what is its true meaning?

The true meaning of the G is that of the phallus, the representation of deity in the Egyptian fertility cults.[185] In the legend of Osiris and Isis, Osiris was murdered and his body was cut into fourteen pieces and thrown into the Nile. Isis found and recovered all parts but one, the phallus, which had been eaten by a fish. So, she made an image of the phallus of Osiris, put it in the temple, and caused it to be worshipped as the image of the slain sun god. That's how it was supposed to have happened back in ancient Egyptian mythology, and Masonry has taken the legend, the symbolism, and the worship for its own.

Albert Pike explained that the G in English-speaking Lodges actually represents a corruption of the Hebrew letter *yod*. "The mysterious YOD of the Kabalah" is the "image of the Kabalistic Phallus."[186]

Who would ever have thought that this pagan phallic worship would be brought into our midst, right into wholesome, "Christian," Hometown, USA, and practiced by some of its finest citizens? I assure you that it was shocking news to me (and is also shocking news to most Masons!). That golden G that hangs on the wall above the head of the Worshipful Master in the East is a symbol of deity alright, but it is not the God of Abraham, Isaac, and Jacob.

7. And, are you saying that Masonic philosophers admit these things and even put them in writing?

Absolutely. In fact, there is so much of this material existing in mainstream Masonic literature that even the most serious students of Masonry will probably never read it all. And, probably 95 percent of all Masons will never read any of it.

8. Then, why don't all Blue Lodge Masons know these things?

Because, in the first place, they are taught the outer, wholesome meanings, and they believe them. Their minds are made up. After that, they never learn the true meanings because they don't read the materials for themselves. If they would find the source books and read them, they would know; but they almost never do.

9. Do you mean that these incredible things are true and that the Masons acting all this out don't know the true meaning of what they are doing?

Blue Lodge Masons, the heart and backbone of American Freemasonry, representing approximately 95 percent of all American Masons, are deliberately deceived as to the true meaning of their own symbols. That's right. They are deliberately deceived about the true meaning of the symbols, as we have seen already. (See Chapter Sixteen, "Freemasonry and Deception.") The vast majority of Masons, even dedicated ones, never go beyond the Blue Lodge, are never exposed to the true meanings, and go to their graves believing the lies. Even those who do go on into the higher degrees, where the occult, pagan nature of Masonry is much more apparent, seldom pay attention or think about it enough to realize the contradictions between Blue Lodge teachings and the truth. Their minds are already made up before they go into the higher degrees, and most of them really don't care about the lesson content; they just want to get the degrees, get it over with, join the Shrine, and get on with the parties and good works. All Thirty-Second Degree Masons receive a copy of Albert Pike's *Morals and Dogma* (or its equivalent), but the vast majority never open it.

10. But, why would the elite leaders at the top of the system want to deceive the rank and file in the Blue Lodge in this way?

I believe that the answer to this perplexing question is that the leaders know that if the rank and file knew the truth about the true nature of Masonry and the real meaning of the symbols, they would not only leave Masonry immediately, they would wish they had never joined it in the first place, which may compel them to dissuade others who are considering joining. I have never seen this explained in Masonic doctrinal writings or even dealt with as a matter of speculation, but this seems to me to be the only reasonable answer and, on this point, I have never been challenged by Masonry's defenders.

11. What other Masonic symbols are there in the Blue Lodge?

There are many, way too many to deal with here. They all have occult meanings about which the Blue Lodge Mason is never told. Besides the square and compass and the G, among the most important of these are the point within the circle, the right triangle (the forty-seventh problem of Euclid), and the all-seeing eye. Let me explain briefly the outer (false) meaning and the inner (true) meaning and cite Masonic authorities for each.

Point Within a Circle:

The Blue Lodge teaching is that the point represents the individual Mason, and the circle represents the limitations on his behavior because of his duties. In other words, he can't do just whatever he wants, he must be responsible and faithful to his responsibilities. The two parallel lines flanking the circle are supposed to represent "the Holy Saints John," in whose names the Blue Lodge is always opened. The true meaning is, of course, occult and sexual.

The point represents the phallus, the circle represents the vagina, and the juxtaposition of the one within the other represents sexual union.[187] The two parallel lines are actually the zodiacal signs of Cancer and Capricorn, where the sun is found during the summer and winter solstices, respectively. They were depicted by the ancient Egyptians as two rigid snakes, heads at the top. Are you thinking that I must be making this up? Well, let's hear from the Masonic authorities.

Albert Mackey: "Phallus, a representation of the virile member, which was venerated as a religious symbol .... It was one of the modifications of Sun worship, and was a symbol of the fecundating power of that luminary. The Masonic point within a circle is undoubtedly of phallic origin ...It is derived from Sun-worship, and is in reality of phallic origin."[188]

"The point within a circle is an interesting and important symbol in Freemasonry, but it has been debased in the interpretation of it in the modem lectures [the wholesome teachings in the Blue Lodge] and the sooner that interpretation is forgotten by the Masonic student the better it will be. The symbol is really a beautiful but somewhat abstruse allusion to the old Sun-worship, and introduces us for the first time to that modification of it known among the ancients as the worship of the phallus."[189]

"They [the two parallel lines] are said to represent St. John the Baptist and St. John the Evangelist; but they really refer to the solstitial points Cancer and Capricorn in the Zodiac."[190]

Albert Pike: "These two Divinities, the Active and Passive principles of the Universe, were commonly symbolized by the generative parts of man and woman ... the phallus and cteis [vagina], emblems of generation and production, and which, as such, appeared in the Mysteries. The Indian Lingam was the union of both, as were the boat and mast, and the point within a circle."[191]

"The Solstices, Cancer and Capricorn, the two Gates of Heaven are the two pillars of Hercules, beyond which he, the Sun, never journeyed; and they still appear in our lodges, as the two great columns—Jachin and Boaz—and also as the two parallel lines that bound the circle, with a point in the center."[192]

The Equilateral Triangle:

The usual, outer interpretation of the equilateral triangle in Masonic teaching is that of the Triune God. The hidden, true meaning is, again, pagan and sexual. With the base line down and the point up, it represents the male reproductive element, the phallus. With the base line up, it represents the female reproductive element, the vagina. When the two are combined to form the six-pointed star, they represent sexual union. Recalling that the square, with the point down, symbolizes the female principle, it is interesting and significant to realize that this square, with a line drawn across its upturned arms, becomes the inverted triangle, also symbolic of the female principle. Additionally, the compass above, with its points connected by a line, becomes the male principle, in union with the female.

The equilateral triangle, a basic symbol of deity, is subtly present in the Blue Lodge in that the Master, Senior Warden, and Junior Warden, the three officers whom Blue Lodge Masons must obey, are arranged in a triangle, and the candles around the altar, representing the sun, moon, and Worshipful Master, three representations of deity, are arranged in a triangle. Again, let's hear from the authorities:

Albert Mackey: "In the higher degrees of Masonry, the triangle is the most important of all symbols ... Among the Egyptians it was a symbol of universal nature, or the protection of the world by the male and female energies of creation [sexual power]."[193]

"Writing of the combination of two triangles, the one base up and other base down, Mackey further explains, "The interlacing triangles or deltas symbolize the union of the two principles or forces, the active and the passive, male and female...."[194]

J.D. Buck: "Back of this trilateral glyph [triangle, representing the Hindu fertility god trinity, Brahma, Siva and Vishnu] AUM, lies the philosophy of the secret doctrine.... Each deity in this triad was regarded as masculine, and as having his sakto or female consort which was represented by the triangle with its base upward, and is the symbol of the door through which every human being comes into the world."[195]

Albert Pike: "... the Triangle, to all Ancient Sages the expressive symbol of the Deity ... Osiris and Isis, Har-oeri, the master of light and Life, the Creative Word."[196]

The Right Triangle:

The right triangle, one containing a ninety degree angle, is an important symbol in Blue Lodge Masonry. It is illustrated in monitors and other Masonic sourcebooks with a rectangle drawn on each of its three sides, depicting what Masons call "the 47th problem of Euclid" (the theorem of Pythagoras). The meaning of the symbol taught in Blue Lodge is that Pythagoras was "initiated into several orders of priesthood, raised to the sublime degree of a Master Mason" during his travels through Asia, Africa, and Europe, and that during his sojourn in Egypt he discovered the relationship between the square of the hypotenuse and the other two sides, shouted "Eureka!" and sacrificed one hundred oxen (which Masonry, always in search of a bigger word, calls "a hecatomb" of oxen). The lesson of the "right-angle triangle," according to the Blue Lodge, is that a Mason is "to be a general lover of the arts and sciences."[197]

Ah, but let's hear what the authorities really say:

Albert Pike: "... the 47th problem of Euclid, a symbol of Blue Masonry, entirely out of place there, and its meaning unknown [to the Blue Lodge Mason] ... The perpendicular is the Male, the Base the Female; the Hypotenuse the [sexual] product of the two."[198]

"The 47th Proposition is older than Pythagoras. [Things are *never* ancient enough to suit Masonic philosophers!] We must suppose that the perpendicular is designed by them to represent the masculine nature, the base the feminine, and that the hypotenuse is to be looked upon as the offspring of both; and accordingly the first of them will aptly enough represent Osiris, or the prime cause; the second Isis, or the receptive capacity; the last, Horus, or the common effect of the other two."[199]

Albert Mackey: "Among the Egyptians it was the symbol of universal nature; the base representing Osiris, or the male principle; the perpendicular, Isis, or the female principle; and the hypotenuse, Horus, their son, or the product of the male and female principle."[200] (It seems to me that Dr. Mackey got his male and female symbols reversed here; but it could have been a typesetter's error, and we get the message anyway).

The All-Seeing Eye:
Ask any Mason what the eye within a triangle represents, and he will tell you that it represents the eye of God, seeing all, knowing all, and watching over us (or, he will say that he can't talk about it). And, either way, he will be sincere, for this is what he has been taught, and he believes it to be true. Ah, but here again, this is only the "exoteric" meaning and not the true meaning. The true meaning of this symbol is with Osiris, the

Egyptian sun and sex god, the actual object of worship in the Masonic Lodge. Let's again hear from the Masonic authorities:

Albert Pike: "The Blazing Star has been regarded as the emblem of Omniscience [all-knowing], or the All-seeing Eye, which to the Egyptian initiates was the emblem of Osiris, the Creator."[201]

Albert Mackey: "It is a very ancient symbol, and is supposed by some to be a relic of the primitive sun-worship.... An important symbol of the Supreme Being, borrowed by the Freemasons from the nations of antiquity ... the Egyptians represented Osiris, their chief deity by the symbol of an open eye, and placed this hieroglyphic of him in all their temples."[202]

12. But, do all these symbols and their meanings really matter; aren't they just a very minor part of Masonry?

In Masonry, symbols not only matter, it could be said the symbols are the only thing that matters—that symbols, in a sense, *are* Masonry. Symbols are the language of Masonry, and their meanings are its lessons. The old English lecturers and their American descendants define Freemasonry as "a system of morality, expressed by symbols and veiled in allegory."[203] And, Albert Mackey agrees that allegory and symbolism are the only things in Masonic teachings that really matter:

"All the legends of Freemasonry are more or less allegorical, and whatever truth there may be in some of them in an historical point of view, it is only as allegories, or legendary symbols, that they are important."[204]

ENDNOTES

183 Albert Pike, *Morals and Dogma*, rev. ed. (Washington, DC: House of the Temple, 1950), 819.
184 Ibid., 11, 850, 851.
185 Ibid., 15, 771, 772.

186 Ibid., 5, 757, 758, 771, 772.
187 There does seem to be something universal about this imagery. I can remember little boys demonstrating it with their fingers in a Kentucky school yard to impress the other little boys, and I can remember seeing, from a docking troopship, Japanese prostitutes doing exactly the same thing on a pier during the Korean War, advertising their trade.
188 Albert Mackey, *Symbolism of Freemasonry* (Chicago: Chas T. Powner Co., 1975), 352, 353.
189 Albert Mackey, *The Masonic Ritualist* (New York: MaCoy Publishing Co., 1903), 62.
190 Mackey, *Symbolism*, 352.
191 Pike, *Morals and Dogma*, 401.
192 Ibid., 506.
193 Mackey, *Symbolism*, 195, 361.
194 Albert Mackey, *Encyclopedia of Freemasonry,* rev. ed. s.v. 'Triangle" (Chicago, New York, London: The Masonic History Co., 1927), 801.
195 J.D. Buck, *Mystic Masonry* (Chicago: Chas T. Powner Co., 1925), 62.
196 Pike, *Morals and Dogma,* 861.
197 Mackey, *The Masonic Ritualist,* 129, 130; Henry Pirtle, The Kentucky Monitor (Louisville, KY: Standard Printing Co., 1921), 148,149.
198 Pike, *Morals and Dogma,* 789.
199 Ibid., 86-88.
200 Mackey, *Encyclopedia*, 800.
201 Pike, *Morals and Dogma*, 15, 16.
202 Mackey, *Encyclopedia*, 47, 48.
203 Ibid., 47.
204 Mackey, *Symbolism*, 315.

PART TWO — CHAPTER EIGHTEEN

Death Oaths and
Masonic Execution

BUT ABOVE ALL THINGS, MY BRETHREN, SWEAR NOT, NEITHER
BY HEAVEN, NEITHER BY EARTH, NEITHER BY ANY OTHER
OATH; BUT LET YOUR YEA BE YEA, AND YOUR NAY NAY,
LEST YE FALL INTO CONDEMNATION.
JAMES 5:12

1. Do Masons have to take blood oaths in order to join?

Yes, they definitely do. With the possible exception of an extremely important man who is made a Mason "at sight," it is not possible to become a Mason otherwise.[205]

2. Are these oaths also called "death oaths?"

Yes, the terms "blood oath" and "death oath" are synonymous. Although some may use the term "blood oath" to mean a ceremony where two people cut themselves in order to bleed and then mix their blood, becoming "blood brothers," that is not what is meant here. When I use the expression "blood oath" in relation to Freemasonry, I mean that the penalty for breaking the oath is bloodshed and death. For this reason, "death oath" is a better term, and the one I normally use.

353

I must make it clear, however, that these are not Masonic terms. The Masonic term for the oath of a degree or order is "oath of obligation;" the short form, commonly used, is simply "obligation."

3. Does a man take only one oath to become a Mason?

Oh, no. There is one death oath for each degree, plus one for the Shrine and any other "side" order or degree a man might seek. This means that a Master Mason (third degree Mason) has taken three such death oaths. A Thirty-second Degree Mason has taken at least thirty-two such oaths. Mr. Evans Crary Jr., Past Grand Master of the Grand Lodge of Florida, who wrote the foreword to Part Two of this book, was a Thirty-third Degree Mason, a York Rite Mason (Knight Templar), and a Shriner. When he turned away from Freemasonry to follow Jesus, he violated forty-four death oaths!

4. What is the nature of the oaths?

They are basically similar. Like everything else in Masonic ritual, they are very formal, wordy, and pompous, and each one involves some form of torture, mutilation, and death. In each oath, the initiate swears that he will not violate the secrecy of the degree, swears to certain peculiarities of the specific degree, and agrees that if he should violate his oath, especially the secrecy provision, he will allow himself to be tortured, mutilated, and put to death, always in horrible ways. One Christian writer expresses it well when he refers to their "horrid oaths and penalties of which a common cannibal would be ashamed." It is interesting to me that even the oath of the Ku Klux Klan is not a bloody, death oath. (Some of the oaths are in Appendix B at the back of this book.)

5. What is the purpose of these oaths?

The purpose of the oaths is to bind the initiate to the organization, to separate him from the outside world, and like any oath, to require him to take seriously the commitment he is making. Such declarations are almost as old as man; promises of any kind are considered to be binding even though they may subsequently be broken.

But, in Masonry, there is an added, unhealthy, unscriptural aspect: Fear. The oath of obligation is designed to instill fear in the initiate, to bind him even more tightly to the organization and to his promises of secrecy, with cruel cords of fear.

6. Do the oaths actually put the man in fear for his life?

Definitely, and this is especially true at first. After a man has taken the first oath (Entered Apprentice Degree), he is better prepared for subsequent degrees, and their oaths aren't so much of a shock; but, in each of the Blue degrees, the candidate is deliberately made to feel helpless and kept disoriented and confused, and with each oath, there is real fear. After a man has already taken ten or fifteen such oaths, the impact is lost, partly because he is not blindfolded and roughed up but also because repetition has taken the edge off the effect of their wording.

7. Can this have a lasting effect on the man who takes these oaths?

Definitely! I believe they are designed to do just that. Whether or not the originators of Freemasonry had this in mind, it is nevertheless true (and at least Satan had it in mind). These oaths (and other parts of the ritual) are a powerful means of mind control, and the men are extremely vulnerable when they take them. At first, they are made vulnerable by disorientation and fear. In the higher degrees, they are just as vulnerable to the occult, pagan poison in the oaths because of pride and deception. Their minds are open to suggestion and programming because they see themselves "moving up" and are proud of it, and there is openness to the lectures of the degrees because this is what they have sought. At the very first, they were vulnerable because of confusion, disorientation, and fear; later on, they are still vulnerable because of openness to what they are saying.

There can be, and often is, a powerful form of mind control accomplished (or at least set in motion) in the death oaths.

8. How do Masons, especially Christians, justify these terrible oaths?

They can't. There is no way to justify this affront to God, the violation of Scripture, and what it does to the men who take these oaths. Until recently, however, they were seldom called upon to defend them because most people didn't know anything about them.

In the 1830s and for decades thereafter, there was widespread public knowledge, at least among Christians, of the oaths and other negatives concerning Masonry. But, in time, that public awareness dissipated like morning fog, and, until the recent reawakening of the church to the realities of Masonry, hardly anyone outside the Lodge was aware of the oaths.

Now, when Masons are asked how they can justify the oaths, some will deny that they have taken any, for that admission would itself be a violation of their oaths. We can see here that one of the things wrong with the oaths is that the men must promise to lie if necessary. Some will answer that they "can't talk about such things." The rest will say that they took the oaths but didn't mean them literally, that they were "just symbolic."

To those who would say, "I didn't take seriously all that stuff about the mutilation and death, I really didn't mean it," I say that you should have meant it; you should have taken it seriously, because you sealed that oath with the words "So help me God, and keep me steadfast in the performance of same." It is a dangerous, sinful thing to "vow a vow" in God's name, call upon Him to make you able to perform it completely, and not mean it.

Some Masons try to explain the oaths away by saying, "Oh, the oaths aren't important in Masonry, they're just part of the ritual and really don't matter." They should remember the question in Blue Lodge ritual, part of the test an initiate must pass. The question is, "What makes you a Mason?" The correct answer is, "My obligation." So, according to the Lodge, the oath not only matters, it is the thing that makes a man a Mason! The same question and answer also appear in the higher degrees.

9. Who would carry out these executions that the oaths call for?

This is one of the most important questions that could be asked about these oaths, yet hardly anyone ever asks. People, including Masons, apparently don't think it through, but this is a terribly important point! The answer is, obviously, that other Masons must do it.

And, that leads us to something of extreme importance that remains un-discussed (at least, no one has ever pointed it out to me), and I believe that not one Mason in one hundred thousand ever realizes it. In taking these oaths, the Mason is also agreeing that he will torture, mutilate, and murder any other Mason who violates the oaths! He is promising to become a Masonic torturer and executioner, if need be. After all, **who else would do it?** Who, but other Masons acquainted with the man and his behavior, would even know that it should be done, let alone have any reason to do it? Who else would even know of the penalties? No one! Think about this, and especially if you are a Mason. There is no other possibility.

10. Has this ever happened? Have men ever actually been murdered for violating their Masonic oaths?

Yes, it has really happened. The first known Masonic execution in the United States took place in 1826 in New York. It may have happened before, in the 109 years since that first

Grand Lodge was organized in England, but the first one on record in this country was in 1826.[206]

11. Who was the victim, and how did it happen?

The murdered Mason was one Captain William Morgan of Batavia, New York, a veteran of the War of 1812, a Christian and a Mason of thirty years. Masonic versions of the story differ, of course, most of them denying any Masonic guilt, even denying that Morgan was ever a Mason, implying that he was motivated by his having applied for acceptance in a lodge and being rejected.[207] But, when one assembles all versions and all available evidence, the following story emerges.

Captain Morgan, a Mason for thirty years, became convicted about the immorality of Masonry, especially for a Christian. He wrestled with the question. It is never easy to renounce instantly something one has accepted, embraced, and served sincerely. He finally decided that he must not only leave Masonry, but that he should write a book exposing it to the public. After he had written the book, but before it was published, both he and his publisher, Col. David C. Miller, were kidnapped by Masons. Morgan was taken to Fort Niagara, New York, and held captive for three days in a powder magazine (today, we would call it an ammunition bunker) while Masonic authorities debated what to do with him. It was decided that he must die; lots were drawn to choose the killers, and three men drew the executioner lots. He was taken out into the Niagara River, bound, and weighted. He begged for his life to be spared, for the sake of his young wife and small children, but he was thrown into the river and drowned.

12. Did this become known right away?

Yes, it became known almost immediately. His publisher, Colonel Miller, escaped and initiated a search for Morgan, but he was not found. His body was found and identified a year later.[208] DeWitt Clinton, governor of New York, offered rewards for his recovery and the capture of the perpetrators. Even before the body was found, a groundswell of angry reaction began to rise, and within months, Morgan's book was published. This triggered a series of other such renunciations by prominent Masons, and there grew a tidal wave of angry public reaction which nearly swept Freemasonry off the American scene. More than 90 percent of all American Masons left the Lodge in anger, and the vast majority of American Lodges closed. Many Grand Lodges ceased to meet; the Grand Lodge of Massachusetts turned in its charter.[209] Numerous books, tracts, and sermons were written condemning Masonry for what it is. Prominent men of all Masonic orders and degrees deliberately went to court and saw to it that all the degrees, all the secrets, all the rituals were read into the court records and so became public knowledge. Since that time, there have been no Masonic secrets.

There was even an anti-Mason political party organized, with its members winning many political offices. In 1832, this party even ran a slate for president of the United States and carried one state (Vermont), this in spite of the fact that their candidate, William Wirt, was a Mason who had supposedly seceded. It was determined later that he hadn't and may have been planted by the Lodge in order to sabotage his own election. In 1836, William Henry Harrison ran for president as an anti-Mason and lost; he ran again in 1840 as a Whig and was elected. Many prominent political leaders, including President Millard Filmore, began their careers in the anti-Mason party. It was definitely no small thing.

13. Was anyone ever convicted of the abduction and murder of Morgan?

Yes, several men were convicted of kidnapping, assault and battery, and false imprisonment. But, no one was ever convicted of the murder, although two of the three made confessions late in life. Henry L. Valance, the man who actually pushed Morgan into the river, confessed to his physician on his deathbed.

14. Have there been any such Masonic executions since Captain Morgan?

Yes, but only God knows how many. Charles Finney, the great evangelist of the nineteenth century, himself a seceding Mason and author of an excellent exposé of Freemasonry, said that he could document more than twenty Masonic executions since Morgan. As recently as 1982, there appears to have been a Masonic execution that made the news. A man was found dead, hanging from Blackfriars Bridge in London, England. He was Roberto Calvi, member of the internationally powerful "P2" Lodge in Rome (the members of this lodge call themselves "Black Friars") and an international banker with strong ties to the Vatican. The story made a brief initial splash in the news and disappeared. According to close associates, Calvi was about to reveal incriminating things about powerful men, all members of the P2 Lodge. The inquest declared the circumstances of his death "open" (meaning that it could be murder rather than suicide). Masonic symbolism associated with the death pointed to European Masonry, and even the London police (most of them Masons themselves) theorized that it looked like a Masonic execution. The "Blackfriar's" name of the bridge from which his body, drugged before his death, was hanged is a further indication of this.

15. Could such a Masonic execution happen in this day?

The answer is "Yes." But I must make one thing clear: The vast majority of Masons are definitely not murderers, no matter what their rank or position of authority; they are, on the whole, good men. I believe that such a thing would be unthinkable, even in the highest levels of leadership of the York and Scottish Rites of Freemasonry. It is my opinion, however, that it is not unthinkable in the levels of international Freemasonry above them, that shadowy level of globalist power brokers who remain largely unseen by the rest of us. Again, the "Black Friars" of the P-2 Lodge of Rome is an example of this level, and the Calvi murder is probably an example of this. These men are capable of such an execution because of their amoral wickedness, cynicism, and greed.

In Blue Lodge Masonry in the South, men take the institution and their oaths of obligation very seriously. They believe that their "secrets" really are secret, and passions can run high. On many occasions I have had my life threatened; however, since I have never been a Mason I have violated no oaths of obligation. The probability of a Masonic execution for violating the obligations is near zero, and then I believe it would only be done by an unbalanced individual, and not sanctioned by any local lodge.

The fact that such things have happened and can still happen, however, is a powerful indictment of the Masonic system which lies to the rank-and-file Masons, takes their money, and makes merchandise of their loyalty.

ENDNOTES

205 Being made a Mason "at sight" is an unusual event, explained in chapter 11.

206 There is reason to suspect (and there are many who believe) that Mozart, a Mason who died very young, was poisoned for revealing Masonic secrets in his piece *The Magic Flute.*

207 Masons, in an attempt to discredit me, accuse me of the same thing. The fact is that I have never applied for acceptance by a lodge of any kind, including Freemasonry. In Morgan's case, how could he have written his book, exposing the secrets of Masonry if he had not been a Mason? Had he been "black balled" he would never have even entered the preparation room, let alone have knowledge of the Blue Degrees.

208 Although the body was somewhat decomposed, it had been significantly preserved by having been weighted and submerged under the cold water. The coroner's jury declared unanimously that it was that of Captain Morgan.

209 Henry W. Coil, *Masonic Encyclopedia* (New York: MaCoy Publishing Co., 1961), 57, 58.

Freemasonry, Presidents and the Founding Fathers

THOU SHALT PROVIDE OUT OF ALL THE PEOPLE ABLE MEN,
SUCH AS FEAR GOD, MEN OF TRUTH, HATING COVETOUSNESS,
AND PLACE SUCH OVER THEM....
EXODUS 18:21

1. Is it true that all U.S. presidents have been Masons?

No, this is definitely *not* true. It is very common for Blue Lodge Masons to say this when trying to justify Masonry, and most of them believe it. It is just another example of the tendency of people to accept favorable generalizations; it is comforting and requires no individual effort or thought. The truth is that Masons among the presidents of the United States are a distinct minority. And presidents who were devoted Masons are a tiny, almost nonexistent minority.

2. Then, how many U.S. presidents have been Masons?

Here, again, we have a problem in trying to nail down facts concerning things Masonic; it isn't always easy to know what it means to "have been Masons."

Ronald Reagan was not a Mason, although he was made an *honorary* one in his office at the White House during his second term. He was never inside a lodge hall and wouldn't have known what to do if he had gone. Not even Masonry's top leaders consider him to have been a Mason. He wasn't.

And, then there is the interesting case of Lyndon Johnson. He took the first degree as an Entered Apprentice and never went back. As a completely pragmatic, self-serving politician, it appears that Lyndon "got his card punched" so he would have Masonic support in politics and then left it all behind. This was most unusual—it is almost never done! A spokesman (docent) at the House of the Temple in Washington, D.C., headquarters of the Supreme Council of the Thirty-third Degree, Southern Jurisdiction, spoke of this as he showed me through the museum.[210] There was a large, decorative portrayal of American presidents who have been Masons, and it included Lyndon Johnson. He said that Johnson really shouldn't be counted as a Masonic president because of his having never gone beyond the Entered Apprentice degree. And, he isn't counted. In the book, *Masons Who Helped Shape Our Nation*, published by the Supreme Council of the Thirty-third Degree, Southern Jurisdiction, there is an illustration of Masonic presidents; and Johnson is not included.

3. Then, how many U.S. presidents are counted; how many have actually been initiated fully into the Masonic lodge?

There have been fourteen U.S. Presidents who have technically been Freemasons; but, as we will see, this figure depends on how we define a Freemason. Barak Hussein Obama is the 44th President of the United States, so only fourteen out of forty-four presidents have been Masons in any way. Even among these fourteen, several seem questionable. James Monroe received only the Entered Apprentice degree in 1775 and never proceeded beyond it through the Blue Lodge; his reasons are unknown.

William Howard Taft was made a Mason "at sight" in 1901 (which means that he was not initiated, a dispensation usually reserved for "important" people who will make Masonry look good). His record indicates that he was not active in any way, being a "member at large" of the Grand Lodge of Ohio.[211]

Warren G. Harding, another extremely pragmatic politician, received only the first degree in 1901 and didn't receive any other degrees for 20 years. After becoming president, he was quickly made a member of the Royal Arch and the Scottish Rite and was made a Knight Templar, all in a short period of time in 1921.

4. Have any U.S. presidents been serious Masons?

Yes, a few have been what I would call serious Masons. Andrew Jackson, although records are less than conclusive, is recorded as having been Grand Master of Tennessee. Gerald Ford certainly embraced Masonry; he was Thirty-third Degree in the Scottish Rite and was a member of the Shrine.

But, the one true Masonic president of them all was Harry Truman. He was a passionately devoted Mason and came up through the system, all the way from Entered Apprentice to being Grand Master of the Grand Lodge of Missouri, before he was either vice-president or president. He was recognized as a Master Ritualist (one who excelled in memorizing, teaching and directing the rituals) and Thirty-third Degree. He never joined the Shrine. While president, he frequented the House of the Temple at lunchtime to play the piano there, and sometimes this could interfere with business. On at least one occasion, it was necessary for a messenger to go to him and say, "Mr. President, would you please stop playing, or use the damper pedal; the Master is trying to open the Lodge [open a meeting of the Lodge there]."

5. But, what about the Founding Fathers of the nation; weren't they all Masons?

Definitely not. Here, again, is a commonly believed generalization that is simply not true. Ask any ordinary rank-and-file Mason, and he will probably tell you that all of them were Masons; and he will be sincere. But, the truth is that while some of the Founding Fathers were Masons, many were not.

The books and pamphlets published by Masonic sources would give one the impression that all those men in Philadelphia were running around in Masonic aprons, giving one another grips and passwords, laying Masonic cornerstones all over town, that the Constitutional Convention "met on the level and parted on the square," and that they opened and closed Lodge every time the Continental Congress met!

Such was simply not the case, Scottish Rite paintings and publications to the contrary notwithstanding.

6. Who are some of the Founding Fathers who actually were Masons?

The most prominent, and the one Masons will always hold up to "prove" that Masonry is good, is George Washington. Besides Washington, other prominent men who were Masons included Benjamin Franklin (who was also a Rosicrucian) and John Hancock, famed first signer of the Declaration of Independence. Franklin was a zealous Mason and one of the first members of the Philadelphia Lodge. Hancock was taken into an English lodge while visiting in Canada and later affiliated with a lodge in Boston. Although not in the category of "Founding Father," Paul Revere is a prominent man in American history; he was definitely a Mason and became Grand Master of Massachusetts.

But, they never mention Benedict Arnold. Masonic historians and propagandists, in painting their pictures and writing their stories of the Masonic Founding Fathers, never mention one of the most famous ones. Benedict Arnold, whose name became a synonym for "traitor," was a Mason and remained one for life.

7. What about Thomas Jefferson, Alexander Hamilton, John Adams, James Madison, Thomas Paine, John Jay, and the other Founding Fathers; weren't they all Masons?

No, they definitely were not, not a single one. In fact, not only these men, but most of the other Founding Fathers you may be able to think of, were not Masons.

Contrary to popular Masonic opinion, and some of what I can only call Masonic propaganda, Jefferson was never a Mason. John Jay was never a Mason. Not only was Thomas Paine not a Mason, but he wrote an essay in which he traced the origins of Freemasonry to ancient paganism, specifically to the Druids.

John Adams, Washington's vice-president and second president of the United States, was not only not a Mason, but was opposed to Masonry.

His son, John Quincy Adams, grew up in the colonies, was a young man during the revolution, was Secretary to Washington's Mission to Russia at age 15, and at age 27 was Washington's Minister to the Netherlands. Because of his youth one might question his credentials as "a founding father"; but he witnessed the Battle of Bunker Hill, held responsible positions in Washington's administration, was sixth president, and certainly played a role in shaping the nation. John Quincy Adams was a passionate anti-Mason.

Daniel Webster felt that the Masonic oaths of obligation should be against the law: "In my opinion, the imposition of such obligation as Freemasonry requires should be prohibited by law."[212]

John Marshall, the "Great Chief Justice," is one of those whom Masonry holds high as an example of Masons who made our nation. Like Washington, he became aware of the Masonic myths being spread abroad while he still lived. Before his death in 1835, he repudiated the practices of Masonry falsely attributed to him and stated that he had been in a lodge only once in the past forty years. He wrote, "The institution of Masonry ought to be abandoned, as one capable of producing much evil, and incapable of producing any good which might be affected by open means."[213]

8. But, how could George Washington have been a part of it; was he just not as pure as we have been taught?

Here was, for me, the most troubling thing in all of Masonry as I began to learn the truth about it, for he has always been a hero to me.

Washington is definitely their number one icon; when the rightness of Masonry is questioned, the very first thing most Masons will do is to tell you that Washington was a Mason. They continuously hold him up before the world as their great representative. That huge ziggurat (my term) that they have built just inside the capitol beltway in Alexandria, Virginia, towering over the countryside, is named for him (the George Washington Masonic National Memorial). The first thing with which the visitor is confronted upon entering that building is a huge inscription of a letter written by Washington, carved into the stone wall. Every lodge hall of any means has a portrait of Washington, wearing his Master's jewel and sash, and that same portrait frowns from the opening pages of most Masonic Monitors. Paintings of Washington in his Masonic apron and Master's jewel, wielding a trowel at cornerstone ceremonies, adorn much of Masonic literature, especially public relations materials.

The more I learned the ugly truth about Masonry, the more troubled I was with Washington's apparently being such an important part of it. So, I began to research Washington's Masonic history, and the more I learned of the truth about it, the more relieved I became. And, I can now say, the truth has not been told-not nearly. Yes, Washington was "as pure as we have been taught;" he was human, to be sure, but he was an honest, admirable, extremely honorable, Christian man of prayer and of exceptional devotion to the Lord.

9. Then, how can we explain his having been a Mason, especially such an active, prominent Mason?

The first thing we need to know is that he wasn't "such an active, prominent Mason." Those paintings of Washington in his Masonic regalia, which practically all Masons believe were painted from life, are spurious. Ask any honest historian (including honest Masonic historians), and he will tell you that Washington never sat (or "stood") for any such portrait. Every painting of Washington from life is known by collectors and curators; and the last one, undoubtedly the most famous, was never finished. Those paintings on lodge walls and in Masonic *Monitors* are apocryphal, painted after Washington's death.

Even while he still lived, there was growing impetus among Masons to canonize Washington and capitalize on his place "in the hearts of his countrymen." The Masonic myth of Washington's commitment to Freemasonry was growing, and Washington, nobody's dummy, perceived this and was troubled by it. It troubled him enough that he took pains to try to clarify the situation and set the record straight before he died.

He failed, but the fact that he tried is significant, and what little evidence survives is enough to establish that the generally accepted Masonic version of Washington's Masonic connection is so vastly overblown as to be simply untrue.

10. Well, was he, or was he not, a Mason?

As much as I wish it weren't true, the fact is that Washington was a Mason of the Third Degree—a Master Mason.

11. Then, doesn't that mean that he was not as pure as we have believed, that he was a part of all that is wrong with the unscriptural, Christ-denying Masonic system?

The answer is an emphatic "No!"

12. But how can this be, when you admit that he was a Mason?

Let me explain. First, I will summarize, and then I will be more specific.

As a young man George Washington, in his own words "joined an English Lodge in Fredericksburg, Virginia."[214] He apparently soon became inactive. We don't know the reason for this; it may simply have been that he was away so much, surveying boundaries in the wilderness and fighting England's battles with the French and Indians. But, whatever the reasons, he apparently soon became inactive and was never active again.

One foundational fact is much more important for purposes of our inquiries than is the extent of his zeal, or lack of zeal, for Masonry. That fact is that the institution of Masonry young George Washington joined in 1752, and which survived until fourteen years after his death in 1799, acknowledged and honored Jesus Christ as the Savior of lost mankind and offered prayers in His name. It was not until the formation of the United Grand Lodge of England in 1813 that Jesus was downgraded to the status of merely one of the exemplars, and prayers became "universal," making no mention of Him. Washington was dead fourteen years before American Masonry took on this Christ-denying character.

But, you may ask, wasn't the Masonry Washington joined still rooted in paganism? Yes, as much as I would like to deny it, the answer is "Yes." But, it was still a very different Masonry from that of Albert Mackey, Albert Pike, Joseph Fort Newton, Daniel Sickles, J.D. Buck, and Manly Palmer Hall—as different as night is from day.[215]

13. Did Washington ever renounce Freemasonry?

What scanty evidence there is concerning this question indicates a "yes and no" answer. There is no conclusive evidence that he completely renounced Masonry before he died; however, it is clear that he was at least ambivalent about Masonry, even the "Christian" Masonry that he knew. He took the trouble to correct, when he could, the growing Masonic myth about him.

He wrote to a friend, correcting the record, indicating that he was troubled over the stories "of my Presiding over the English Lodges in this country." He said that he presided over none and that he had not even been inside a lodge hall "more than once or twice within the last thirty years," quite a different story from that of the Masonic myth.[216] In addition, Washington, before his death, warned the nation to beware of secret societies.[217] He didn't mention Masonry specifically, but neither did he specifically exclude it.

Was Washington a dedicated, Bible-believing Christian? Absolutely! Was he an active, zealous Mason? Definitely not! Was he "founding master" of a lodge in Alexandria?[218] No, nor was he ever Master of any other lodge. Had he attended lodge since his induction as a young man? No. In his words he had not even "been in one, more than once or twice in over thirty years." But, did he ever renounce Masonry completely? There is no evidence that he ever did, although it is reasonable to assume that had he lived to see the changes and the murder of Morgan as John Marshall did, he would have joined Marshall in renouncing Masonry completely.

14. What about the other Founding Fathers who actually were Masons; did they belong to the same, Jesus-confessing Masonry as Washington?

Yes, they certainly did. And, this, I believe, casts an entirely different light on Masonry's claims on the Founding Fathers.

ENDNOTES

210 I want to be on record as saying that I have been treated very graciously when I have visited the House of the Temple, as I have been when dealing with them by phone or mail.
211 See chapter 9, "Freemasonry's Membership: How Men Join."
212 W J. McCormick, *Christ, the Christian and Freemasonry* (Belfast, Ireland: Great Joy Publications, 1984), 112.

213 Ibid., 111,112.

214 That is what such a lodge was called in early American history, because they were chartered by the Grand Lodge of England; a "Scottish Lodge" was one chartered by the Grand Lodge of Scotland.

215 Many a Mason over the years, including prominent leaders, has clung to his belief in the Bible as the inspired Word of God and in Jesus as unique Savior. All Masons didn't instantly abandon Jesus and His Word as of the day in 1813 when the Grand Lodges of England united. For example, even that zealous and influential Mason, Rob Morris, founder of the Order of the Eastern Star, while Grand Master of Kentucky, suspended a lodge Master for saying that the Bible was "a good sort of history, but not sacred." Morris was later overruled, and the suspended Master restored; but, this is an eloquent illustration of the lack of unity, and theological complexities, involved in American Masonry, especially in the first, formative century.

216 Letter from Washington to Reverend G. W. Snyder, dated 25 September 1798.

217 Finney, Charles G., "The Character, Claims and Practical Workings of Freemasonry" (Southern District of Ohio: Western Tract and Book Society, 1869), 222.

218 Letter from Washington to Reverend G. W. Snyder, dated 25 September 1798.

Freemasonry and Divided Loyalties

NO MAN CAN SERVE TWO MASTERS: FOR EITHER HE WILL HATE
THE ONE, AND LOVE THE OTHER; OR ELSE HE WILL HOLD TO
THE ONE, AND DESPISE THE OTHER.
MATTHEW 6:24

1. Is there any conflict between a Mason's oaths of loyalty to the Lodge and his other commitments of loyalty?

Yes, and this conflict is one of the most insidious things about Freemasonry. By taking his oaths of obligation, the Mason puts himself in the position of swearing to put his loyalty to the Lodge above all other commitments of loyalty.

2. How then can the Mason justify this?

He can't. If he thinks about it, he finds himself in the position of having to violate one commitment or the other. Whatever he does, it will be wrong; but most Masons don't seem to realize this.

3. What do you mean by that?

Let me answer with an example. If a Mason has sworn to conceal the secrets of all brother Masons and is subsequently called as a witness in a trial in which another Mason is accused of a crime of which the first Mason has knowledge, what does he do? He is sworn in court to tell the truth, "So help me God"; yet, he has already sworn, in the Lodge, to conceal the man's secrets, including crimes, and he swore, "So help me God" there also. What can he do? He must violate one solemn oath or the other. If he lies in court, he violates his oath as a witness (and, incidentally, is guilty of perjury); if he tells the truth, he violates his Masonic oath.

There is definitely a problem of divided loyalty.

4. Do Masons actually swear to conceal the crimes of other Masons?

Absolutely. They cannot become Masons any other way. It is his oaths of obligation that make him a Mason, and his oaths include such swearing, both in the Blue Lodge and in the higher degrees.

5. Just what kind of vows do they make about concealing other men's crimes?

In the Master Mason degree (third degree), the climactic degree of the Blue Lodge, the candidate must swear to conceal the secrets of a brother Master Mason, "murder and treason excepted." This, of course, binds the Master Mason to conceal all other wrongdoing, including rape, mayhem, stealing, etc. In some places, the words "and this left to my own discretion" are added, thus making it "honorable" to commit perjury concerning, or to otherwise conceal, even murder and treason.

In the higher degrees, such as the seventh (Royal Arch) degree, he swears the same oath but adds the words, "without exceptions."

6. Do these men really mean these things?

They should, for they swear, "So help me God, and keep me steadfast in the performance of the same." But, to answer your question directly, I would say that many really mean them, while many are really just going through the motions. But, even those who don't mean them must have lingering thoughts that trouble them. If they don't, they certainly should.

7. Can this become a problem in the courts?

Yes, obviously, and here is one of the most ominous aspects to Freemasonry's long arm. If a man is accused of a crime, and a witness called against him is a Mason, this witness is obviously on the horns of a divided loyalty dilemma. He must either perjure himself for the accused, or tell the truth and violate his Masonic oath.

If even one member of the jury is a Mason, he is obliged to "go to the relief" of the accused. If the accused gives the Masonic sign of distress, the jurist is obliged to vote for acquittal and, at the least, hang the jury.

8. What is this sign of distress?

This signal is called the "Grand Hailing Sign of Distress." It is supposed to be given only when a Mason believes his life is in danger (as it well could be in some court trials) and consists of standing, raising the arms above the head, lowering them to the sides in a certain way, and saying, "Oh Lord my God, is there no help for the widow's son?"[219] I should also point out that the accused doesn't have to interrupt court by standing up to shout this out; it can be conveyed in subtle ways.

9. When this distress sign is given, what is another Mason supposed to do?

He is supposed to help the man, so long as there is a better chance of saving the distressed man's life than of losing his own. Here is an obvious flaw in Masonic selflessness but still a real problem in a court case.

10. Are there any judges who are Masons?

Definitely, and here is the gravest problem of divided loyalties. The Masonic judge has sworn on a Bible (or on some "holy book") to lie if necessary in order to protect other Masons. Yet, he has also sworn on a Bible to uphold and defend the Constitution and to render fair and impartial judgment of all who come before him accused. What does such a Masonic judge do when the accused standing before him is another Mason? Here is an impossible case of divided loyalty, and its implications go to the very heart of our system of law and justice.

11. Does this ever happen?

Yes, it is bound to happen. In spite of Masonry's claims to exalted morality, Masons do wrong things all the time, like the rest of us, and sometimes they get caught. Even if such a situation occurs only rarely, it is still a problem. Even if the judge, prosecutor, defense counsel, or witness tells the truth and does the honest thing, the problem of divided loyalty still exists.

12. What happens in such a case?

There are many possibilities, all the way from a Masonic policeman who decides not to write another Mason up, through a prosecutor who decides not to prosecute, an investigator who "loses" evidence, to a judge who renders biased judgment, or a governor who grants unjust clemency.

And, all these things have happened at one time or another.

13. Has it happened recently?

Such events must be everyday affairs in this country with overloaded police departments and courts, and with thousands of crimes committed every hour. Most, of course, go undiscovered or unreported. Of those reported, most don't make the news. However, there was a case in New York state a few years ago that seems to be a valid example. A Mason, director of a boys' camp for the Order of DeMolay, was accused of sexually abusing a number of the boys under his care. The parents filed criminal charges. When the case was finally tried, the defense counsel, the prosecutor, and the judge were all Masons. The charges were reduced to a relatively meaningless misdemeanor, and the camp director walked away with a gentle slap on the hand.

Another case that made the news in recent years took place in Cincinnati, Ohio. A man, a Mason, accused of installing an illegal wiretap, testified that he subsequently went to a superior who was also a Mason and asked him to get the charge dropped or reduced. During the conversation, the accused man showed his Masonic ring and asked, "Is there no help for the widow's son?" The charge was reduced.[220]

14. Do these Masonic vows produce divided loyalties in other areas of life?

Yes, and the possibilities are almost limitless. Officers and noncommissioned officers in the armed forces are supposed to perform their duties fairly and impartially and are sworn to uphold and defend the Constitution against all enemies, foreign or domestic. Many of the men are Masons, and some of the women belong to the Eastern Star or some other adoptive Masonic group. Can they live up to their commitments as military leaders and to their Masonic vows of favoritism at the same time? No. It is not possible, and this is a growing morale and discipline problem, one with enormous potential for ill.

15. Do all Masons take vows that produce divided loyalties?

Definitely. Beginning with the very first degree, each oath binds the man more tightly to the Masonic system and separates him still more from the rest of the world. In fact, in some of the higher degrees, a man swears allegiance to his order or rite above all other commitments, bar none. Think of the implications of that!

Even in the Blue Lodge, doctrinally, the man is required to obey the Worshipful Master and the wardens, and, in some jurisdictions, this applies "no matter what."

16. Can it be a problem within the home?

Absolutely, and this is probably the most serious area in which commitments to Masonry can undermine relationships. The moment a Mason takes his first oath of obligation, he is separated from his wife, in very real ways, for life. Not only has he become bonded by death oath to something of which she can never be a part, but she has become "profane," and if she asks him certain questions about what he does in the Lodge, he must lie.[221] Divided loyalties? Yes, serious ones, where there should be none, and they have no remedy except for him to leave the Lodge.

ENDNOTES

219 Like so much in Masonry, the details of this sign vary from one place to another, but this sign is everywhere considered to be one of Masonry's most important "secrets."

220 Associated Press, "Masonic Loyalties enter testimony in wiretap trial," *Cambridge, Ohio Daily Jeffersonian* (8 December 1989): 5.

221 To get an idea of what it means to be classified as "profane," read 1 Timothy 1:9, 10.

Freemasonry and the Occult

WHEN THOU ART COME INTO THE LAND WHICH THE LORD
THY GOD GIVETH THEE, THOU SHALT NOT LEARN TO DO
AFTER THE ABOMINATIONS OF THOSE NATIONS.
THERE SHALL NOT BE FOUND AMONG YOU ANYONE THAT
MAKETH HIS SON OR HIS DAUGHTER TO PASS THROUGH THE
FIRE, OR THAT USETH DIVINATION, OR AN OBSERVER OF TIMES,
OR AN ENCHANTER, OR A WITCH, OR A CHARMER,
OR A CONSULTER WITH FAMILIAR SPIRITS, OR A WIZARD,
OR A NECROMANCER. FOR ALL THAT DO THESE THINGS
ARE AN ABOMINATION UNTO THE LORD.
DEUTERONOMY 18:9-12

THE SECRET [HIDDEN] THINGS BELONG UNTO
THE LORD THY GOD.
DEUTERONOMY 29:29

1. Does Freemasonry have anything to do with the occult?

Yes, in fact, one might fairly say that Freemasonry is the occult. Many of Masonry's leading men have been occultists, and Masonry is often defined as an occult science. But, let me hasten to explain; I can say this on the basis that virtually every kind of occult activity is carried on among Masons with no rebuke from the hierarchy, and the occult philosophy runs through the entire system.

2. What do you mean when you say that the occult philosophy runs all through Freemasonry?

First, we must be sure that we understand the terms. It is clear to me that the occult permeates Masonry, from top to bottom; but, for you to understand me, we must first define the word "occult."

3. Then, what does *occult* mean?

The word "occult" is derived from the Latin words "occultus" meaning "secret" and "occulere" meaning "to conceal or hide." The word "occult" then, refers to things hidden or concealed. It covers an enormous amount of murky, dark, sinful, and destructive things, but it basically has to do with the seeking of hidden things, such as secret knowledge and understanding that most people don't possess.

4. What's wrong with seeking knowledge?

Nothing is wrong with seeking knowledge; it is not only right and reasonable, it is scriptural. God gave us the ability to think and learn, and He expects us to use it. What is wrong with seeking knowledge within the occult is two-fold: the means used are wrong; and the purpose is usually wrong.

5. What do you mean by that? Why does it matter how and why we seek knowledge?

In occult things, the means are usually, if not always, supernatural avenues, forbidden by God; so the "how" of it matters very much. What also makes the occult so wrong is the "why" of it. The occult is all about power—not the power of God, but supernatural power possessed and exercised by the person, by tapping into and controlling the power of (demon) spirits.

6. But, some people get involved in the occult in order to help others. How could this be wrong?

Because wrong is wrong. Although people sometimes dabble in the occult for unselfish reasons, it is still wrong—a thing forbidden by God. And He forbids it, incidentally, for the same reason that He forbids all other sin: it hurts us. Satan may grant certain knowledge or supernatural powers to those who seek him, but he always exacts a very high price.

7. Then, what are these occult things that God forbids?

As I said, there are so many things included under the generic term "occult" that a definition is difficult. It can be summed up, perhaps, as a seeking after hidden things, especially secret or hidden knowledge and the supernatural power it bestows. However, God is nowhere in it; it resides completely in Satan's dark and deadly realm.

8. What are some examples of occult activities?

Examples of the occult include all forms of divination (seeking hidden knowledge), such as fortune telling, astrology, psychic phenomena and spiritism (consultation with spirits for information and power). It also includes magic, witchcraft, and charming.

A useful way to keep it straight is to remember that anything supernatural not done in Jesus' name, or which does not glorify Him, is done with Satan's power and is therefore very wrong and very dangerous. There are only two sources of supernatural power and experience: The Holy Spirit of God, and evil spirits. It helps to remember that the Holy Spirit will only glorify Jesus, never anyone else. (See John 16:13-14.) People with occult Satanic powers glorify themselves, Satan, or both. This is true of the latter group, even when they are good people attempting to do good things, and do not realize that they are doing something wrong.

9. But, what does all that have to do with Masonry?

You might say that it has everything to do with Masonry. You see, in Christian circles, "occult" is a negative word representing sin of the worst kind, an abomination to God. But, in Masonry, "occult" is a positive word, one that denotes favor. The favor which the occult enjoys in Masonry is an outgrowth of the basic nature of Masonry. We have already seen that the true (esoteric) meanings of Masonry's lessons and symbolism are hidden from the masses, and can be known and possessed only by the elite few. Keep that always in mind.

Masonry, according to the claims and teachings of many of its authorities, is an occult science. This is a valid claim because all of esoteric ("true") Masonry is a search for enlightenment, a seeking for the knowledge that will purify and redeem the seeker, and give him access to supernatural knowledge and power.

10. Do any leading Masons admit being involved in the occult?

Definitely. Among Masonry's most authoritative teachers and philosophers are occultists of international reputation. Until his death in recent times, Manly Palmer Hall was one of the leading occult teachers in the world. He is the author of "Lost Keys of Freemasonry" and other influential Masonic books, and a Mason who received Masonry's highest honors. Manly Palmer Hall is a man of whom the Masonic institution is extremely proud.

11. But what, specifically, is it that ties Masonry to the occult?

Masonry defines itself as a search for "light." This means enlightenment, the acquisition of knowledge that redeems and empowers. And, typical of the occult world, one is to go on searching (through many lifetimes, actually, by means of reincarnation) and, yet, never really find the light. You see, the occult has no absolutes; one must go on seeking and seeking.

In the occult world, based on evolution of man and his gradual perfection by his own efforts, fulfillment is in the seeking, not the finding. This search for the secret knowledge goes on and on, as the individual becomes gradually perfected, redeeming himself.

At risk of being repetitious, I must point out that God and His gracious provision for our redemption through Jesus are nowhere in all this seeking. It is all something that we must do for ourselves.

12. Then, what is this knowledge they seek that is so important?

First, they seek knowledge that supposedly once was possessed by men in some past age when things were supposed to have been much better. Somehow, this knowledge was lost (they usually blame it on the Christians and Jews), and now things are crummy. So, there is this endless quest to rediscover that knowledge and wisdom, a "treasure" they often call "the hidden wisdom of the ancients."

They often think the keys to this lost wisdom are to be found in little green people in flying saucers, or buried beneath the sea in Atlantis, somewhere in the mountains of Tibet, or in the mind of some witch doctor worshiping bats in a Mexican cave. Such are places I would never think to look for anything useful, but occultists seem irresistibly drawn to them.

So, in the occult world, the endless search goes on for "the lost and hidden wisdom of the ancients."

13. What is the other knowledge that occultists seek?

Second, and much more important, they seek the "lost" knowledge of "the ineffable name." This exalted Masonic language really just means that they want to know the name of God. And this search, which is at the very heart of Masonry's occultism and the subject of its most important legends and symbols, is the essence of witchcraft: man's rebellion against God.

14. What do you mean? What does God's name have to do with witchcraft?

It is a basic principle of occultism in general, and witchcraft, in particular, that if one can learn the true name of a spirit, one can have that spirit's power. So, if knowing the true name of a minor evil spirit can give you that spirit's power to see into the future, think what it would mean (to the occult mind, at least) to possess the knowledge of the true name of God! You would have God's power—all of it! You could be "like the most High" and maybe even bump God and take His place in the universe. As you probably know, this stupid idea is what caused all of Satan's interpersonal problems with God and created the Kingdom of Darkness.

So, there you have it. This is serious stuff—and the heart of all the occult search for "lost" knowledge and the power it brings. They believe that the "lost word," the "ineffable name" of God, was known to the priesthood of the pagan mystery religions back in those ancient "good old days," but Christians, Jews, and other narrow-minded bigots stoned or burned all the magicians who knew it, so it was lost. Things have been downhill for mankind ever since, so their story goes, and the search to rediscover it by the occultists goes on.

15. You surely don't mean that people who go see a fortune teller, call the psychic hotline, or play with a ouija board are trying to obtain God's power!

Of course, I don't mean that. But, all who even dabble in such apparently harmless occult matters are entering the same dark world of the occult, forbidden by God. And, incidentally, such "harmless" dabbling isn't harmless; it can be deadly. Many a dedicated occultist began his dark career with the "harmless fun" of the Ouija Board "game" or a visit to a palmist or astrologer, seeking hidden knowledge.

16. But how do you know that Masonry is so involved in the occult?

I assure you that it is no secret. Anyone who cares to inquire will know this. Masonry's authorities are unanimous in the belief that Masonry is a search for that "light," that lost wisdom, that beauty and perfection of the ancient priesthood and its religious system, the mysteries of Isis, Osiris, Mithras, Ashtoreth, and Baal. Their books, lectures, and degrees are full of it.

If I quoted 1 percent of it here, it would be too much for me to write and too much for you to read. But, I will include a few and rest my case.

Author's Note: When confronted with statements like these that follow, Masonry's spokesmen will say that what prominent Masonic scholars and philosophers have said and written are not necessarily "official" declarations of Masonic doctrine; and, of course, that is true. However, the writings of these men are taught as truth to Masons in their lodges, their degrees and Masonic bodies. In the not-so-distant past, Scottish Rite candidates in some jurisdictions were required to demonstrate at least a working knowledge of Pike's *Morals and Dogma* in order to receive the 32nd Degree. These men are venerated in the Masonic world, and are held up before the Craft as exemplars. For more on these honored men and their writings, see Appendix D, "Masonry and Its Controversial Authorities."

And now, with this said, let's hear some of what they have to say to us.

Albert Pike:

"Though Masonry is identical with the ancient Mysteries, it is so only in this qualified sense: that it presents but an imperfect image of their brilliancy, the ruins only of their grandeur...."[222]

"The Occult Science of the Ancient Magi was concealed under the shadows of the Ancient Mysteries ... and it is found enveloped in enigmas in the rites of the Highest Masonry."[223]

J.D. Buck:

"There is a Grand Science known as Magic, and every real Master [Mason] is a Magician. Feared by the ignorant, and ridiculed by the "learned" the Divine Science and its Masters have, nevertheless, existed in all ages.... Masonry in its deeper meaning and recondite mysteries constitutes and possesses this Science, and all genuine initiation consists in an orderly unfolding of the natural powers of the neophyte, so that he shall become the very thing he desires to possess. In seeking Magic, he finally becomes the Majus." [224]

"The tradition of the Master's Word, of the power which its possession gives to the Master [Mason]; the story of its loss and the search for its recovery; the tradition of the Ineffable Name...."[225]

"The Freemason is ... the nearest to the Ancient Wisdom.... He may dig deeper and find not only the Keystone of the Arch, the Ark of the Covenant, the Scroll of the Law, but, using the spirit concealed in the wings of the Cherubim, he may rise ... and, meeting Alohim face to face, learn also to say 'I am that I am'!"[226]

"But this is the Ineffable Name, which every Master [Mason] is to possess **and become** [emphasis mine]."[227]

Joseph Fort Newton:

"The three really great rituals of the human race are the Prajapati ritual of ancient Hinduism, the Mass of the Christian Church, and the Third Degree of Masonry. ... they testify to the profoundest [sic] insight of the human soul—that God becomes man that man may become God."[228]

Manly P. Hall:

"When the Mason learns that the key ... is the proper application of the dynamo of living power, he has learned the mystery of his Craft. The seething energies of Lucifer are in his hand."[229]

I rest my case.

ENDNOTES

222 Albert Pike, *Morals and Dogma,* rev. ed. (Washington, DC: House of the Temple, 1950), 23.

223 Ibid., 839. It can be revealing to see what words people capitalize; the capitals are in the originals.

224 J.D. Buck, *Mystic Masonry*, 3rd ed. (Chicago: Chas T. Powner Co., 1925), 34.

225 Ibid., 132, 133.

226 Ibid., 45.

227 Ibid., 62.

228 Joseph Fort Newton, author of *The Builders* and *The Religion of Freemasonry* quoted in Henry Pirtle, The Kentucky Monitor (Louisville, KY: Standard Printing Co., 1921): xx.

229 Manly P. Hall, *The Lost Keys of Freemasonry* (Richmond, VA: MaCoy Publishing Co., 1976), 48.

Freemasonry and Mormonism

EVEN SO EVERY GOOD TREE BRINGETH FORTH GOOD FRUIT;
BUT A CORRUPT TREE BRINGETH FORTH EVIL FRUIT.
MATTHEW 7:17

1. Does Mormonism have anything to do with Masonry?
Yes, it does. As a matter of fact, Mormonism cannot be separated from Masonry.

2. Why do you say that Mormonism can't be separated from Masonry?
Mormonism is, in many ways, a doctrinal sprout that grew from the stem of Masonry. In their rituals and terminology, there are many similarities.

3. How are Mormonism and Masonry similar?
They are similar in terms of being secretive about their internal affairs, and both are cultic in many ways.

4. What do you mean, that both are cultic? Are you saying that both Mormonism and Masonry are cults?
I didn't say that, but it is probably true. Mormonism certainly qualifies as a cult by almost anyone's definition, and

many students of cults classify Masonry as one also. At the very least, both are what I call cultic.

5. What do you mean by the word "cultic"?

By cultic, I mean that they have at least some characteristics of cults; both Mormonism and Masonry have at least some cultic traits.

6. What are the traits considered to be cultic?

Characteristics considered by most observers to be cultic include secrecy; exclusion of outsiders from the fellowship of the group; complete commitment to an essential doctrine; possession of a secret doctrine, secret rituals and practices from which the public is excluded; blind obedience to a leader (or leaders); the belief that only that group has the truth; the belief that to leave the group will bring destruction of some kind, especially eternal damnation; and shunning, or outright persecution by the group, of any person who leaves. There are others, but these make the point clear.

7. Is Masonry a cult?

Most students of cults classify Masonry as a cult. As a matter of fact, Jack Harris, a former York Rite Mason and Past Master of his Blue Lodge, wrote a book on Masonry from the Christian point of view, and he titled his book *Freemasonry: the Invisible Cult in Our Midst.*

8. Is Mormonism a cult?

There seems to be unanimous agreement that Mormonism is a cult (except, of course, among Mormons). On most authorities' lists of cultic traits, Mormonism would score 100 percent.

9. But, except for the fact that both Masonry and Mormonism have some characteristics of cults, what do they have to do with one another?

When Mormonism was in its first, formative years, Joseph Smith, Mormonism's founder and first "prophet," and his brother Hyrum both became Masons. It seems that they became Masons in a somewhat unorthodox way (Joseph took all three Blue Lodge Degrees in one day!); nevertheless, they did it and learned the Blue Lodge rituals.[230]

10. So Joseph Smith and his brother Hyrum became Masons; is that all that makes Masonry and Mormonism "inseparable"?

Oh, no. There is much more. It was not long after Joseph Smith became a Master Mason that he got the "revelation" for the secret temple ceremony. The rituals of the Mormon Temple are so similar to those of Blue Lodge Masonry that there can be no doubt that Joseph lifted most of it directly from the rituals of the Lodge.

11. What is it about the two rituals that are the same?

Many things are alike, but a few examples will suffice. Elements apparently stolen by Joseph Smith include the presentation and wearing of an apron, whispering of "secret" information "on the five points of fellowship" (i.e., "foot to foot, knee to knee, breast to breast, hand to back, mouth to ear"), similarities in the oaths of obligation, the penalties and penalty signs for each, and the symbolism of the square and compass, which must be embroidered in significant places on their "magic" underwear.[231]

12. Are these similarities in ritual and symbols all that tie Mormonism to Masonry?

No. Not only were both Joseph and Hyrum Smith Masons, but so was Brigham Young, Smith's successor. As a matter of fact, the first five presidents of the Mormon Church (its first five "living prophets") were Masons.

13. Is Masonry strong in Mormonism today?

No, at least it is not on the surface. As a matter of fact, for a long time the Mormon hierarchy has forbidden Mormon men to become Masons.

14. Why have the Mormon leaders not wanted their men to be Masons?

Because of the secrecy that prevails in Mormonism, it is difficult to know. It appears that they feared the divided loyalty that would almost certainly result.

15. What about the leaders themselves? Are any of them Masons?

There has been ongoing "talk" to the effect that, while forbidding Masonry to their rank-and-file members, the top Mormon leaders have not only been allowed to join the Lodge, but that it has been required. The persistent rumor has it that those selected for the highest levels of Mormon leadership have been taken out of their home areas, been secretly taken into the lodge, and then returned home. I believe this, but, obviously, it would be almost impossible to document.

16. What if a man who is already a Mason wants to join the Mormon Church? What happens then?

Until recently, such a man had to resign from the Masonic Lodge. Now, however, this requirement has been dropped. A Mason can join the Mormon Church and go right on being a Mason; so, it appears that Mormon men could now join the Masonic Lodge. The bonds between Masonry and Mormonism seem to be growing ever tighter.

17. But, back to Joseph Smith; didn't the Masons have something to do with his death?

Yes, and that is an extremely interesting part of his story. Joseph Smith, with his brother Hyrum, died in a blazing gun battle while they were being held in jail. According to most accounts, when Joseph saw that he had no chance, he gave the "Grand Hailing Sign of Distress," lifting his hands above his head and crying out, "Oh Lord, my God, is there no help for the widow's son?" Apparently there was none, for he was immediately shot down. It is also interesting that part of those in the crowd shooting at Joseph and Hyrum were their "brother" Masons.

18. So, is that the story of Mormonism's ties with Masonry?

Yes it is, except for one fascinating thought. Joseph Smith joined the Masonic Lodge in 1842 at the very peak of public knowledge and awareness of the wrong things concerning Masonry. When almost everyone knew about Masonry, especially the things wrong with it, when the rest of the nation was leaving the Lodge and rising up against it, Joseph rushed, eyes wide open, to embrace and join it! This, I believe, says a great deal about the character of Joseph Smith, as well as that of his brother Hyrum.

ENDNOTES

230 Joseph and Hyrum not only became Masons, but, almost immediately, there was trouble. Because of the Mormon practice of polygamy, most Grand Lodges took a stand against admitting Mormons, so the charter for Joseph's lodge was withdrawn. This didn't stop him, though; he just got busy and organized his own, chartering them himself. The ensuing conflicts over Mormons in Masonry lasted many years, and, in a sense, continue to this day.

231 Not all Mormons are initiated into the Temple rites. Those who are initiated are given "magic" underwear, which must be worn next to the skin, night and day, to protect the wearer from harm. It would certainly appear that in the case of Joseph and Hyrum Smith, it didn't work.

Freemasonry, the New Age, and the New World Order

IF THEREFORE THE LIGHT THAT IS IN THEE BE DARKNESS,
HOW GREAT IS THAT DARKNESS!
MATTHEW 6:23

1. Does Masonry have anything to do with the New Age?

Yes, like Mormonism, the New Age and Masonry are definitely interrelated. As a matter of fact, they seem, to me, to be inseparable.

2. How, then, is Masonry related to the New Age?

First, I suppose, it is necessary to again define some terms. "New Age" is about as difficult to define precisely as "the occult." We are bombarded today with New Age propaganda, news items (sometimes it isn't easy to tell these two apart!), reports, and advertisements. We all have some awareness of it, but, if asked to define it, we would find it difficult to know how to answer.

Perhaps, for our purposes, the best way to think of the New Age is as a philosophical and religious system that had its modern beginnings at least a century ago. It is basically occult and esoteric (Yes, those terms also describe Masonry), featuring a great deal of spiritism (e.g., contact with familiar spirits, automatic writing, spirit guides, etc.). It is a "feel good" movement, denying such unpleasant matters as sin, judgment, and hell. It recognizes a coming "messiah" whom they call Lord Maitrayah (variously spelled, but pronounced "Mah-tray-ah") who soon will come to Earth from "somewhere out there" to usher in the "New Age" (hence the name) of Aquarius, an indefinite period of peace, good will, prosperity, and all-around happiness.[232]

Sounds too good to be true, doesn't it? Well, it is too good to be true; there is no truth in it.

3. Is there a New Age headquarters or a leader of the New Age?

No, there isn't. There are many New Age groups with their individual leadership structures, and they cooperate a good deal, but each one wants to be in charge, and there is no central authority, recognized as such by all the others. Of course, behind the scenes, they all have one "central authority" whose name is Lucifer, but most of them don't realize it.

4. Do they recognize Jesus as Lord?

Definitely not; like Masonry, New Agers take the usual vapid line that Jesus was a wonderful man, a "master teacher" (remember the Rainbow Girls and their burial service?), a "highly evolved avatar," and so on. But, they deny His uniqueness as "the Way, the Truth, and the Life." They, like Masonry, humanize and water down their concept of Jesus Christ, and, like Masonry, they don't seem to realize that a watered-down Jesus is no Jesus at all.

5. In what other ways is the New Age related to Masonry?

In doctrinal ways, they are closely related, being basically occult in their beliefs. Both teach about the "Christ Spirit," a spark of deity in everyone that merely needs to be discovered and released, the perfectibility of man, the basic goodness of man, etc. Doctrinally, Masonry and the New Age are in the same big bag. You see, the New Age, as we know it, isn't more than about one hundred years old. One of its first leaders was Madame Blavatsky, founder of the Theosophical Society. She was a close friend and frequent companion of Albert Pike, author of the ultimate Masonic classic, *Morals and Dogma*, and virtual father of modern, occult Freemasonry.[233]

6. What other ties, if any, are there between Masonry and the New Age?

Until a few years ago, the official journal of the Supreme Council, Thirty-third Degree, Southern Jurisdiction, by far the most influential Masonic periodical publication, was called *The New Age*. The name was changed to *Scottish Rite Journal*, apparently because of "bad press" from Christian writers and broadcasters. Masonry has in no way distanced itself from the New Age occultism and world view; but, by changing the name of the magazine, that relationship isn't so readily apparent.

7. Who is Alice Bailey?

During her busy lifetime, Alice Bailey was spiritual successor to Madame Blavatsky as the most prominent New Age writer and teacher of more recent times.

8. Was Alice Bailey in any way connected to Masonry as Madame Blavatsky was?

Yes, she was, at least in her heart and in her relationships with Masonry's "mystics," such as the late Manly P. Hall. As a matter of fact, she wrote something extremely significant about Masonry and the New Age in one of her many books. In *The Externalisation of the Hierarchy*, Mrs. Bailey wrote that there would be three primary channels for preparing the American people to receive the New Age messiah, Lord Maitrayah: the traditional ("dead") church system, the schools (educational system), and Freemasonry. She said that Masonry would be thus valuable and effective because it understands the occult principles of initiation and the mystery religions.[234] It appears that she was right.

9. How does all this fit in with the New World Order?

Here, again, is a rather broad, amorphous phenomenon. To try to clarify and neatly define the New World Order is like trying to stack soft jello, but we must try.

The New World Order is a generalized goal or dream of a great many powerful people, a future time when there will be a one-world government and a one-world banking system, all with an elite group in charge. Most of them also want a one-world religion, and that will be New Age paganism, the worship of nature, fertility, and sex.

Sound familiar? It should because I just described the ancient mysteries, that old wisdom religion, that old veneration of the phallus and all that goes with it.

Yes, we are back to Freemasonry and the revival it seeks; we have come full cycle.

10. Is Lucifer included anywhere in all this New Age/New World Order/Masonic paganism?

Absolutely, and he is there right in the middle of it all. He is clever enough to stay in the shadows (that is, after all, a natural environment for him), but he has been there all along, guiding, inspiring, orchestrating the whole thing.

11. Are any of Masonry's leaders worshipers of Lucifer?

Yes, of course; there are many among the "mystics" and occultists of Masonry, as a private matter of personal conviction. But, it seems also to be true that Masonic leaders at the very top (that strange, misty level of international power and influence that we might call "the illuminati" level of power) are all Luciferians and sincere ones. They believe that Lucifer is really the "good" god, that Jehovah was jealous of Lucifer's beauty and wrote a bunch of lies about him in the Bible, that someday Lucifer will come out on top, and, when he does, his followers will be with him.

12. What is meant by "illuminati"?

The term merely means, "the illumined, or enlightened ones," the ones who have found "the light" and, as a result, have the knowledge and wisdom to be competent to control the rest of us. They really believe that they know best what we need and think they should have the power to run it all.

13. Is "the Illuminati" an organization with a leader, a headquarters, etc.?

No, not as such, at least not to my knowledge. In the late eighteenth century, there was such a society of European elitists organized by Adam Weishaupt in Bavaria. Their "illuminism" was well received in certain Masonic circles, spread even to America, and was a matter of great concern to George Washington, who warned the nation against it in his last years of life. Today's power brokers are Weishaupt's philosophical descendants, no doubt, but they have built their own organizations (e.g., Trilateral Commission, Council on Foreign Relations, Bilderbergers, etc.).

14. Do any of Masonry's leaders and writers ever come right out and admit that they serve Lucifer?

That is seldom done. We get occasional glimpses of this in their writings, but, for the most part, they have always seemed aware that it would do them more harm than good to come out in the open.

We saw the statement by Manly P. Hall in chapter 20, in which he spoke of the Mason's possessing "the seething energies of Lucifer." Albert Pike wrote, somewhat cryptically, of Satan in *Morals and Dogma*: "Lucifer, the Light Bearer! Strange and mysterious name to give to the Spirit of Darkness! Lucifer, the Son of the Morning! Is it he who bears the light, and with its splendors intolerable blinds feeble, sensual, or selfish souls? Doubt it not!"[235]

This can only be described as an attempt to "set the record straight" on poor, misunderstood, maligned Lucifer and to give him the honor he deserves .

15. What is Palladian Masonry, or the Palladian Rite of Masonry?

I can only say very, very little about Palladian Masonry, for there is only very, very little known about it. It may not even exist, but there are some indications of Masonic rites, above the level of the Thirty-third Degree, of the most closely kept secrecy. If they exist, their members are carefully selected from those of the highest Masonic degrees and bodies, their theology is Luciferian, and their secrecy sealed with assurance of certain death for any would-be seceder.

As I said, there may not be such a group (or groups), but, if there is, three things are certain:

1. These men would possess enormous power, both financial/political power and Satanic spiritual power, the true "Maji" of which Manly P. Hall, J.D. Buck, and other occult Masonic philosophers wrote;
2. It would be virtually impossible to learn much about it, for to betray it would be to die; and,
3. Such a Masonic Rite, if it exists, is at the very center of dreams of and plans to establish, global government and bring in the New Age and the New World Order.

16. Where is all this leading?

The forces of darkness are more out in the open every day. These people mean business. It appears that the End-time conflict is approaching showdown time, and we can no longer find any middle ground. I believe that we will all be either a part of a great End-time falling away, or a great End-time harvest of souls and we no longer have any latitude for dabbling in evil, with one foot in light and the other foot in darkness.

The choice is clear. The choice is ours. The time is now.

ENDNOTES

232 As a matter of fact, some years back the New Age people bought a full-page ad in the *New York Times*, announcing that he had already arrived on earth. He is yet, however, to make public appearances.

233 There is some evidence that Pike and Madame Blavatsky were lovers. They were frequently seen, arm in arm, around Washington during Pike's long tenure as Sovereign Grand Commander, Supreme Council of the Thirty-third Degree, etc.

234 A. A. Bailey, *Externalisation of the Hierarchy* (New York: Lucis Publishing Co., 1957), 510-512.

235 Albert Pike, *Morals and Dogma*, rev. ed. (Washington, DC: House of the Temple, 1950), 321.

Part Two – Epilogue
RECENT DEVELOPMENTS

Freemasonry has existed for nearly 300 years with little change to its foundational principles. In the early years of the 21st Century, however, even those are being stirred and buffeted by the winds of change. At the time of publication of *Please Tell Me*, declining membership was a significant problem. Since that time declining numbers have continued, and represent an increasingly critical problem. This problem is driving significant changes. In 1993 the average age of an American Mason was 70.[236] At the time, it was projected that if membership continued to decline at the current rate, by 2020 there would not be enough members left to sustain the Craft in the U.S.; for all practical purposes, American Freemasonry would cease to exist. The membership problem has been, and is, an ongoing topic of discussion, from rank-and-file Masons to Masonic leaders, from coast to coast. It is increasingly an agenda item in closed meetings and open conferences, and has been publicly expressed in the *Scottish Rite Journal*.[237]

Prince Hall (Black) Masonry

Prince Hall (black) Masonry, heretofore scorned and rejected as "clandestine" (illegitimate) by traditional (white) Masonry, is now finding increasing acceptance. Prince Hall Masonry is now officially recognized by the Grand Lodge of

New York as legitimate Freemasonry. Some lodges in other jurisdictions are receiving black initiates. To some extent this changing policy concerning blacks is the result of changing attitudes in the culture at large; but a significant factor in changing attitudes and policies, toward Prince Hall Masonry and blacks as individuals, is the growing crisis of falling membership numbers. Meanwhile, as we have seen, Prince Hall lodges have taken whites and Hispanics into overseas military lodges, and it appears that Masonic racial segregation has a diminishing life expectancy.

A Need for Radical Change

Behind the Lodge doors, conferences have taken place as every conceivable move was considered in the effort to reverse the trend of Masonry's disappearing membership. Recruiting, which had never been officially approved, but which had been going on in various forms for a long time, has been intensified. In some places recruiting has been done openly, but to no avail; the downward trend in membership has continued.

A radical change was needed. And, in the year 2000, a radical change took place—and it shook Freemasonry to its roots!

Enter the Shrine

Historically, to enter the Shrine it has been necessary first to be a Master Mason in good standing in the local lodge. In addition to this, it has been necessary to complete either the Scottish Rite and become a Thirty-Second Degree Mason, or to complete the York Rite and become a Knight Templar. Then, after six months in either the Scottish Rite or the York Rite, a man was eligible to apply to the Shrine. This is the way it has been, ever since the Shrine found its present form.

More than the rest of the Masonic world, however, the Shrine was feeling the pain of falling numbers. Fewer men were entering the Blue Lodge and becoming Master Masons. That means that fewer still were going to the trouble and expense to enter the Scottish or York Rite and take the higher degrees. The meaning of this for the Shrine becomes obvious and inevitable: there, at the far end of the manpower pipeline, so to speak, the number of applicants for the Shrine was becoming a trickle.

With membership drying up, all of Masonry was feeling it in terms of finances and hope for the future. In the Shrine where, historically, huge amounts of money have been received, and where so much money has been spent on their own conventions, parties, travel and luxurious perquisites, the financial pain was particularly acute.[238]

Something Had to Change

The handwriting was on the wall, and there was no solution in sight. The long-range prospect for Freemasonry as a whole was gloomy. For the Shrine, one might say, the situation was desperate. So, in July 2000, seeing no other way to avoid extinction, the Imperial Council changed Shrine law to allow any Master Mason in good standing to go directly into the Shrine, by-passing the higher degrees of the Scottish and York Rites.

The result was a resurgence in applicants for the Shrine; but the effect on the Scottish and York Rites was the opposite! In the past, a significant number of the men in the York and Scottish Rites have gone through the higher degrees only as a means of joining the Shrine. Suddenly, with men going from the Blue Lodge directly into the Shrine, numbers of applicants for the Scottish and York Rites dropped still more.

A Potentially Fatal Wound for the Higher Degrees

The leadership in the Scottish and York Rites could not believe what they were seeing and hearing. They were shocked! They had been "blind-sided" by the Shrine! They were betrayed! And they were furious.

So, what could they do? Because the Shrine had lowered its standards in order to gain more applicants, and in so doing had pulled the rug out from under the York and Scottish Rites, it appeared that the only thing for them to do was to lower their standards also. Recruiting became increasingly aggressive, and standards were lowered, in order to make it easier for applicants to enter the Lodge and obtain degrees. The various rites, bodies and jurisdictions competed with one another in making the process easier and the standards lower. In the sense of standards and meaning for the new Masons, as the Craft struggled to stay alive, there was only one way to go: Down. Easier standards led to still easier ones, and as the standards for obtaining those degrees were lowered, the degrees had less meaning for those who obtained them. In terms of philosophical and religious meaning, the entire Masonic system seems to be in an irreversible tailspin.

A Revealing Event in Pennsylvania

A remarkable (and revealing) example of this took place at various locations in Pennsylvania on October 10th 2010. This event was sponsored by the Grand Lodge of Pennsylvania, and was advertised and promoted in advance as "A One-Day Masonic Journey."

The one-day event featured cooperation by the Blue Lodges, the Scottish Rite, and the Shrine. In one tightly scheduled day, men were rushed through a series of events which resulted in their becoming Master Masons, Scottish Rite Masons of the 32nd Degree, and Shriners—all in one day! All of it was done in eleven hours, and "seeker-friendly" took on an entirely new meaning. All that the applicants had to do was to bring their check books. Prior to the melt-down of traditional Freemasonry triggered by the Shrine, the "honors" that those Pennsylvanian men received in eleven hours, and with nothing at all required of them, would have taken several years. It would also have required a lot of travel, many hours of instruction, study and testing, and a significant amount of memorizing. The Masonic ancestors of those "instant Masons" would not be able to believe what took place in that one day in Pennsylvania in the Fall of 2010. They simply would not have been able to believe it! If Albert Pike were raised from the dead and told of it, he would probably put on all of his regalia, medals and gold chains, and commit ritual suicide before the altar in the Temple Room!

What significance could any of those "accomplishments" have for those "instant Masons"? The obvious answer is "little-to-none."

The Odd Couple: Serious Masonry and the Shrine

Freemasonry as it exists today can trace its beginnings to 1717 in a London pub. Of course, some Masons claim that the institution dates from 1,000 BC and the building of Solomon's Temple; and others even stretch it back to Adam and Eve. But let's stick with the facts here.

Freemasonry (for purposes of this comparison, I will call legitimate Masonry "serious" Masonry) will soon celebrate its 300th birthday. Although its standards for entry and the earning of its degrees have been lowered considerably in the last 50 years because of reduced interest on the part of men to apply, serious Masonry has traditionally held high standards for entry and for earning its various degrees. In the Blue Lodge, at least, much study and teaching have been required, with considerable memorizing of its catechism and obligations.

The Shrine, by comparison, is a relative newcomer to the Masonic world, having been organized in 1872 in New York. From the beginning the Shrine has refused to be serious about anything but fun; and, from the beginning, serious Masonry has viewed it with disapproval and scorn. Although the Shrine attached itself to serious Masonry, serious Masonry viewed the Shrine as the illegitimate child at the family reunion. In the Grand Lodge of England, Mother Lodge to American Masonry and the rest of the world, the Shrine is seen as literally illegitimate. Masons under authority of the Grand Lodge of

England are forbidden to enter the Shrine, and this upon pain of dismissal.

In its early days the Shrine appears to have been only tolerated by serious American Masonry. But the Shrine leaders had a truly brilliant idea: to build and operate free hospitals for crippled children—who could disapprove of a group which does that? As a result of an increasingly favorable image of the Shrine in the eyes of the public, serious Masonry has gradually become more and more tolerant of it. This tolerance, it seems, was the result of the realization that serious Masonry could use the building and operation of the children's hospitals by the Shrine to bolster its own image. The Shrine, it seems, was adopted into the world of serious Masonry because, in terms of public relations, the Shrine is the Masonic goose that lays the golden eggs.

Today there is even a Shrine room at the House of the Temple, and a large Shrine exhibit in the George Washington Masonic National Monument, that looms over the beltway in Alexandria, Virginia. And so, as serious Masonry has progressively taken unto itself a portion of the Shrine's "good works" benefit, the Shrine has concurrently taken unto itself a portion of serious Masonry's respectability.

It will be a crowning irony if the Shrine, the viper nurtured in serious Masonry's bosom for its own advantage, should ultimately deliver the bite that kills serious Masonry.

But, one must wonder, even if the new Shrine policy should bring about the death of the York and Scottish Rites, surely the Blue Lodge would survive. But maybe not. Since the Shrine may ultimately kill the higher degrees by taking Masons straight from the Blue Lodge, what is to prevent them from abandoning that policy, and taking applicants right off the street? This could—in fact, probably would—eventually cause the death of the Blue Lodge. And I won't be surprised if they do it.

The Last One Standing—a Crowning Irony

It would be a crowning irony if serious Masonry in the U.S. should sicken and die. The "step child" Shrine would be the last one standing, heir to it all, thumbing its nose at the serious Freemasonry of Pike, Mackey, Newton, and Hall, while it grows in numbers and wealth, and the collective memory of a long-ago connection between real Masonry and the Shrine fades into a blank screen.

It could happen.

ENDNOTES

236 Thomas M. Boles, 33rd Degree, "Where Do You Do Your Shopping?, *Scottish Rite Journal* (July 1993): 53.
237 S. Brent Morris, 33rd Degree, "Unite in the Grand Design," *Scottish Rite Journal* (May 1990): 46-49.
238 John Wark and Gary Marx, "Shrine," *The Orlando Sentinel* (29 June 1986, A-1; 30 June 1986, A-1; 1 July 1986, A-1).

Female "Brothers" in the Lodge

One of Freemasonry's fundamental tenets is, and has been since the beginning, the exclusion of women. This is one of the "Ancient Landmarks" of Masonic law. The original charges compiled by Anderson and Desaguliers, modern Masonry's founders, were explicit in this regard, saying, "the persons admitted members of a Lodge must be good and true *men*,... no bondmen, no women" (the emphasis on "men" is in the original).

If you ask most Masons why they don't accept women in the Lodge, they will be stumped for an answer; they may say something like, "Well, uh, we just never have." If you ask one of the few who study and enquire, the justification usually given goes something like this: "Well, since speculative Masonry is based on the customs of the old operative stonemason guilds, and since their work was so strenuous, lifting and moving those big stones, women couldn't perform it, and couldn't belong to their guilds. The same tradition has carried over into speculative Masonry, and that's why we don't take women into the Lodge." Both of these men, incidentally, will be sincere. The truth, however, is probably something darker.

The true reason for Masonry's historic exclusion of women is probably rooted in the occult. Since the true (esoteric, hidden) meaning of Masonry's rituals and symbols is phallic, based on the ancient worship of the sun, and since its rays were thought of as phallic, penetrating the passive {female} earth from above and causing the earth to conceive and bring forth new life, and since the phallus is a piece of reproductive equipment God didn't issue to women, they couldn't participate in this symbolic impregnation. This being the case, a woman cannot be made a Mason, simply because a woman cannot be made a man.

There seem to have been a few bizarre exceptions to the "no women" rule. The first known was Elizabeth St. Leger (later Mrs. Richard Aldworth). As a young girl in Ireland, during Masonry's earliest days, her father and brother were members of a lodge that met in her home (other versions have it meeting in a tavern, etc). At any rate, she overheard, one night, a meeting and its ritual, she was fascinated, and listened regularly until discovered by the men. When they discovered her they considered killing her; but they decided instead to initiate her into the Entered Apprentice Degree, swearing her to secrecy, under penalty of death, with the usual oath of obligation. Portraits of her, in Masonic apron and badges, have hung in many Irish Lodge halls ever since.

There are other stories of women who became Masons, in one way or another. Henry Wilson Coil, in his "Masonic Encyclopedia," lists a total of seven; but he doesn't necessarily accept them all as historically valid. Catherine Sweet, of Kentucky, was apparently the only woman ever to be a Master Mason. Her story is similar to that of Elizabeth St. Leger in that she arranged to spy on the initiations of all three Blue Lodge Degrees, learned them "better than the men," and, when discovered, was taken in herself and "initiated, passed and raised," becoming history's only female Master Mason.

PART TWO — APPENDIX B

Death Oaths

Since the very first revelations of the secrets of Freemasonry, the oaths of obligation have been probably the number one lightning rod of negative public reaction. And, I suppose, they should be. This was true during the high tide of anti-Masonic feeling and activity following the murder of Captain Morgan in 1826; and it has been true in the latter part of the Twentieth Century, and the early part of the Twenty-First century during the "second awakening" to the true nature of Freemasonry.

As you already know, there is one of these horrible oaths of torture, death, and mutilation for each degree. Even some of the adoptive Masonic orders for the "gentler sex" have such oaths. So, to reproduce them all, or even a tenth of them, here, would be too much for both of us. I wouldn't want to write them, and you definitely would not want to read them. And, even if you did read them all, you would soon lose your awareness of which one you were reading, for they sound so much alike.

Here are some of the penalty portions of commonly earned degrees. You will see the similarities, as well as the barbarity, of these "solemn obligations" imposed by this supposedly civilizing, character-building Masonic system. You need to know that the oaths, like all the rituals, will vary in some small details from one jurisdiction to another; however, they are remarkably uniform when one considers all the possibilities for modification and distortion, with thousands of lodges spread clear around the world. Examples follow.

"All this I most solemnly, sincerely promise and swear, with a firm and steadfast resolution to perform the same, without any mental reservation or secret evasion of mind whatever, binding myself under no less penalty than that of having my throat cut across, my tongue torn out by its roots, and my body buried in the rough sands of the sea, at low-water mark, where the tide ebbs and flows twice in twenty-four hours, should I ever knowingly violate this, my Entered Apprentice obligation, so help me God, and keep me steadfast in the due performance of the same" (Entered Apprentice, or First, Degree).

"Binding myself under no less penalty than that of having my breast torn open, my heart plucked out, and given as prey to the birds of the air and the beasts of the field should I ever knowingly violate this my Fellowcraft obligation. So help me ..." (Fellowcraft, or Second, Degree).

"Binding myself under no less penalty than that of having my body severed in twain [this is just exalted Masonic wording for "cut in two"], my bowels taken from thence and burned to ashes, and scattered before the four winds of heaven ..." (Master Mason, or Third, Degree).

Even that fun-loving order, the Shrine, Masonry's party boys and ambassadors of good will, participate in these graphic oaths: "In willful violation thereof may I incur the fearful penalty of having my eyeballs pierced to the center with a three-edged blade, my feet flayed [cut across in thin strips], and be forced to walk the hot sands upon the sterile shores of the Red Sea until the flaming sun shall strike me with livid plague ... etc., etc." (Ancient Arabic Order, Nobles of the Mystic Shrine).

Furthermore, even the women, the civilizing gentler sex, take part in these horrible oaths:

"I further promise and vow, with a firm and steady purpose to perform and keep the same under no less penalty than having my body severed in fourteen pieces and thrown in the river, if

I violate any part of this my obligation."[239] The Commandress then directs, "You will kiss the Bible three times, the Koran once, and the Red Stone of Horus once" (Ritual, National Imperial Court of the Daughters of Isis, North and South America).

Because of growing public awareness of such bloody, atrocious death oaths, some Masonic jurisdictions are making changes, omitting the more offensive portions. Most, however, retain the "ancient" obligations, unchanged. And, even if all their oaths had the parts requiring torture, death, and mutilation removed, it wouldn't make their oaths scriptural, nor would it change any of the basic abominations of the system.

ENDNOTES

239 National Imperial Court of the Daughters of Isis, *Ritual*, (Chicago: Ezra Cook, undated).

The "Lost Word" and Its Significance

Throughout Masonic writings, rituals, lectures, and degrees, there are references to something called the "lost word" (also called "The Master's Word" and "The Grand Masonic Word"). One very soon becomes aware that there must be something terribly important about this word because it figures prominently in so much of what Masons say, write, and do. If you read and listen, you soon get the impression that the fate of western civilization, if not the entire human race, centers on this mysterious word. And, if you really read carefully, you finally learn that, in Masonic philosophy at least, it does mean that!

Having learned that, you will probably want to know why this lost word is so important. Most simply put, the "lost word" is the name of God. That's right, the name of God. You probably thought there was no mystery about his name since He has identified Himself plainly, elaborately, and repeatedly, in the Bible. It seems to me to be a non-issue also; but Masonry has a completely different view of the matter. They believe that it has been lost, and that it must be found.

Masonry's position is that God's "true" name was once known to a select, enlightened, elite priesthood in those long-ago, "good old days," when the world was pagan, the mystery religions were in full flower, and everyone was happily worshiping the phallus. Then, as time went by, stupid, unenlightened, narrow-minded bigots (you guessed it—Christians) came along and, failing to appreciate the "grandeur, beauty and perfection" of all that orgiastic, sex-worshiping, they got rid of all of the sorcerers, magicians, and other masters of black arts who knew the word. And, so, tragedy of tragedies, it was lost.

The Power in a Name

But why, you might wonder, is mankind's inability to remember a name such a problem? Well, here, in the answer to this question, is the very heart of all occultism, especially witchcraft. In basic occult philosophy, if one knows the true name of a spirit, one then possesses that spirit's power. Not only that, however; with the knowledge of the spirit's name, the occultist can control that spirit.

Consider then a minor demonic spirit, flitting about some suburban neighborhood in Hometown, USA, performing wicked little deeds for Satan. If knowing that spirit's name would give you its power, just think what it would mean if you could know the "lost" name of God, Himself! Obviously, it would mean (as the occultists believe) that you would then have, and be able to use, all the power of God. In fact, you could take over and become the God of the Universe, yourself. This was Lucifer's big mistake; and intelligent people the world over are going to great expense and effort today, trying to repeat his stupid mistake for themselves.

By now, you should be wondering how this lost word fits into Masonic philosophy and teaching. The answer is that the search for the lost word is a uniting thread which runs throughout Masonic degrees, teachings, and writings. Masonry defines itself as a search for "light" (knowledge), and the acquisition of knowledge (enlightenment) is the heart of the Masonic plan of redemption. J.D. Buck, one of Freemasonry's occult exemplars, has declared that in Masonry "Initiation and Regeneration are synonymous terms."[240] It should not be surprising, therefore, that the quest to find and possess the knowledge of the lost "Grand Masonic Word" is the centerpiece of the initiation into the Master Mason degree; and the Master Mason Degree is the truly climactic degree in pure Freemasonry.

In the Third Degree, the initiate must participate in the reenactment of the legend of Hiram Abiff, entering into Hiram's death, burial, and resurrection. In the drama, this Hiram is the only one who knows the "Master's Word" and, with his murder by three "ruffians" (could this be a veiled reference to Trinitarian Christians and their Triune God? Maybe I am too sensitive about such things.), the knowledge of this all-important word is lost. Truth is lost. Light is lost. Forever! What was a king to do?

In the story, while Hiram is dead and in the grave for three days and nights (Satan never has any original ideas), King Solomon decides that, when Hiram's body is found and restored to life, the very first thing that Hiram says will be the "new" Grand Masonic Word, i.e. the replacement for the real one.

Well, the body is found, dug up, restored to life, and raised up from the grave by Solomon with the Master Mason's grip. When Hiram is "raised" from the grave, the first thing he says is "Mah Hah Bone." This strange expression, according to the legend, then becomes the substitute for the real name, the true "lost word," and Masons the world over have been seeking to be initiated into this redeeming knowledge ever since.

You may still be wondering what this all really means to us. Well, it means very little—or it means everything—depending upon how we view it. In that it is revealing in terms of the true, occult nature of Masonry, it matters a very great deal. It also means a great deal because sincere Masons all over the world take this silly story seriously and are deceived by it. However, in terms of reality and truth, it is not only meaningless, it is completely absurd.

There Was a Simple Solution All Along

Ever since I first read the legend of Hiram and studied the Master Mason initiation, I have had a question for which I have found no logical answer in all of Masonic lore. You have probably already thought of it, but I'll point it out anyway. If the lost word was so all-important, if it was the key to life, death, and eternity, the doorway to happiness, redemption and power, and if it was lost when Hiram was killed, then why, when Hiram was restored to life, didn't Solomon just ask him what it was? Why fool with a substitute? Why didn't Solomon just say, "Hey, Hiram! Welcome back to the land of the living! Praise the Lord brother—we're so glad to have you back! Now, tell us, just what is that word that all this fuss has been about?" I mean, why plunge humanity into an endless quest, searching and groping forever for something called "Ma Ha Bone" when Hiram could have just told us the real one?

Well, there it is. And now you know the lost word and its meaning.

If you would like to know more about the legend of Hiram Abiff, the "lost word," or the initiation ritual of the Master Mason's degree, you will find all that in Part One of this book.

ENDNOTES

240 J.D. Buck, *Mystic Masonry*, 3rd ed. (Chicago: Chas T. Powner Publishing Co., 1925), p. 44.

Freemasonry and
Its Controversial Authorities

If you have read this far in this book, names like Albert Pike, Albert Mackey, J.D. Buck, and Manly P. Hall are as familiar to you by now as those of your neighbors. Most people, however, have never heard of them. As a matter of fact, most Masons have never heard of them. Some, or all, of these references are on the shelf of every lodge library; but most Masons not only don't read them, they have no interest in reading them. Most Masons, confronted with some revealing statement by Albert Pike or Albert Mackey, are likely to look blank and reply, "Albert who?" Even Lodge secretaries, custodians of the Lodge's Masonic library, may never have read most of the Masonic classics cited in this book, although they are gathering dust on their own library shelves.

But this is changing, and Freemasonry has a growing problem. As more and more of the unflattering truth about Freemasonry is publicly revealed, by books such as this, by preaching and teaching, by radio and television commentators, and by increasingly frequent public controversies, such as the gigantic one still going on within the Southern Baptist Convention, ugly truth is escaping. And, once such truth escapes into the public awareness, it spreads in all directions. As more questions are raised, interest grows; and as a result of the growing interest still more questions are asked. The jinni is out of the bottle, so to speak, and Masonry can't get it back into its place.

In earlier times it seems to have been a traditional (and wise) policy, at Masonry's top levels of leadership, simply to remain silent when awkward or embarrassing things make the news. They know how quickly the public forgets. All that was necessary was simply to remain inconspicuous and silent while that predictable process ran its course. Today, however, it isn't working; there is just way too much truth escaping and getting the public's attention.

So, What Is Masonry's Leadership to Do?

Now that the public (including a great many Blue Lodge Masons) is being educated to the truth about the secret doctrines of Masonry, and becoming acquainted with the utterances and doctrinal teachings of such Masonic exemplars as Albert Pike, Albert Mackey, Joseph Fort Newton, J.D. Buck, and Manly P. Hall, these revered Masonic philosophers are becoming a problem—a serious embarrassment; and silence hasn't worked. So what are the Masonic leaders to do? They have tried two basic stratagems in recent times, and neither is holding water.

One Defense

Confronted with the writings of their own revered authorities today, one defense is to dismiss the writings casually, saying that these men don't speak for all of Masonry. They will say that the works of such men as Pike, Mackey and Hall are valued works by visionary Masonic philosophers, but that they are not "official" Masonic doctrinal works. And yet you can look in any Masonic library, catalog of Masonic books, or lodge's or jurisdiction's recommended reading list and these men's works will be prominently featured there (unless they have been removed in recent times for "damage control"). If this argument were valid, these works, at the very least, would be kept in a separate room, or on a separate shelf, with a warning as to their unofficial status.

By the same token, you can write to, or call, any Grand Lodge and tell them you are interested in a serious study of Masonry and ask for a list of ten top books or authors recommended for study. Unless they suspect that you are an "anti-Mason" trying to embarrass them, you will probably find those that are most often quoted in this book making every recommended reading list.

Blue Lodge Masons, whether newly raised or aged veterans, don't think in terms of "official" or "unofficial" publications. They think only in terms of the Masonic literature that they are urged (or required) to read. And if the Lodge leaders require or recommend a source it is "official" as far as the rank-and-file are concerned.

Another Defense

A second way to deflect the effects of growing awareness of these Masonic classics is to dismiss them, not as "brilliant-but-unofficial," but as heresies, teaching things contrary to pure Masonic philosophy. But this position won't survive even a minute of clear thinking. If this were true, all those books would never have been placed on their library shelves and reading lists in the first place; or, at the least, they would have been removed long ago. Also, they would disappear from the catalogues of MaCoy, Ezra Cook and other Masonic publishers because no one would be buying them.

And, Finally

Finally, I can demolish this defense with just one undeniable fact, and it is this: For at least the past 150 years, not one Masonic authority, not one major leader, not one spokesman for any significant rite, body or other segment of Masonry has publicly

423

denounced a single one of the Masonic classics quoted in this book. There has not been a single word of public utterance officially condemning them as heretical. If the writings and teachings of these men are unorthodox, heretical, or in any way offensive to Masonry's top leaders, they haven't announced it! This should be enough to give the lie to their denials; but the case against them gets even stronger. Not only have these Masonic philosophers not been denounced by Masonic officialdom; they have instead received the highest public endorsement and praise! I will cite just two examples and rest my case.

Albert Pike

Albert Pike is probably the most influential Mason of the last 150 years. In fact, his position and presence during his lifetime, and for many years following his death, were so dominant that it might almost be said that, during those years Albert Pike **was** Freemasonry—at least in the Scottish Rite. He was "Supreme Pontiff of Universal Freemasonry"; and his other Masonic titles and honors would fill a small book. His classic work, "Morals and Dogma," is perhaps the most significant Masonic book ever written. This ponderous, thousand-page tome is the ultimate source book for the "esoteric" (true, hidden) meaning of Masonic symbolism and doctrine. It is also the most closely kept, and the most difficult of all Masonic books for the non-Masonic researcher to obtain. And, since it has been obtained by some researchers, it has become the most embarrassing, hard-to-explain-away publication with which Masonry is confronted. Much of the ongoing public debate over Masonry centers on quotations from "Morals and Dogma."

So, who, and what, was Pike? Was he a fringe group heretic in the eyes of Masonry's leaders? Are the discussions of his writings therefore irrelevant? Not a chance! If you travel to the magnificent House of the Temple in Washington, D.C. (often referred to as "The House that Pike Built"), you will be at the headquarters of the Supreme Council of the Thirty-third Degree, Southern Jurisdiction. There, inside that beautiful monument to Egyptian paganism, you will find three statues of Pike. There, also, is the Albert Pike museum. And, as a matter of fact, old Albert himself is there—buried in the wall! A special act of Congress was required in order to bury him there.

The recent Sovereign Grand Commander, C. Fred Kleinknecht, successor to Pike's canopied Masonic throne, wrote an article in the January 1989 issue of *The New Age* (now published under the title *Scottish Rite Journal*), concerning the official view of *Morals and Dogma*. Grand Commander Kleinknecht wrote, "Pike's great book is not the book of an hour, a decade, or a century. **It is a book for all time**" (emphasis mine). Kleinknecht closed his article with this ringing declaration of support for Pike and his book: **"Abandon *Morals and Dogma*? Never!"** (emphasis mine).

This reads like a challenging battle cry, and I believe it was! Why? Because this very public declaration was made a year after the publication of my book, *The Deadly Deception*, in the midst of growing, excited public debate concerning the true nature of Masonry and the writings of its authorities. It was a time when vastly growing numbers of Christians were becoming aware of the issue, speaking out about it and writing on the subject. The air waves virtually crackled with heated debate on radio and television talk shows. Not since the murder of Captain Morgan was there a time when the tranquil world of Masonry was so shocked and shaken by sudden public awareness of its nature. Heated debate was boiling, quotations from Masonic books were circulating widely, and *Morals and Dogma* was easily the most controversial of the Masonic classics being discussed. It would not be an exaggeration to say that Pike and his book were a major focal point—and at times **the** focal point of the entire swirling conflict.

Politically and diplomatically, the wise course for the Scottish Rite, and the rest of Masonic officialdom, would have been to maintain a low public profile, adopt a "no comment" position, and wait for the public to forget. But, no—instead, Kleinknecht rose up, as it were, from his canopied Masonic throne in the Temple Room, threw down the gauntlet, and took the "Here I stand!" position in defense of Pike and his book. He did this as unequivocally and sincerely as Martin Luther had done it 500 years earlier, concerning reformation. And remember—these words were not spoken in a private conversation with a friend—not even in an interview with a researcher or a journalist. These words were written and proclaimed to the World, in his own, official publication. Remember also, that when he wrote and published the article, C. Fred Kleinknecht was the sitting Sovereign Grand Commander, speaking "ex cathedra"—i.e. as an official pronouncement from his official seat of authority. For this I respect the man. He could have done the politically wise and expedient thing and deflected or ignored the issue; the public has a short attention span, and soon forgets. But he didn't do that. Instead, he rose up, planted his feet, and took a very public stand for what he believed. Although his beliefs were, and are, the very antithesis of mine, I must respect him for publicly refusing to compromise or deny his own.

Manley Palmer Hall

The late Manly Palmer Hall was a Thirty-third Degree Mason, the quintessential Masonic mystic, and an internationally renowned occultist. He is the one who wrote that a Mason "has the seething energies of Lucifer in his hand." His pronouncements, like those of Albert Pike, have been prominent in the ongoing debates over the true nature of Masonry. He has not been denounced and decried by Masonic officialdom; rather, he has been publicly praised, and has received Masonry's highest honors. Upon his death in 1990, he was given a glowing tribute in *The New Age/Scottish Rite Journal.* And, interestingly, the tribute to Hall included concurrent praise for Albert Pike. It will be useful, I think, to quote from some of it here; it speaks condensed volumes:

"Illustrious Manly Palmer Hall, often called 'Masonry's Greatest Philosopher,' departed his earthly labors ... August 7, 1990.... [He] received the Scottish Rite's highest honor, the Grand Cross, in 1985 because of his exceptional contributions to Freemasonry, the Scottish Rite and the public good. Like Grand Commander Albert Pike before him, Illustrious Hall did not teach a new doctrine, but was an ambassador of the ageless tradition of wisdom.... The World is a better place because of Manly Palmer Hall."

So, does Masonic officialdom denounce these writers as heretics, fringe radicals or philosophical renegades? Do they warn Masons against their "heresies"? No! In fact, they celebrate them—they publicly and enthusiastically praise and endorse them. Masonic officialdom is proud of these men and their writings—and don't let anyone tell you otherwise!

I do recommend to the reader a visit to the House of the Temple. It stands majestically on the east side of Northwest 16th Street in Washington, DC, between "R" and "S" Streets. It is beautiful—an awesome thing of polished marble, polished mahogany, walnut and other beautiful woods, stained glass and polished brass. From the outside you will see, high above the entrance, a window with a golden image of Egyptian deity. It is easily seen from the street or the stone pavement in front of the building; but if you aren't looking for it you will probably not notice it.

The outside doors are massive and bronze. Once inside, you will be greeted by a courteous docent (guide), who will lead you through the various parts of the building. Among other things of interest there are museums dedicated to Masonic icons such as the one devoted to Albert Pike. On the top floor is the beautiful Temple Room, where the Supreme Council of the 33rd Degree conducts its rituals. There you will see its enormous pipe organ, and the famous "serpentine" windows. The House of the Temple is definitely worth the trip; however, I recommend that you pray before going in and after leaving; it is definitely a thing of beauty, but it is also devoted entirely to "the unfruitful works of darkness."

Bibliography

"Busy, Brotherly World of Freemasonry," *LIFE Magazine* (8 October 1956).

Bailey, A. A., *Externalisation of the Hierarchy* (New York: Lucis Publishing Co.), 1957.

Baskin, Wade, *The Sorcerer's Handbook*, (New York: Philosophical Library), 1974.

Blanchard, Jonathan, *Scottish (Scotch) Rite Masonry, Illustrated*, vols. I and II (Chicago: Chas T. Powner Publishing Co.), 1972 (Original publication 1887, 1888).

Buck, J.D., *Mystic Masonry*, 3rd ed. (Chicago: Chas T. Powner Publishing Co.), 1925.

Chase, George W., *Digest of Masonic Law*, 8th ed. (Boston: Pollard and Leighton), 1869.

Claudy, Carl H., *Introduction to Freemasonry* (Washington, DC: Temple Publishers), 1939.

Claudy, Carl, "Spirit of Masonry" *The Kentucky Monitor* (Louisville, KY: Standard Printing Co.), 1921.

Coil, Henry W., *Coil's Masonic Encyclopedia* (Richmond, VA: MaCoy Publishing Co.), 1961.

Duncan, Malcolm C., *Duncan's Masonic Ritual and Monitor*, 3rd ed. (New York: David McKay Co.), undated.

Epperson, Ralph. *A Review of the Book Entitled Morals and Dogma*, Rev ed. (Tucson, Arizona: Publius Press) 1995.

Finney, Charles G., *The Character, Claims and Practical Workings of Freemasonry*, (Southern District of Ohio: Western Tract and Book Society), 1869.

General Grand Chapter, Order of the Eastern Star, *Ritual of the Order of the Eastern Star*, 22d ed. (Chicago), 1911.

Hall, Manley P., *The Lost Keys of Freemasonry* (Richmond, VA: MaCoy Publishing Co.), 1976.

Hascall, L.C., *History of the Ancient and Honorable Fraternity of Free and Accepted Masons, and Concordant Orders* (Boston and London: The Fraternity Publishing Co.), 1891.

Knight, Thomas C., *Knights of Columbus, Illustrated* (Chicago, IL: Ezra Cook Publications), 1974.

MaCoy, Robert, *Adoptive Rite Ritual* (New York: MaCoy Publishing and Masonic Supply Co.), 1942.

Mackey, Albert, *Encyclopedia of Freemasonry*, rev. ed. (Masonic History Co.: Chicago, New York, London), 1927.

Mackey, Albert, *Jurisprudence of Freemasonry*, rev. and enlarged ed. Book II (Chicago: Chas T. Powner Co.), 1975.

Mackey, Albert, *Lexicon of Freemasonry*, 2nd Ed, (Charleston, SC: Walker and James), 1852.

Mackey, Albert, *Manual of the Lodge* (New York: MaCoy Publishing Co.), 1903.

Mackey, Albert, *Symbolism of Freemasonry* (Chicago: Chas. T. Powner Co.), 1975.

Mackey, Albert, *The Masonic Ritualist* (New York: MaCoy Publishing Co.), 1903.

Masonic Dictionary (Chicago: Consolidated Book Publishers), 1963.

McCormick, W J., *Christ, the Christian and Freemasonry* (Belfast, Ireland: Great Joy Publications), 1984.

McQuaig, C.F., *The Masonic Report*, (Norcross, GA: Answer Books and Tapes), 1976.

Morgan, William, *Illustrations of Masonry*, printed for the Proprietor, republished (Batavia, NY) 1827.

National Imperial Court of the Daughters of Isis, *Ritual*, (Chicago: Ezra Cook, undated).

Newton, Joseph Fort, *The Great Light of Masonry, Masonic Bible* (A. J. Holmes Co.), 1968.

Newton, Joseph Fort, *The Builders*, (Cedar Rapids, IA: Torch Press), 1915.

Newton, Joseph Fort, *The Religion of Freemasonry, an Interpretation,* (Kingsport, TN: Southern Publishing) 1969

Order of the Eastern Star Recognition Test (Chicago, IL: Ezra Cook Publications), 1975.

Parchment, S.R., *Ancient Operative Masonry* (San Francisco: San Francisco Center-Rosicrucian Fellowship), 1930.

Pierson, A.T.C., *Traditions of Freemasonry* (New York: Anderson and Co.), 1865.

Pike, Albert, *Morals and Dogma of the Ancient and Accepted Scottish Rite of Freemasonry,* rev. ed. (Washington, DC: House of the Temple), 1950.

Pirtle, Henry, *The Kentucky Monitor,* 9th ed. (Louisville, KY: Standard Printing Co.), 1921.

Secret Societies Illustrated (Chicago, IL: Ezra Cook Publishers), undated.

Shriners Recognition Test (Chicago, IL: Ezra Cook Publishers), undated.

Sickles, Daniel, *Ahiman Rhezon and Freemason's Guide* (New York: MaCoy Publishing Co.), 1911.

Still, William T., *New World Order* (Lafayette, LA: Huntington House), 1990.

Storms, E.M., Should a Christian Be a Mason? (Fletcher, NC: New Puritan Library), 1980.

Taylor, M., "Masonic Burial Service, "*Texas Monitor* (Houston, TX: Grand Lodge of Texas), 1883.

The Mystic Shrine, an Illustrated Ritual of the Ancient Arabic Order, Nobles of the Mystic Shrine, rev. ed. (Chicago: Ezra Cook Publishers), 1975.

Wagner, Martin L., *Freemasonry, an Interpretation,* republished, (Grosse Pointe, MI: Seminar Tapes and Books), 1912.

Wark, John and Gary Marx, "Shrine," *The Orlando Sentinel* (29 June 1986, A-1; 30 June 1986, A-1; 1 July 1986, A-1).

Webb, Thomas Smith, *Freemason's Monitor* (LaGrange, KY: Rob Morris Publishers), 1862.

Wilmshurst, Walter, *The Meaning of Masonry,* (New York: Bell Publishing) 1980

Index